AT RISK

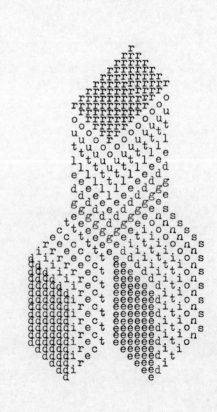

AT RISK: AN ACCOUNT OF THE WORK OF THE BATTERED CHILD RESEARCH DEPARTMENT, NSPCC

EDWINA BAHER

CLARE HYMAN

CAROLYN JONES

RONALD JONES

ANNA KERR

RUTH MITCHELL

Executive Head
RAYMOND CASTLE

ROUTLEDGE DIRECT EDITIONS

ROUTLEDGE & KEGAN PAUL
London, Henley and Boston

First published in 1976
by Routledge & Kegan Paul Ltd
39 Store Street,
London WC1E 7DD, Broadway House, Newtown Road,
Henley-on-Thames, Oxon RG9 1EN and
9 Park Street,
Boston, Mass. 02108, USA
Printed and bound in Great Britain
by Unwin Brothers Limited,
The Gresham Press, Old Woking, Surrey
A member of the Staples Printing Group
Reprinted 1976 and 1978

ISBN 0 7100 8313 0

CONTENTS

FOREWORD by Rev. Arthur Morton, Director, NSPCC   vii

PREFACE by Professor C. Henry Kempe, MD   viii

ACKNOWLEDGMENTS   x

INTRODUCTION   1

Part one   9

1   METHODS USED IN THE THERAPEUTIC STUDY   11

2   BATTERING AS A PHENOMENON: THE INJURIES AND PROBLEMS OF DIAGNOSIS   18

3   COMPOSITION OF THE SAMPLE   29

4   THE CHILDREN   36

5   THE PARENTS   65

Part two   95

6   OVERALL MANAGEMENT OF CASES   97

7   PROTECTION OF THE CHILDREN   106

8   THE PRIMARY THERAPEUTIC RELATIONSHIP   133

9   THE USE OF OTHER WORKERS - PROFESSIONAL AND UNTRAINED   158

10   EVALUATION OF PROGRESS IN FAMILIES   167

vi Contents

Part three   181

    11 PSYCHOLOGICAL ASPECTS OF BATTERING PARENTS   183

    12 A PSYCHOLOGICAL STUDY OF BATTERED CHILDREN   198

    13 GENERAL DISCUSSION AND RECOMMENDATIONS   210

        APPENDICES   219

        BIBLIOGRAPHY   233

        INDEX   242

FOREWORD

ARTHUR MORTON
Director, NSPCC

I was first privileged to meet Professor Kempe and his colleague Professor Steele in Denver at Christmas 1964. I was so impressed with the work they were doing with the Battered Child Syndrome that I returned to Britain convinced that we must establish a similar programme here.

Two and a half years later, the Central Executive Committee of the NSPCC authorised me to make a prolonged visit to the United States, together with the late Dr David Thomas, Honorary Consultant Psychiatrist to the Society, to hold discussions with American Paediatricians and others, about their work, prior to setting up the battered child research and treatment project in this country.

We were deeply impressed by what we saw and on our return secured the consent of the Central Executive Committee to setting up a research and treatment project whose work and findings are described in this book.

It is customary in the field of social work to stress the importance of the pioneering role of voluntary societies. It is scarcely possible to conceive of a more important piece of pioneering than that undertaken by the NSPCC in regard to the tragic problem of the Battered Child Syndrome, the first results of which are recorded in this book.

PREFACE

C. Henry Kempe, MD
Professor of Pediatrics and Microbiology
University of Colorado Medical Center
Director, The National Center for the Prevention and
Treatment of Child Abuse and Neglect
Denver, USA

The authors of this volume, all members of the NSPCC, Battered Child
Research Department, have, in a comprehensive way, presented results
of their treatment of abusive parents. The philosophy of a total
family approach uses a variety of treatment modalities and very much
includes the needs of the child. The findings have broad implications for general adoption of these methods by local child protection authorities as well as by private agencies in the field of
family care.

This study shows the important role the Health Visitor has to
play in case finding, and the valuable contributions made by
physicians in the field of General Practice, and by the Pediatric
and Surgical Consultants, in providing a setting where a true
interdisciplinary decision can be made regarding, first, a comprehensive family diagnosis; second, an agreement on the odds for
successful treatment, and third, the development of a realistic
treatment plan as offered by the authors and their lay associates.
Next, they show that the availability of immediate crisis intervention for those families thought to be treatable and accepted into
the study was of great importance in easing the stress on the
families at risk. The provision of daycare, the development of
mothers' groups and the 24-hour on-call service readily provided
by the team, all are examples of the broadening of the therapeutic
spectrum which must become part and parcel of all child protection
agencies in the very immediate future. Of great importance is
the confirmation of the fact that the abused child himself requires
treatment from the start, and that it is not enough simply to pay
attention to the needs of the parents. Regrettably, access to
fathers was less than optimal, and in this, as in some other
British studies, middle-class and upper-class socio-economic groups
are not represented. The authors believe, with us, that cases in

that area of the population are handled quite differently by
physicians and that they generally don't come to the attention of
the NSPCC and, hence, could not be expected to be represented in
the sample.   Further, the geographic location of this study made
such an inclusion unlikely in any case.

The collaborative effort of a dedicated team understanding the
needs of a family and responding generously to those needs, was
initiated through the cooperation and support of the Executive
Committee of the NSPCC, under their Director, the Reverend Arthur
Morton, and was initiated by Miss Joan Court and her Deputy, Mr
Raymond Castle, who has since succeeded her.   To these people
and to their many active collaborators, including their lay
helpers, goes a great deal of credit for being able to strike out
in new directions in providing a therapeutic model of comprehensive family care.   This is something that voluntary agencies can
sometimes do more readily than governmental ones.   But it is
clear that tax-supported, public child protection agencies on
both sides of the Atlantic, are rapidly coming to appreciate the
importance of sharing the decision-making process among social
workers;   physicians;   health visitors;   the police;   and, often,
the court.   In the final practical analysis, child abuse is
defined simply - it is not what social workers, doctors, nurses, or
police feel it is, but what the judge says it is.   Through increasing knowledge, we now know better who is treatable and who
is not;   what the needs of the child are in a complex and often
very frightening family situation;   and we can urge the courts to
face once again the question as to what the rights of children are.
It should be stressed, as this study makes clear from the onset,
that when one intervenes in the process of child abuse or the
'failure-to-thrive syndrome' one is not acting on behalf of the
child against the parents, but rather for the abusive parents as
well.   With the exception of a relatively few sadistic parents,
who are child torturers in the Dickens sense of the word, child
abusers are, themselves, in very deep pain;   and by their rescue
one does not only protect the child and other children to come,
one often strengthens a marriage and, when things go well, one
ends up with either an intact family, very much improved, or with
the understanding that a child they cannot love will never succeed
in his family and that an effort must be made to find permanently
other arrangements through termination of parental rights and
adoption.

The very great caseload carried by protective service workers
makes it quite clear that additional modalities of treatment must
be provided.   These include crisis nurseries;   therapeutic day
care facilities;   mothers' groups of Parents Anonymous;   lay
helpers in the form of mothering aides;   and, perhaps in the near
future, the provision of residential care for entire families for
comprehensive family treatment, but not requiring the usual prolonged separation of the child from the parents in foster care.
It is hoped that these will become standard fare for protective
service departments throughout the Western world.

It is to the credit of the authors that they have given a good
push in that direction.

ACKNOWLEDGMENTS

Special acknowledgment is made to the following people who have
generously given their help at different times during the project:
Joan Court
Peter Davis
Elizabeth Elmer
David Fruin
Charles Garvin
Colin Gibson
Susan Higginson
Diane Humphries
Ruby Le Peltier
Gabrielle Marchbanks
Shirley Rutherford
Peter Scott
Angela Skinner
Christine Smakowska
Anne Tindale
Jessie Waters
Colin Weaver
together with many members of staff, friends of the project, co-
operating agencies and the parents and children who were our
clients.
    The project has been assisted by grants given by the Calouste
Gulbenkian Foundation, the Joseph Rowntree Charitable Trust, The
Chase Charity, Friends of the Violet Melchett Infant Welfare
Centre and a Five Year Urban Aid Grant administered by the Royal
Borough of Kensington and Chelsea.   The Scientific Advisory
Committee under the Chairmanship of Professor Thomas Oppé, MD,
FRCP, DCH was set up to advise the project team.

INTRODUCTION

In 1962 Professor C. Henry Kempe, an American paediatrician, and
his associates published an article entitled The Battered Child
Syndrome. Kempe was the first to use this term 'to characterise
a clinical condition in young children who have received serious
physical abuse, generally from a parent or foster parent'. The
report drew attention to the considerable number of young children
suffering unexplained injuries and it made a deep impact on the
medical, legal and social work professions, government and the
public in America and other parts of the world. The following
year, two orthopaedic surgeons, Griffiths and Moynihan (1963),
published the first study of the syndrome in Britain which likewise
aroused considerable interest and led to an increasing awareness
that the problem was far more common than had previously been
realised.

The National Society for the Prevention of Cruelty to Children
followed with concern this growing knowledge on the battered child
syndrome and in 1968, encouraged by friends of the society in
America and with the support of leading paediatricians in Britain,
set up its own research unit in London, which, in the words of the
Director, was intended to 'strive to create an informed body of
opinion about the battered child syndrome and to devise methods of
treatment'.

The establishment of the Department was made possible from a sum
set aside from the amount raised for the Society's Building and
Development Appeal by supporters during the previous three years
and the Society has borne the main running costs of the Department
throughout its existence. Grants to cover the cost of specialist
personnel, ancillary staff, office and other equipment and specific
research tasks were subsequently obtained from the Joseph Rowntree
Charitable Trust, the Calouste Gulbenkian Foundation and the Chase
Charity. Financial assistance for the running of the therapeutic
day nursery was received from the Friends of the Violet Melchett
Infant Welfare Centre and from a Five-Year Urban Aid Grant administered by the Royal Borough of Kensington and Chelsea.

From the outset the need for a multi-disciplinary approach to
the problem was recognised. Thus a Scientific Advisory Committee,
was set up for the guidance of the project, under the chairmanship

of a consultant paediatrician, Professor Thomas Oppé.   The Committee
included members of the medical, legal and social work professions.
  During 1968 Miss Joan Court, a psychiatric social worker with
research experience, was appointed to head the project, to assemble
a team of social workers and a project co-ordinator, and to embark
on a programme of research and treatment.   It was agreed that the
team should be given complete freedom to decide on the kind of
social work techniques and practices to be employed to safeguard
children and to meet their parents' needs;   and that each social
worker's caseload should not exceed ten cases.   The stressful and
emotive nature of the work to be undertaken was recognised and provision was made for the social workers to meet regularly with a
consultant psychiatrist for support and consultation.
  At this time in Britain the battered child syndrome had been
defined primarily in physical terms, while its social and psychological facets had received only cursory attention.   There was a
dearth of knowledge about the management of such cases.   An
article by Arthur Hughes (1967), who played a leading role at the
NSPCC in setting up the Research Department, emphasised the importance of providing comprehensive services and long-term support to
the families of battered children.   There were no Child Abuse
Reporting Laws in operation, as there were by this time in the USA
(see Paulsen, 1968), and it was against a background of poorly
defined responsibilities, confused ethical, legal and treatment
issues, that the project commenced.
  The first year of the project was spent at the Society's head-
quarters and served to orientate the newly appointed project staff.
Plans were made for the main therapeutic study to begin as soon as
a suitable building had been found.   As a preliminary to this
study, the team concentrated on reviewing the world literature on
the battered child syndrome and evaluating and integrating the
practice insights accumulated by others already dealing with the
problem.   In addition, a Retrospective Study of seventy-eight
cases of battered children which were handled by the NSPCC Inspec-
tors during a twelve-month period was undertaken (Skinner and
Castle, 1969).   Important implications for treatment emerged from
this study.   For example, there was considerable evidence to
suggest that agency pressures together with the emotive nature of
the problem created anxiety in workers which restricted their
ability to offer help.   In a sample where the incidence of re-
battering was as high as 60 per cent, we were forced to conclude
that procedures for handling these cases were ineffective and that
an authoritarian approach which added to existing family tension
could be one factor precipitating further battering.   It was noted
that some battering parents responded favourably to a non-punitive
relationship with a skilled social worker, who was able to devote
considerable time and attention to their problems and also focused
attention on their emotional needs rather than on routine inspection of the child (Skinner, 1970).
  These observations were in keeping with the treatment philosophy
of Helfer, Kempe and their colleagues at the University of Colorado
Medical Center, Denver, whose work was a great source of inspira-
tion for the team.   However, from the outset, we were aware of
the considerable differences between our setting and that of

Kempe's team, affecting the type of service and resources available.
For example, Kempe's team was largely hospital-based, which ensured
direct and swift access to families of children with non-accidental
injuries.   In contrast we were a community-based team, highly dependent on other agencies for prompt referral.

In the summer of 1969, after a long search for suitable accommodation, we moved into homely, rambling offices above a shop in West
London.   The premises were large enough for individual offices and
we chose our own decorations and furnishings.   We named the building 'Denver House' in tribute to Professor Kempe and his team.   We
were particularly fortunate that Professor Kempe and his wife, Dr
Ruth Kempe, a psychoanalyst and psychiatrist with considerable knowledge of child abuse, were based at Denver House while spending a
sabbatical year with the NSPCC during 1969-70.   In addition to
advising us on the handling of our first cases and conducting his
own research, Professor Kempe undertook an extensive educational
programme throughout the country.   Dr Ruth Kempe, who worked with
us on a sessional basis, assisted in selection of additional staff
for the Department, participated in case conferences and discussions, and offered individual supervision and support to social
workers.

Our first task was to make ourselves known in the area and build
up community relations.   Shortly after we moved to Denver House an
exploratory study of the possibilities of earlier diagnosis of
inflicted injuries to young children was conducted in the Casualty
Departments of two local hospitals (Okell, 1971).   This indicated
that a number of cases of abuse were being misdiagnosed as accidents
and proved a useful exercise for project staff.   It familiarised
us with the hospitals in our area and with meeting families of
injured children, and helped us to sharpen our diagnostic skills in
differentiating between inflicted and accidental injuries.

An Inter-Agency Co-ordinating Committee was established which
met regularly at Denver House.   Members of this Committee, representing the main local agencies, initially participated in working
out with the team criteria for referral, referral procedures and a
common policy on crucial issues of case management, such as primary
responsibility for casework, police intervention and the instiga-
tion of Juvenile Court proceedings.   Subsequent committee meetings
were primarily devoted to tackling difficulties encountered by the
Department in connection with case management and liaison and to
keeping members informed of the Department's work.

At the outset of the study it was agreed that referrals would be
accepted from hospitals, Health Departments, Children's Departments
(this was before the reorganisation of the local authority personal
social services), general practitioners and other social work
agencies from a defined geographical area.   At all times this was
restricted to three London Boroughs as it was felt that a larger
area would not have facilitated close inter-agency liaison and communication, or the provision of an on-demand, intensive, twenty-
four hour service which was thought to be essential in these cases.
The criteria for referral, some of which were modified during the
course of the project, are outlined in chapter 1.

Prior to the opening of intake, our treatment philosophy and
proposed casework strategy were fully discussed with the co-operat-

ing agencies in the context of the action research which we would
be undertaking.   It was explained that in addition to studying
the families referred to us for treatment, our aim was to develop
and assess methods of therapeutic intervention and to see what
could be achieved with these families if workers were able to
operate in near ideal conditions.   Hence we reserved the right to
close intake at any time if pressure of work endangered the
quality of our service.

In January 1970 all the co-operating agencies in the research
area were notified that we were ready to accept referrals and the
first phase of intake began.   This lasted until 31 March 1971,
when in view of the sudden pressure of referrals, the temporary
loss of the Deputy Head of the Department, who took several months'
study leave in the USA and imminent holidays for other team
members, we decided to close intake.   A locum social worker was
employed for the next few months to ensure that the intensive
support offered to clients would not be diminished.

During the next ten months prior to re-opening intake, considerable effort was directed at making revisions in our research
design (see chapter 1).   Extensive case records had accumulated,
which contained a wealth of data but not in a form that was conducive to analysis.   Thus, with the help of several experienced
research consultants, we developed more systematic methods of data
collection and adopted a more concise method of casework recording.

Also, during this period the composition of the team changed.
In September 1971 Mr Raymond Castle replaced Miss Joan Court as
Head of the Department.   By the beginning of 1972 the Department
consisted of the Head of the Department, the Deputy Head and a
Research Officer (who were no longer available to take on new
cases), three research social workers, a project co-ordinator,
three secretaries and a telephonist.   Another research social
worker joined the Department later in the year to replace a team
member who took maternity leave, but who subsequently returned to
the Department to help with research tasks on a part-time basis.

By this time, in addition to the social work team, a number of
other workers were employed by the Department.   We obtained the
services of two part-time clinical psychologists, one of whom was
later replaced by a full-time graduate assistant (chapters 11 and
12).   A consultant forensic psychiatrist, whose role is discussed
in chapter 9, worked for the Department on a sessional basis.

In November 1971 we opened a therapeutic day nursery for some
of our battered children and their siblings.   It was conveniently
situated near Denver House and was staffed by a matron and three
NNEB trained nursery nurses.   To complete the team we employed
two carefully selected lay workers, a drop-in foster mother and a
mothering-aide, whose roles are discussed in chapter 9.

In February 1972 the second phase of intake began and a treatment control group was instituted (see chapter 1).   As social
workers in a specialised research unit we had already experienced
the inevitable dilemma of being unable to take on families for
treatment who badly needed help, but did not meet our criteria for
referral.   During the first phase of intake, the pattern of
referrals had been irregular and there had been lulls which created
a good deal of anxiety about refusing help when we were not working

staff for the first of the special treatment units subsequently
established by the NSPCC outside London.   We would agree with
Galdston (1971) that 'the balance of a service and research approach
allows the group to leaven the burden of anxiety with learning and
satisfaction from sharing the experience.'

Part one

9

Chapter 1

METHODS USED IN THE THERAPEUTIC STUDY

The subjects of the study were families in which a child, under the age of four, normally cared for at home by at least one natural parent, received injuries which were not consistent with the explanation or where there were other factors indicative of injury by other than accidental means. It was agreed that all referrals should be medically supported. Because a firm diagnosis of abuse is rarely possible (Simons et al., 1966; Silver et al., 1969), it was recognised that a few cases would transpire to be genuine accidents and that some short-term crisis work would be inevitable.

As the Department was unlikely to have a large and accumulating sample of battering parents from which a random selection of cases could be made, sample selection was not attempted. It was hoped that the total population of battered babies diagnosed in the catchment area during the study period, would be referred to the Department, but it was realised that this would not represent the true incidence of the syndrome in the area while many cases were being misdiagnosed or were remaining undetected (for example, see Okell, 1971).

THE SAMPLE

The first phase of intake was from January 1970 to March 1971. During the fifteen months, twenty-four cases were taken on by the Department for treatment although additional cases were accepted for diagnostic assessment and short-term crisis work. In fact, during this phase of intake the project workers did not always rigidly adhere to the criteria for referral and several cases were taken on for treatment in which the children had no current injury on referral, but whose mothers had admitted handling them roughly in the past and expressed a continuing fear of injuring them again.

Out of these twenty-four cases, four were eventually eliminated from the sample for research purposes, although they continued to receive treatment. Three cases were eliminated because the families were not thought to be 'batterers' and one because staff losses interfered too much with data collection. Thus, the first phase of intake yielded twenty cases for analysis.

Intake remained closed for almost a year not only because of our desire to maintain a high quality service by controlling the flow of referrals but also because of staffing problems.   We took advantage of this hiatus and extended it in order to make revisions in our research design.   The changes included the development of more systematic methods of data collection and the institution of a treatment control group.   Controls were gathered by referring alternate cases to other social work agencies in the area, which would normally have had responsibility if our specialised project had not been established.   Our intention was to collect comparative material on the routine services offered to battering families and the rate of reinjury.   Obviously it was felt unethical to leave a control group untreated as it had already been established that in the absence of intervention there is a high risk of re-battering (Helfer and Pollock, 1968).   The control cases were followed up after one year with the aim of crudely comparing their management with those treated by the Department.   Unfortunately, the rate of referrals during this period from February 1972 until September 1973 was low and only nine controls were gathered (see Appendix C).

Of the equal number of cases taken on for treatment by the Department, four were excluded from the sample because premature closure of the Department meant that insufficient time was available for a full treatment service to be provided and a comparative analysis made.   This not only affected data relating to treatment but information about the family history as well.   We knew from experience that data gathered around the time of referral was often seriously incomplete or incorrect.   Further contact with families invariably meant that information gained early in treatment would be modified or supplemented by subsequent comments from the parents. The amount of contact could not be standardised as the frequency of visiting and the overall length of treatment were to be determined by the therapeutic needs of the families.   However, we felt that a minimum period of one year was required to allow the worker to gain the confidence of the parents and thus gather reliable information from them and clarify any inconsistencies in earlier accounts of events.   Thus, this phase of intake yielded only five more cases.

Unless otherwise stated, the therapeutic study is based on an analysis of data from twenty-five cases, twenty from the first phase of intake and five from the second.   It should be noted that the sample referred to in the psychological section of this book is not the same as the therapeutic study sample, although there is some overlap.   The psychologists have incorporated material in their chapters, partly derived from their contact with some of the parents in the therapeutic study and partly from other battering families.

COLLECTION OF DIAGNOSTIC DATA

From the beginning of the therapeutic study, detailed records were kept on all cases.   All interviews were process recorded and full accounts kept of what the workers actually did for the families and how they responded.   Decision-making relating to the management of the cases was carefully documented and minutes of all case conferences were kept on the files.

Schedules were then devised by the social work team to cover virtually all aspects of family functioning, mainly at the time of referral.   Over four hundred variables were examined in this way. This work represented an attempt to arrange the data contained in the case records into some kind of systematic order and quantifiable form.   A thorough literature survey undertaken before the study began highlighted topics thought to have special significance for the syndrome and these were developed in considerable detail. Source material of prime importance was the work of Kempe and colleagues at the University of Colorado Medical School (Helfer and Kempe, 1968) and that of Elizabeth Elmer at the University of Pittsburg (Elmer, 1966).   The topics included the mother's pregnancy with the battered child; the birth and developmental progress of the battered child; the nature of parent-child interaction; the quality of the parents' own early experiences, including disruptions of their mothering; the degree of social isolation; the support derived from close relationships; the dynamics of the marital relationship; and acute and chronic stress in the family.

Many items on the schedule were precoded.   However, where it was felt that this process would fail to capture the full significance of a complex topic or it was difficult to foresee the categories into which data would fall, workers were asked to provide their comments in an open-ended format.   The coding frame was subsequently devised from the available information.   This also guarded against the distortion of data.   The original schedules were conceived as a rudimentary version to be piloted on the first series of cases and then refined for subsequent use.   However, various unforseen problems emerged in the course of the project which made the idea of redrafting the schedule unprofitable and the unwieldy original version was retained.

In addition to completing diagnostic schedules on each case, workers were asked to write vignettes of each parent and the child around certain headings.   Also, the workers were asked to describe how they were affected by the parents and the child and to assess the part played by each parent in battering.

COLLECTION OF DATA ON TREATMENT

Only a small part of the data on treatment was captured in schedule format.   This related to the referral process and the first interview, and to readily quantifiable material such as the number of contacts between clients and worker, the location of visits, the use of the on-call service, and the type and length of separation between the parents and their children.   A separate schedule was devised to document the progress of Adult Court and Juvenile Court proceedings in cases where legal action was taken.   In addition very detailed summaries covering the first three months of treatment were completed in all cases.   They were focused on specific topics including overall case management and liaison with other agencies; protective placements for the battered child and siblings; and the development of the primary therapeutic relationship.   This last topic took account of the casework techniques used; the parents' accessibility, motivation and presenting

problems; the parents' sensitivity and development of trust; the
way in which workers handled the question of abuse and how the
parents responded, and the workers' approach to the marital situation.   In addition, the progress of each case through subsequent
phases of treatment until the closure of the Department was outlined
for discussion.

As qualitative material comprised the bulk of our data for
assessing treatment, some attempt to gauge family functioning after
a reasonable period of treatment was also thought to be desirable.
The period chosen was eighteen months.   This seemed to combine the
minimum length of treatment, according to professional opinion with
the maximum number of cases, enabling twenty-two families to be
assessed in this way.   Fifty key variables were selected from the
original diagnostic schedules on family functioning and re-examined.
For the bulk of our cases we were thus able to compare family
functioning in important areas at the point of referral with a
point in time some eighteen months later.   This gave us some indication of changes which might be associated with treatment up to
that point, although many families had been in treatment for a
longer period.   Subsequent evaluation was based on our collective
impressions.

To obtain data on the treatment controls, questionnaires were
sent out one year after referral to workers in other agencies who
were currently carrying the cases.   Primarily we were interested
in finding out by this time, whether the children had been re-
injured and whether the treatment service had been discontinued.
According to experience, both eventualities were quite likely (see
for example, Skinner and Castle, 1969).   Information was also
requested on residential and day placements for the children, the
use of legal proceedings, overall treatment and management, and
how the families responded to what was provided.

DATA ANALYSIS

A system of carefully checking all data for accuracy was instituted
to ensure that items had not been missed or coded incorrectly.
The main diagnostic schedules were then analysed, beginning with
the quantification of items which had not been precoded.   Occasionally, where information was obviously insufficient for virtually
all families, the item was discarded without further consideration.
A few other variables were excluded from this schedule when it
became clear that the comments were insufficiently focused to
allow codification.   Where there was doubt about an item, it was
included, and over 95 per cent of the original questions were
retained.

As we were dealing with such a large number of variables, the
Statistical Package for the Social Sciences (Nie, Bent and Hull,
1970), a packaged system of computer programmes, was used.   This
provided ease of operation, economic tabulating ability and great
flexibility in handling data.   It was advantageous that one of
the full-time research staff was able to learn to operate the programme and avoid external errors and misunderstandings at this
crucial stage of the analysis.

Simple frequency tables were obtained for each variable providing us with a detailed profile of our families which has been drawn upon repeatedly throughout the text.   For convenience we have given a specific meaning within this study to certain phrases.   In order to avoid barraging the reader with figures and percentages, the following terminology has been adopted:

Most	Over 70%
Over half	51-70%
Under half	30-49%
A few	Less than 30%

Wherever these words occur in the text, it can be assumed that they refer to figures within the defined ranges.   Where more detail was required simple figures have been given rather than percentages.

The substantial number of variables with a response rate of less than 80 per cent were viewed with considerable reservation.   From the remaining items, those giving reasonably clear-cut impressions were selected.   Those variables which resulted in a wide spread of responses were either omitted or else commented on cursorily.   A small number of selected cross-tabulations were carried out in order to examine possible associations between variables and some new variables were created by combining existing variables.   While realising the statistical limitations of our data, for a few selected items dealing in the main with more straightforward demographic topics, some tests of significance were carried out for interest and have been reported on.

The quantified data relating to treatment were processed and analysed in a similar manner.   The bulk of the material on treatment, however, was analysed by hand.   The summaries documenting various aspects of the treatment process were dealt with in separate sections and time periods.   Each treatment topic was examined case by case for the first three months of treatment and each aspect of treatment was then summarised for the sample as a whole.

The latter periods of treatment were broken down as follows: three to twelve months, thirteen to twenty-four months and twenty-five to thirty-six months respectively.   These periods were analysed in less detail than the beginning period which tended to be more eventful.   Here we were mainly concerned with charting the broad changes in techniques and worker-client interaction, the main emphases of the cases having already been ascertained from the first three-month period.

With small numbers, it was not possible to think of identifying distinctive sub-groupings within the sample.   In the main, we looked for trends in the cases on aggregate.   This was particularly true for material describing family events and what the families were like, both currently and in the past.   In considering the treatment material, largely qualitative descriptions of processes, the individual case differences and possible sub-groupings were more apparent.   However, in order to draw even tentative conclusions about treatment we were often forced to look at what occurred in the majority of cases.   To give a glimpse of the variety and range of differences between families and to demonstrate the essentially heterogenous nature of our sample, case illustrations have been used.   To avoid identification, family details have been scrambled without distorting important research data and confidentiality has been preserved.

One striking feature is the common lack of information on the fathers and father figures in the study.   This stems from the difficulties encountered in our attempts to make direct contact with them.   Although it was our initial intention to include fathers in the treatment process, this was rarely achieved and in a substantial number of cases, fathers were never seen on their own.

CRITIQUE

The study aimed to examine at close quarters, over a substantial period of time, a small group of battering families and the social work treatment that they were offered.

This part of the project was devised and carried out in the main by social workers who acted as both therapists and researchers. We were primarily concerned with examining the battered child syndrome from the vantage point of social work practice and the combining of the casework and the research function was felt to offer the best prospects for this (Howe, 1974).   This gave rise to two serious drawbacks.   Firstly the most obvious drawback was that of bias.   Little was done to counter interviewer bias in this study and this imposes serious limitations on the validity of the findings.

Secondly, difficulties arose when there was conflict between the desired therapeutic action, e.g. supportive comments, and the need to probe for information.   Generally the therapeutic function took precedence, thus limiting the amount of data collected and accounting for the high rate of non-response on many items.   Unlike many clients encountered in our previous social work experience, battering parents presented exceptional problems in this respect. In other settings we have found more clients gaining gratification from talking about themselves and their lives.   Our abusive parents were relatively inarticulate, guarded, and on the whole were most unforthcoming about their personal histories.   They seemed to view discussion about many areas of their lives as a source of discomfort and pain rather than relief.   It is doubtful in fact whether more direct questioning on our part would have yielded any more information than that which was gathered slowly over time as trust and confidence developed in the client.   Certainly we would doubt the accuracy of data gathered under pressure from this particular client group.

The data examined were not very different in kind from that utilised in many social work transactions and ranged from 'hard' facts to 'soft' impressions.   The differences are apparent in the vast quantity of material which the study considered and the thoroughness with which information was gathered, recorded, and checked, where possible, against other data for accuracy.

A large part of any social work process entails the use of subjective assessments by the social worker of the client and his situation.   It also includes some kind of on-going appraisal of the effectiveness of both the client's and the worker's action in mitigating the client's problems, and what else needs to be done.

Social workers are trained to carry out these tasks as far as
possible with objectivity and skill, but the judgments employed in
the process are usually unverifiable.   This presents serious
problems to the social work researcher as so many of the crucial
data, being impressionistic, do not lend themselves to rigorous
analytical treatment.   None the less, as MacDonald (1959) points
out:

> Practice theory in social casework is necessarily to be con-
> structed on the observations of social case-workers.   The
> theoretically significant 'observables' are not simple facts
> like age and sex or even social class, nor are they client
> statements taken literally.

Hence a good deal of 'soft' impressions have been included in
the analysis with whatever relevant factual information could be
obtained.   This entailed the coding and quantification of subjective data and some elementary statistical treatment of it.

> This may be done intuitively and the result expressed verbally
> without benefit of numbers, but it is clear that where proce-
> dures for combining data into scores are definitely prescribed,
> errors of subjective interpretation and bias are eliminated in
> some degree (Peak, 1953).

Such figures can be misleading in so far as numerical presenta-
tions tend to be endowed with unjustified authority.   The same
applies to the so-called 'hard' data for different reasons;
namely that the small number of cases employed, the absence of
acceptable controls, and the method of sample selection by no
means eliminate the likelihood of the chance distribution of key
variables in the study.   Loeb (1960) remarks that many social
research reports should begin with the anecdotal phrase, 'Isn't it
interesting that ...?'   This is precisely the level at which our
figures should be understood.   However, we have tried to avoid
vague generalisations and where possible to quantify our impressions.   Too often there has been a failure in social work literature to carry objectivity even as far as this.   As Selltiz (1965)
states:

> The meaning of the data should not be speculated about when it
> is possible to test the speculations in the data themselves.
> Often ... the statements which the researcher sets forth as
> interpretation can be checked against his own data.   If con-
> firmed, it can be stated not as speculation but as a finding
> within the limitation of his study.

Without this stage being attempted, valid generalisation which is
the ultimate goal of research, cannot be made.

Chapter 2

BATTERING AS A PHENOMENON: THE INJURIES AND PROBLEMS OF DIAGNOSIS

This part of the study is based on twenty-five families. Although in all, thirty-three families were treated by the Department, five were excluded from analysis on methodological grounds. Another three cases were excluded because, after careful retrospective assessment, it was decided that these cases had been incorrectly diagnosed and did not fit our definition of the battered child syndrome.

In the first case of a two-year-old with no injury on referral, it emerged that the parents had raised the risk of abuse with their general practitioner in order to get a day nursery place. Long-term assessment of the child contrasted markedly with the features usually found in battered children and the behaviour problems of the parents emerged as the main difficulty. Efforts were made to secure the parents appropriate help in their own right but this was not obtained until they were eventually both placed on probation for petty larceny.

Another two-year-old presented with no current injury but a history of two previous injuries. This case was referred by a health visitor, who had been concerned about the family for over a year on account of the mother's depression and rejection of the child. On referral, the mother felt that her depression was in a state of remission and her interaction with the child seemed sensitive and warm. She expressed considerable guilt about her past rejecting behaviour and responded well to focused help, during which there were no indications of risk to the child.

The third family was referred because of a one-year-old's serious head injury. Although there was evidence of financial and marital stress and the child was helped by the arrangement of a day nursery place, in the course of treatment, the worker did not feel it to be a battering situation. This opinion was based on the warm quality of both parents' care and handling of the child, the absence of previous injuries and the evident plausibility of the parent's account of the accident.

The above three cases illustrate some of the difficulties of differential diagnosis and the need in cases of doubt, for a full assessment. This may entail a relatively lengthy period of work with the family before a firm decision can be reached. Social work

can still be of considerable value to families if the injury to the
child transpires to be the result of accident as demonstrated by
the above cases.   A non-accusatory approach to treatment offers
maximum opportunities for intervention, however uncertain the
initial diagnosis.   In a study of accidents and abuse, Okell (1971)
makes the following comment: 'Judging by the reception given to
interviewers by most parents, it was apparent that they welcomed a
chance to talk about what had happened to their child, and sought
reassurance themselves.'

TABLE 2.1   Sources of referral (N = 25)

	Number
Hospital	14
Health Department or Maternity and Child Welfare Clinic	7
General Practitioners	0
Social Services Department	2
NSPCC	2

    Over half of the children attended hospital with their referral
injury and the majority of our referrals came from hospitals.
Over half were in-patients at the time of referral although not all
of these cases were referred to us by the hospitals concerned.
Not all of the children in hospital on referral had serious
injuries and two without any form of physical abuse had been admitted as a protective measure, a practice which we would fully
endorse.
    Health visitors in the area were also active sources of case-
finding.   The number of cases included in the study which health
visitors referred does not reflect the amount of interest shown in
the project by many health visitors and the considerable number of
case consultations and discussions which took place.   Unfortunately, similar comments cannot be made about general practitioners,
who apart from one or two exceptional individuals, rarely made any
contact with the project (Silver et al., 1967).

CLASSIFICATION OF INJURIES

We gave much consideration to the various ways of grouping the
injuries to the children.   Finally, we concentrated on broadly
classifying the injuries by degree simply in terms of the total
extent of damage to the child's body on referral.   This system
gives no indication of the location or multiplicity of injuries
which are however, fully documented in Appendix A.   We did not
feel it was desirable to weight cases according to the age of the
child or the implications of the injury as, for example, did
Skinner and Castle (1969) when bruising to a young child's face
was rated as 'serious'.

Injuries were classified according to degree as follows:

Minor: Injuries confined in area and limited to superficial tissues.   This category could include light scratch marks; small, slight bruises; minute burns; and small welts.

Moderate: Surface injuries of an extensive or more serious nature and small subcutaneous injuries.   This could include cases of extensive bruising; large welts, lacerations; small haematomas and minor burns.

Severe: All bony and deep tissue injuries including, fractures, dislocations; subdural haematomas; serious burns and damage to internal organs.

Five families in which the child had not sustained an injury at the time of referral, were admitted to the study.   Three were cases in which the referred child had a history of previous injury and another was a young baby whose three-year-old sister had been injured in the past.   The fifth was a two-week-old child whom the mother had threatened to kill.   A careful review of these cases by the team led to the firm conclusion that all of the children in question were in danger of abuse and, for this reason, they have been included in the analysis.

TABLE 2.2 Degree of injury (N = 25)

None	Minor	Moderate	Severe
5	4	2	14

Okell (1972) has remarked that 'the degree of injury gives little indication of the degree of pathology in the family' and hence the future risk to the child.   In addition, the element of chance operating in the type of injuries sustained by the child should be stressed.

There is much to suggest that the battering parent is overwhelmed by, and responding primarily to, the force of his own feelings rather than the 'objective' stimulus provided by the child (Boardman, 1962).   In this view the parent's awareness of the object of his attack and his immediate environment is clouded by frustration and rage.   The outcome of the attack, that is the degree of injury to the child, may then be more dependent on chance factors than is often imagined.   Two cases illustrate this point well, both involve very young babies and the following accounts by the mothers of their feelings and actions are remarkably similar.

'Her little brother was so difficult, my husband was working all the time and I felt so alone.   She just kept on crying even when I picked her up, she just would not stop.   So I threw her on the bed and she bounced against the wall.   I think she might have hurt her leg then but she did not seem to cry after that. Another time I was changing her and her brother was all over the place wanting me to see to him.   He was very jealous of the baby.   She kept wriggling and crying and I lost my temper.   I lifted her up and dropped her down again on the bed hard.   She bounced against the window-sill and hit her arm.   Then she just screamed and screamed and kept on crying and I felt awful.

One night the baby was crying again and I just could not
stand it and I just threw her into her cot and she hit her head
on the back of the cot.   I knew it was wrong and did not want
to hurt her, but I just could not stand it any more.'
The above child was referred with multiple injuries and was on the
hospital danger list for several days, whereas the following incident resulted in one minor facial bruise.

'I can remember exactly how I used to feel even though I never
feel as bad now.   I used to really hate her, particularly when
I felt depressed because she used to get miserable as well ...
as though there is some kind of bond ... she is still like it
when I am moody, but I never feel as bad as I did then.   That
time I hit her, I bruised the side of her face and then threw
her really hard into her cot.   If she had carried on crying I
would have done it again too.   I did not feel guilty, I felt
justified because she was being such a nuisance.   I am convinced that I would have gone on and really hurt her if I had
not tried to tell someone about it.'

Although chance factors can greatly affect the outcome of a
battering incident as the two cases illustrate, chance cannot be
relied upon to protect a child from serious or fatal injury as the
syndrome is invariably characterised by repeated attacks on the
child, a point which both of these mothers make.   As Gwinn et al.
stated in 1961, 'the importance of this problem lies in the fact
that it is not self-limiting.'   Unlike the second mother, the
first felt unfortunately that she had no one to turn to and the
child was injured on several separate occasions.

LONG-TERM EFFECTS OF INJURIES

Two children died as a result of their referral injuries.   One
child died shortly after referral, and the other during the third
year subsequent to referral.

Three children sustained permanent physical handicap as a consequence of their referral injuries.   Two of these children suffered
serious residual brain damage, which in one case seriously affected
mobility and in the other caused physical retardation and also
audio/visual impairment.   The third child is thought to have
suffered minimal residual brain damage which did not appear to lead
to permanent physical handicap.   However, this child has a very
slight limp and a minor bone deformity in one arm as a result of
other injuries sustained at the time of referral.

One child was assessed as being severely mentally retarded as a
result of brain damage caused by his injuries.   Perception, cog-
nition, affect and behaviour appear to have been adversely affected,
and there are some features of autism.   Another two children have
been assessed as backward in intelligence, and it is felt that this
may be the result of brain damage due to injuries.   Certainly,
other aspects of their emotional development seem to show disturbance, but it is not known whether this is connected with brain
damage or environmental factors.   In all, four children suffered
long-term effects from their injuries.

THE REPEATING PATTERN OF INJURIES

A check of available official records revealed that eight children
had known histories of previous injury.   Five of the eight had been
injured on more than one occasion and one had an alarming record of
seven previous incidents of abuse.   Using the same criteria adopted
for the classification of the degree of injury on referral, the
childrens' previous injuries were classified according to maximum
severity as follows: three serious; two moderate; three minor.
These figures do not include cases of children presenting on referral with multiple injuries.   As can be seen from Appendix A, such
cases were common and single injuries the exception.   There is
much to suggest that multiple injuries were in many cases occasioned
by more than one battering incident within the month prior to
referral.   Often medical evidence, particularly radiological
findings (Caffey, 1957), give clear, though not always conclusive
(Silverman, 1968) indications of this when injuries appear to be at
different stages of healing.   Such evidence is a very important
aid to diagnosis, emphasising the need for a thorough medical examination, including a full skeletal survey (Griffiths and Moynihan,
1963), in all cases of suspected abuse.   The following case illustrates the need for diligence in this matter and 'the reluctance of
many physicians to accept the radiological signs as indications of
repetitive trauma and possible abuse' (Kempe et al., 1962).

    Four months before referral to the project, a one-year-old
began attending out-patients regularly as he had developed fits.
At the time facial bruising was noted and a head x-ray revealed
intercranial pressure, but no evidence of skull fracture or subdural haematoma.   A diagnosis of abuse was not made and the case
was treated routinely.   The referral injury consisted of a flake
fracture of the elbow for which the child had been taken to another
hospital, where he was admitted.   Shortly after referral the child
was discharged and re-attended the clinic at the original hospital,
when no further signs of trauma were observed.   At the next out-
patient appointment however, the child could scarcely walk and
bruising to his body was noted.   The child was not admitted to the
hospital immediately but sent instead for a full skeletal survey,
after which the mother left the hospital with the child.   The
x-ray results revealed a recent fracture to the leg and evidence of
several older long bone fractures which had not come to light in
previous examinations.   The child was then admitted from home
later that day.

EARLY CASE FINDING

In general, diagnosis proves difficult in many cases of abuse and
onerous in all.   Lack of firm evidence and professional avoidance
of the problem inhibits appropriate action.   In a substantial
number of cases referred to the project there were opportunities
for earlier intervention which could have averted subsequent
injuries.   There were such occasions as in the above case, when
previous injuries were receiving attention, but also many instances
where the parents had sought help themselves overtly for abuse or

in a disguised form.   Fourteen parents had sought help in the
past, more than one month prior to referral.   Ten parents had
actually sought help in the month before referral.   Some were
explicit about their fears of the child's being harmed.

A father rang the family doctor three days before this case was
referred, complaining that his wife had been smacking her one-month-
old baby.   The general practitioner did not visit or arrange for
the child to be seen, but discussed with the father by telephone
the possibility of arranging temporary care for the child with
relatives.   Two days later the father rang again as the child
appeared to be ill and was having difficulty breathing.   The doctor
visited immediately and arranged admission to hospital, whereupon
it was discovered that the child had extensive head injuries
probably caused earlier that day.

In another family, although neither parent mentioned the danger
of abuse, there were clear indications from them that they were
having great difficulty in coping with the child.   The child had
multiple injuries on referral and this gives an even more pointed
example of professional failure to act.   A day nursery matron
noted serious bruising on a six-month-old baby who had just started
to attend her nursery.   She reported what she saw to the social
services department but no action was taken.   The following day,
both parents visited the social services department and requested
that this child be received into care.   The request was refused.
Four days later, a social worker in another agency learned from the
parents that the baby had been left alone.   She reported this to
the social services department, who arranged for one of their
social workers to visit and the child was received into care.
Facial bruising was obvious at the time but a full medical examination was not arranged until the following day.   This revealed
serious head injuries and damage to the limbs and the case was
referred to our project.

THE BATTERING INCIDENT AND INITIAL
EXPLANATIONS GIVEN BY THE PARENTS

In the majority of our cases it was the parents who drew attention
to the fact that something was wrong with the child or their relationship with him which led to a diagnosis of suspected abuse.
In four families this was not done and the request for child protection was initiated by a friend, a neighbour, or health visitor
without the parent's knowledge.

An initial admission of abuse as distinct from an expressed fear
of harming the child when there was no injury on referral, was rare
and occurred in only three cases.   Two involved 'moderate' injuries and the third a severe injury.   Other explanations were more
common during the first examination of the child as can be seen
from Table 2.3

TABLE 2.3   Reasons parents gave for seeking help (N = 25)

Sudden appearance of inexplicable physical symptom	8
Accident to child	5
Admitted abuse	3
Fear of injuring child (no injury on referral)	2
Difficult behaviour of child	2
Unable to care for child	1
Parents did not seek help	4

As discussed below, the initial information was often elaborated upon by one or both parents.   Sometimes it was changed.   However, in spite of much questioning by different personnel, only a further two parents, both with severely injured children, actually admitted causing harm to their child.   Thus, of the twenty cases of children with injuries on referral, only five parents admitted that the injuries were inflicted.   O'Neill et al. (1973) found in a study of 110 abused children that 'in ninety-five cases the history was inaccurate or deliberately evasive.'

In our opinion, admission of abuse was dependent on the emotional state and attitude of the parent rather than the techniques of the questioner.   We had the opportunity of considering a wide variety of cases in which the approach of the person enquiring about the injuries, varied from the accusatory to the placatory. Both approaches figured in the few cases of admitted abuse.   In the majority of cases neither approach led to an admission on the part of the parents (Kempe et al., 1962).   The account which parents give about the cause of an injury and the way they give it is usually of great diagnostic value.   Careful attention to this area often highlights the implausible nature of stories about accidents.

A father took his three-month-old baby with multiple injuries to hospital saying that she had 'fallen down' that morning and had been crying a lot since then.   When informed of the serious damage, and questioned more closely, he said that the other child in the family, a toddler of eighteen months, was very rough with the baby and often hit her with his toys.   He later described an incident in which the toddler allegedly pulled the baby off a low bed.   Several days later he admitted inflicting the injuries.

Such tentative and hazy suggestions about accidents, rarely backed up with much detail, are typical.   Sometimes the suggested accident is not improbable, but changes in the account also occur.

Several explanations of the cause of a fractured skull in an eight-month-old were offered by the parents.   None of them was felt to be adequate and the parents remained vague about what had happened.   They thought that the child might have fallen out of bed.   Later father said, 'maybe she hit her head on the fender', adding defensively, 'you can't stop them crawling around you know'.

Another common feature in the parents' account is the lack of curiosity and lack of expressed anxiety about the cause of injury (Holter and Friedman, 1968). Explanations are rarely proffered willingly (Griffiths and Moynihan, 1963) and most parents do not enter into the search for a possible cause. Instead, they seem to be trying to avoid any sense of responsibility for the child's injuries and sometimes refuse to suggest any possible explanation at all. This happened with the parents of a two-month-old baby. The child had a head injury, scratch marks on the face, and bruises on the stomach. In spite of repeated questioning, the parents were cool and impassive even though the child was critically ill. They refused to make any comment about what might have occasioned the injuries and simply maintained throughout that they 'did not know'.

DETERMINING WHICH PARENT
INFLICTED THE INJURIES

As there were few cases of admitted abuse, the task of determining which parent inflicted the injuries was problematic. In over half of the twenty cases with referral injuries, both parents were assessed as having the potential for abuse. After careful eval-uation, we concluded that nine mothers and three fathers had inflicted injuries but in the remaining eight cases we could not arrive at a firm decision by the end of the project. For example, one father of a two-year-old with a serious fracture dis-closed in the course of treatment that he had been plagued by fantasies of inflicting violence on the rest of the family. After a good relationship had been established with the social worker, he was asked whether he had ever hurt any of the children. He replied openly and convincingly that he had not. The mother appeared to enjoy the children but did show marked impatience with the abused child on occasions. The accounts of the injury given by both parents were hazy and identification of the abuser was not possible.

In our study with a ratio of three to one, it appears that abusive behaviour is more prevalent amongst mothers than fathers. In other studies, the preponderance of mothers was less pronounced. De Francis (1963) and Simons et al. (1966) independently found ratios of three mothers to two fathers in their samples and Skinner and Castle (1969) report a ratio of four to three. Steele and Pollock (1968) feel that the ratio is related to the respective amount of time each parent is spending with the child, as does Kempe (1971):

Depending on the make-up of the group under study findings vary. For example, in one public Denver Hospital serving a population with high paternal unemployment and, therefore, increased exposure of unemployed fathers to small children, the ratio of mother to father battering is 1:1. In another public hospital serving a highly employed group, we found that for 80 battering mothers there were only 20 fathers (4:1).

In our view, it is not only a question of which parent is most exposed to the demands of the child over a long period. Sudden

changes in family circumstances, as in one of our cases where a
mother was admitted to hospital, may leave a vulnerable parent
coping with the child on his own for the first time.   Brief
exposure to an isolated caretaking role in a parent for whom this
is unfamiliar may be enough to precipitate abuse.

PROVOCATION BY THE OTHER PARENT

Certainly, we would agree with Steele and Pollock (1968) that both
parents play a part in abuse.   'Usually only one parent actually
attacks the infant.   The other parent almost invariably contributes,
however, to the abusive behaviour either by openly accepting it or
by more subtly abetting it, consciously or unconsciously.'
   We found little evidence to suggest that both parents had
directly collaborated in any battering incident.   In most cases,
however, there were indications that the non-abusing parent had
played a part in provoking the other partner to attack the child.
Such provocative behaviour usually took the form of denigration of
the abuser's parenting abilities.   It was also associated with
the non-abusing parent's attitude to the child.   This tended to
be dismissive or over-identified so that either the abusing parent
was actively encouraged to reject the child or else resented the
pride of place which the child had in their partner's heart.
   Mrs X found great difficulty in coping with a home and two
   children.   Her husband was angered by this and constantly complained that she was a 'useless mother'.   He often told her
   how his own mother had managed five children and a nursing
   career without a husband to support her.   Mr X was fond of the
   children and tended to idealise the youngest one.   However, he
   only had time for them when he felt like it, expecting his wife
   to know when he was tired and keep the children quiet.   He
   never chastised the children himself but if they troubled him
   he would rage at his wife, sometimes resorting to blows.
   It is not difficult to discern the provocation in the above case
which led the mother to injure severely the youngest child.   In
most of our families, similar factors were operating, though not to
this degree.   In addition, the non-abusing parent usually failed
to protect the child by default.   Obvious signs of a breakdown in
the relationship between the abuser and the child were ignored and
signs of injury to the child overlooked in most cases.

FURTHER AIDS TO DIFFERENTIAL
DIAGNOSIS

Lack of concern and apparent absence of guilt on the part of the
parents in most cases of abuse are in contrast to the kinds of
reactions usually displayed by parents of children who are involved
in genuine accidents.   For instance, in a study of children suffering from accidental burns and scalds, Martin (1970) makes the point
that nearly all of the parents, unlike battering parents, not only
provided an accurate account of the accident, 'but also show marked
guilt'.

It would be wrong however to give the impression that most battering parents do not display any emotion when questioned about their child's injuries.   The reluctance to talk and a guarded, defensive attitude is often present but can give way to consider-able distress.   Usually, however, the distress is related to their own fears and is occasioned by the questioning itself rather than any display of concern for the child's condition.

One mother was initially unforthcoming and apparently calm. She gradually became very upset and tearful about the circumstances wnich caused the injury, but ignored the child, a two-year-old who was obviously in pain and frightened by the unfamiliarity of the hospital setting.   She asked no questions about the medical treat-ment which the child required, and was apparently unperturbed by the prospect of his admission.

Lack of concern for the child is one dimension of the parent-child relationship which can be observed at the initial examination when abuse is suspected.   The other obvious diagnostic feature of the relationship is the actual interaction, or lack of it, between parent and child at the time   (Gregg, 1968).   The quality of this may be characterised by disregard, disdain or even anger.   At best, awkwardness and badly timed responses on the part of the parent towards the child are often seen.   Also, abusive parents often attribute characteristics to the child which do not fit with the observations.   For example, a parent may say a child is clumsy when he is obviously agile (Kempe, 1969).

A final diagnostic pointer worthy of note and mentioned in several other studies, for example, Cameron et al. (1966), Gregg and Elmer (1969), are delays between the injury and the time at which parents seek medical attention.   This area is only worthy of consideration in cases of serious injury and in our sample, con-taining fourteen such cases, we found that in nine cases there had been delays of over two hours.   Often the delay was longer and stretched up to twenty-four hours.

TRIGGER FACTORS IN THE CHILD

We looked for comments about specific behaviour in the child which might have triggered the battering incident.   Our information is extremely limited as few parents talked openly.   Some workers felt confident about intimations on the part of the parents of what irritated them when the child was injured, without direct state-ments about the injury.   Others felt unable to comment on this area as the parents had given no indications about trigger factors.

In accordance with Steele and Pollock (1968), crying was seen as the most common trigger factor and the child's assertiveness or temper tantrums mentioned in a further three cases.   'He's always getting into things.'   'He's getting too big for his boots.' 'She's so stubborn and wilful.'   The last three quotations refer to older children and crying obviously occurs more frequently with babies.   However, crying can still be a potent source of provoca-tion with older children.

'I noticed Judy had started to rock like Ian and was learning bad habits off him.   Ian had been whining all the time, I was

feeling a bit depressed still after the baby's arrival, I'd
been in the flat for three days without going out and had
toothache on and off.   It must have been in the afternoon
when I suddenly lashed out at Ian, hit him in the chest and
winded him.   He started to cry and my husband called out "Do
keep that kid quiet because of the neighbours."   I put my hand
over his mouth to shut him up and suddenly I realised he'd
stopped breathing and was quite limp.'

What is worth bearing in mind on the subject of crying and
equally other difficult behaviour of the child, is that the parents
make the rules.   As Henry (1972) states:

In our culture the illegality of crying focuses on two ideas:
that the child will be spoiled and that the parent will be
exploited.   These can be disregarded however, if the parent
decides that the reason the child is crying is 'serious'.   The
right to decide what is serious is reserved to the parent.

It can be seen that when parents have talked fully about abuse,
they mention a variety of pressures on them at the time of the
incident.   Their personal state or mood, 'toothache', 'depression', 'feeling miserable', comes into it along with anxiety about
the neighbours or siblings, in addition to any specific irritants
in the child.   It seems that, as Boardman (1962) states, 'An
adult who inflicts injuries is not reacting to the specific
behaviour of the child, but to his own feelings.'

It would therefore be misleading to seek in the behaviour of
the child at the time of the incident a simple cause and effect
relationship or condition and response.   Nor is it necessarily the
case that the child's behaviour is seen as the 'last straw'.
Although it may act in this way in some cases, parental frustration
is usually more generalised.   As one mother said, 'these last few
months there have been problems, problems and more problems.'

We agree with Oliver et al. (1974) that 'it is a mistake to
place great emphasis on the immediate precipitants of abuse.'   In
our view the whole history and context of the parents' lives must
be viewed in order to discern the matrix of abuse 'since abuse
undoubtedly results from a complex of pressures and reactions'
(Elmer, 1966).   This includes, their early background, marriage,
social situation, and the development of their relationships with
the battered child from conception, which will be discussed in the
succeeding chapters.

Chapter 3

COMPOSITION OF THE SAMPLE

Our sample is small and therefore subject to local bias, but it
includes the majority of cases available in our catchment area for
the duration of intake.   In spite of limitations, we decided to
compare the demographic characteristics of our sample with the
general population and the findings of other researchers in child
abuse.   We have tried to make our comparisons as valid as possible
by using data, where available, from comparable samples.   For
example, we have used some local borough statistics and weighted
the figures according to the proportion of referrals from each
borough.
    It was surprising to find that, in spite of the high possibility
of bias, in many respects our families did not differ from other
comparable families in the locality.   This observation may help
to dispel some of the stereotypes associated with the battered
child syndrome.   It also underlines the dangers of attempting to
identify abusive families from only superficial characteristics.

TABLE 3.1 Sex of the children (N = 25)

Male	13	52%
Female	12	48%

    Most researchers have not found any marked differences in the
sex distribution of battered children and the distribution in the
normal population.   Gil (1970) studying the national trends in
the USA found a slight preponderance of boys over girls in the
lower age range of reported cases, as did O'Neill et al. (1973)
and Skinner and Castle (1969) in Britain.   In our sample, boys
were no more subject to serious injuries than girls.

TABLE 3.2   Age of the children (N = 25)

0-12 months	13-24 months	25-36 months	37-48 months
13	4	6	2
52%	16%	24%	8%

x^2 = 20.12 p < 0.001
(Mean - 17 months; Mode - 9 months; Median - 12 months)

The main feature is the significantly high frequency of children under the age of one year in a project open to children of any age up to four.   Others have noted this feature and Skinner and Castle (1969) support the view that 'the younger the child, the more likely it is to be battered.'   A variety of factors could be in operation in respect of this picture.   An obvious point is that young infants are simply physically more vulnerable, and less mobile than older children.   Against this, injuries to younger children are more easily concealed.   Perhaps a more important factor stems from the view that battering is a response of frustration on the part of parents who are unable to meet their children's needs.   The younger the child, the greater the dependency.

TABLE 3.3   Ages of the children and the degree of injury (N = 25)

Age of child	Degree of injury	
	Severe	Not severe
Under 2 years	14	3
2-4 years	0	8
Total	14	11

x^2 = 11.1 p < 0.001

When the age of the child was compared with the degree of his injury as rated in the previous chapter, it emerged that the seriously injured children were all under two years of age with the majority under one.   This was a statistically significant tendency suggesting that younger children are not only at greater risk of injury but their injuries are likely to be more serious.

TABLE 3.4   Family size (N = 25)

Number of children in family	1	2	3	4	5
Number of families in sample	13	7	3	0	2
	52%	28%	12%	0%	8%

The proportion of only children in the study was surprising. This tends to counter the view still expressed by some authors that child abuse is a product of large families where parents are over-burdened by the sheer numbers of children for whom they have to care.

TABLE 3.5 Ordinal position (N = 25)

Ordinal position of battered child	1st	2nd	3rd	4th	5th
Number of children in sample	15	6	2	1	1
	60%	24%	8%	4%	4%

It is not surprising that the majority of the battered children were first-born as nearly half the sample were only children. Of the rest, half were the younger of two-child families.

THE SIBLINGS

In the twelve families with more than one child, ten contained siblings under four years of age and three of the families had three children under four. Although by sheer size of family, the factor of 'maternal overload' emphasised by Elmer (1971) is not apparent, a number of families were coping with two or more children born in quick succession.

Two of the twelve families had siblings with a recorded history of previous injury, thought to be the result of abuse. Both injuries would fit into the category of 'moderate' according to our classification.

THE PARENTS

All of the mothers in the sample were the natural mothers of the battered child. Battered children living with adoptive or foster parents had been excluded from the study at the outset by our criteria for referral. It would, however, have been possible for families with a natural father and step-mother to have found their way into the sample. This did not occur.

Of the males in the households on referral, twenty-two were the natural fathers of the battered child, another two were established step-fathers and only one male was in a transient relationship with the rest of the family. Thus, 88 per cent of the children were living with both natural parents, a slightly higher percentage than found by Skinner and Castle (1969). Nineteen of the couples were legally married.

TABLE 3.6 Ages of parents (N = 50)

Ages of parents	Fathers	Mothers	Total
Under 21 years	2	5	7
21-25 years	8	10	18
26-30 years	6	8	14
31-35 years	4	1	5
36 years and over	5	1	6

The age range of the fathers was wide and the distribution was not skewed towards the younger end.   The mean, mode and median age for fathers was twenty-eight years.   Mothers were concentrated in the twenty to thirty years age group.   Thus our parents were not particularly youthful.   The mean, mode and median age of the mothers was twenty-five years, showing on average a three-year difference between the fathers.   Although the difference between the average ages of the mothers and fathers is not striking, age differences in individual families were often more marked.

There is some controversy over the youthfulness of abusive parents.   De Francis (1963) and Gil (1970) both question the assumption that abusive parents are chronologically immature, but their large national samples include children up to eighteen years of age.   Smith et al. (1973) report mean ages of 23.5 years for mothers and 27.0 years for fathers respectively.   These figures appear unexceptional and the comparable figures for the controls in their study are not given.   However, Smith et al. do stress the low mean age at which their mothers conceived their first child which concurs with our findings discussed in chapter 4.

TABLE 3.7 Ethnic origin of parents (N = 50)

Place of birth	Present study	Borough figures
England and Wales	25	34
Scotland	1	2
Northern Ireland	1	0
Irish Republic	9	2
India and Pakistan	5	1
Caribbean	2	1
Africa	2	1
Mediterranean	1	0
Other	4	9

Table 3.7 compares the country of origin of the parents in our study with the figures for the local population provided by the

1971 Census GLC (1974).   Unfortunately, we were unable to obtain
figures for electoral wards and have used data for the three
boroughs as a whole.   This was weighted in accordance with the
proportion of our referrals received from each borough.   The percentages were then taken to a base of fifty (our sample size) and
shown as whole numbers.   In view of our sample size, we felt that
whole numbers give a more realistic presentation of data than percentages.   Although a statistical analysis was not possible given
the spread of nationalities in such a limited sample, the battering
parents do appear to be more cosmopolitan in origin than other
residents in the local community.   The most interesting feature
is the relatively high proportion of parents born in Ireland and
India and Pakistan.   However, the three inner London Boroughs in
which our study took place contain a great many neighbourhoods
where different ethnic groups are variously represented.   It is
clear from our observations that our sample came predominantly
from certain parts of the borough and ward figures could have provided a more valid comparison.

SOCIAL CLASS

Another area of controversy for researchers in child abuse is
social class.   The dispute often has more to do with the differences in emphasis and interpretations of findings than with the
findings themselves.   Thus Steele and Pollock (1968) assert that
abuse is not confined to any one social class, whilst for Gil
(1970) abuse is over-concentrated amongst the poor.
   We compared our sample with the findings of Smith et al. (1973)
and also national figures provided by the 1971 Census (Office of
Population Censuses and Surveys, 1974).

TABLE 3.8   Social class of families (N = 25)

	Social class				
	I	II	III	IV	V
Present study	0	1	12	10	2
Smith et al.	0	3	26	56	53

$x^2 = 13.00$ $p < 0.01$

   Smith et al. (1973) attach considerable importance to low
social class as a feature of abusive families.   Our findings do
not concur with this view and although our sample differed from
the general population in terms of class composition, the difference was not significant.

TABLE 3.9 Social class of families (N = 25)

	Social class		
	I & II	III	IV & V
Present study	1	12	12
National figures	6	12	7

$X^2 = 4.8$ $p > 0.05$

We combined the upper and lower ends of the social class scale and compared our sample with national figures (Government Statistical Services, (1974)).   The result was not statistically significant but did show a trend.

TABLE 3.10 Socio-economic groups (N = 25)

	Socio-economic groups						
	3,4	1,2 13	12,14	8,9	5,6	7,10 15	11,16 17
Present study	0	2	1	8	3	6	5
Borough figures	2	3	1	5	6	4	4

Key based on Registrar General's Classification of Occupations, Office of Population Censuses and Surveys (1970).

SEG	Occupation
3, 4	Professional workers
1, 2, 13	Employers and managers
12, 14	Self-employed workers (non-professional)
8, 9	Skilled manual workers and supervisors
5, 6	Non-manual workers and supervisors
7, 10, 15	Personal service workers, semi-skilled manual workers, agricultural workers
11, 16, 17	Unskilled manual workers and unclassified occupations

We classified our families in terms of socio-economic groups, a more carefully graded system of classification than social class, in order to compare them with the local (as opposed to national) figures which were presented in this form (GLC, 1974).   On inspection, our sample shows very little difference from the local population.   For comparison, we amalgamated the socio-economic groups into manual and non-manual occupations but the result was not statistically significant.

SUMMARY

The battered children in our sample were almost equally distributed between the sexes and there was no correlation between the sex of the child and the degree of his injury.   Although the project accepted referrals of children up to the age of four years, just over half were under one year of age and all of the severe injuries were sustained by children under two.   Most of the battered children were either only children or the youngest of two.   All of the mothers and twenty-two of the fathers were the natural parents of the battered child.

In terms of demographic features, there was little evidence to suggest that our sample of twenty-five abusive families differed markedly from the population from which they were drawn.   There was a slight difference in composition between our sample and the national population in respect of social class.   Socio-economic differences were even less noticeable when our sample was compared by socio-economic groupings with the local population.   Our parents were not predominantly young and the families were not large.

Nearly half of the parents were born outside the UK although only 18 per cent were non-white.   The wide variations in the countries of origin of the parents can partly be explained by the very mixed neighbourhoods in which our cases were concentrated. However, this observation does not explain why referrals came mainly from certain areas of the boroughs rather than others.   It could be that some local agencies were more alert to the problem of abuse than others.   Certainly, cases tended to be referred from the vicinity of Denver House rather than the farther corners of the boroughs.

In addition, certain social stresses could be associated with abuse, and certain neighbourhoods may contain a higher rate of stress, principally in terms of poor housing.   From the findings presented in chapter 5 there is evidence to suggest that inadequate accommodation was an important feature in the social circumstances of our families.

Chapter 4

THE CHILDREN

1 PREDISPOSING FACTORS TO BATTERING

We felt that it was important to find out about the kinds of stress
experienced during the ante-natal period and any complications of
the pregnancy and delivery to see whether these factors might have
affected the mother's anticipation and perception of the baby and
the development of the early mother-child relationship. Detailed
information on the conception, gestation and birth of the battered
child and family events during this time was derived from the
medical records and from the mothers themselves. Whilst not
underestimating the importance of the fathers' feelings about the
pregnancy, we were unable to obtain sufficient direct information
from them for inclusion in the study, as has proved to be the case
on many other topics. It is noteworthy that the mothers were much
more forthcoming on the subject of the pregnancy in contrast to
other aspects of their personal lives.

Attitudes to conception

One of the most striking findings to emerge is that for the majority of mothers the pregnancy was an unplanned, unwelcome event,
which was approached, in the main, with resignation and helpless-
ness. Only five children were apparently planned and wanted,
whereas half of the mothers freely admitted that their children
were unwanted. It is recognised that a sizeable proportion of
all pregnancies are unplanned and unwanted and that such pregnancies are more common amongst working-class women than others and
especially prevalent, for example, amongst those who conceive
before marriage (see Bone, 1973). Nevertheless, we feel that the
predominantly negative attitudes to conception amongst the mothers
in our study had far-reaching implications for the kind of relationship they established with their children. Twelve of the
children in our sample were conceived out of wedlock; eight were
born illegitimate. This is in keeping with the findings of Smith
et al. (1974) that the occurrence of premarital conception and
illegitimate births amongst battering mothers of every age group

in his sample is higher than national norms, even when social class
adjustments are made.   Likewise, in a study of severely ill-
treated young children by Oliver et al. (1974), the rate of illegitimacy was considerably higher than in the local population
studied.

In spite of their adverse reactions to conception it appears
that most of these mothers felt powerless to change their situation.
Only four mothers sought a termination of the pregnancy;   three
were refused termination by their doctors and one changed her mind.
Two of these mothers tried to have their babies adopted immediately
after the birth.

A number of mothers described how they had felt very negative
towards their babies throughout the pregnancy, including one who
commented, 'I did not feel ready to be a mother.   I was not old
enough to give, give, give, all the time.   I needed to take too.
I felt nothing.   It did not feel like having a person inside me.
Somehow I felt it would go away or once it was born, it would not
be there.'

There is no doubt that the prospect of having a child at that
particular point in time was traumatic for many of the mothers and
aroused considerable doubts and fears about their ability to cope
with parenthood.   Eighteen mothers reported feeling very distressed during the pregnancy, typically describing themselves as
weepy and depressed, very anxious generally, and fearful about
actually giving birth.   Only four of these mothers were noted to
have emotional problems by medical personnel involved in their care
and one received in-patient psychiatric treatment.

Major stresses during pregnancy

In view of the negative reactions to becoming pregnant expressed by
many mothers and the circumstances surrounding conception, it is
hardly surprising that the pregnancy itself emerged as the major
source of stress in eighteen cases.   It is interesting that in a
study of infant accidents (Elmer, 1972) amongst the abusive
mothers, pregnancy ranked fifth as a social stress and superceded
death of a family member which took eleventh place, whereas the
non-abusive mothers ranked death far ahead of pregnancy which was
in twelfth place.   Also, Elmer (1971) has found a close association between child abuse and burdens related to pregnancy and the
spacing of children which has led her to draw attention to the concept of 'maternal overload'.   This certainly seems to apply in a
number of our cases in the sense that the mothers had conceived
young or conceived a second child quickly.   Seven of our mothers
had given birth to another child within ten months prior to con-
ceiving the battered child and in five of these cases the period
was less than five months.

Marital problems and housing problems emerged as other major
sources of stress in over half the cases.   In ten cases, the
relationship between the parents became increasingly strained as
the pregnancy advanced;   one father left home for a period of time
and two fathers deserted altogether.   Five couples who were precipitated into marriage or cohabitation by the pregnancy clearly

experienced difficulties in adjusting to the new role of marital
partner and parent in the space of a few months.

Many of the parents were living in poor, cramped accommodation,
unsuitable for the arrival of a new baby.   Hence they spent much
of the pregnancy desperately seeking an alternative, which must
have added to their general insecurity and anxiety.

The three stresses already discussed formed a common pattern in
many cases but no other types of stress featured prominently across
the sample as a whole.   Rather it appears that a whole configura-
tion of events proved stressful at the individual case level with
the result that very few families experienced a trouble-free
pregnancy.

Sources of support

Bearing in mind the fact that many of the mothers reported that
they were in a distressed, anxious state throughout the pregnancy,
another important finding is the extent to which they lacked a
supportive network.   The workers' overall impressions were that
few mothers were able to get support from their partners, extended
family, friends, neighbours or professional workers.   Indeed it
seemed that the majority of mothers had no one with whom they
could share their fears and anxieties about the pregnancy and on
whom they could rely for emotional support.   Only six fathers
were perceived as supportive and in only four cases was support
seen to be available from the extended family.   Furthermore, it
emerged that during the pregnancy a quarter of the mothers had
actually lost a usual source of support which affected them considerably.   This ranged from desertion by the father or the traumatic loss of a maternal grandmother through suicide, to a mother's
only friend moving away from the area.

This marked lack of support is a finding common to other studies
of abusive parents.   However, Elmer (1972) suggests that the
absence of support cannot be wholly attributed to environmental
deficits but must also be associated with the mothers' reluctance
to trust and make use of any supportive resource.

In this context it is interesting to look at the kind of ante-
natal care sought by the mothers.   It is well known that the
successful outcome of a pregnancy is aided by both the quality and
availability of maternity, obstetric and paediatric services.
Yet, however good and however readily available these may be, they
can only come into play if a mother chooses to make use of them and
does so at the optimal time.   In our study it certainly seemd that
in many cases the mothers' reluctance to make use of available
resources combined with their negative attitudes towards the pregnancy affected the care they sought for themselves.   Three mothers
did not receive any ante-natal care and nearly half the mothers
only received it occasionally.   It has been suggested that abusive
mothers may perhaps avoid seeking ante-natal care because they are
unconsciously denying the fact that they are pregnant (Court,
1971).   This seems to be true for a number of mothers in the
latter group who did not seek confirmation of their pregnancies at
an early stage and who only sought ante-natal care in the seventh

month, by which time they could presumably no longer continue to
deny the fact of their pregnancy.   Medical records revealed that
common disorders of pregnancy such as toxaemia were diagnosed in
ten mothers who received at least some ante-natal care and that
another mother had a threatened abortion.

Details of confinement and the neonatal period

We were keen to learn about our mothers' confinement experiences
with the battered child and events during the neonatal period.
For many this was a recent experience as half the children in the
sample were born in the year prior to referral.   However, we were
disappointed in many cases by the lack of detailed information
about the confinement available from medical records.   This is
one example of the disadvantages of collecting data retrospectively,
but in spite of the difficulties we encountered, some interesting
facts emerged.
    All but one of the mothers gave birth to their babies in hospi-
tal.   Fourteen mothers had normal deliveries, four mothers were
induced and seven mothers had abnormal deliveries (breech deliveries, forceps deliveries and caesarian sections were classified as
abnormal).   Half the mothers still recalled the birth as a very
painful, frightening experience for which they were ill-prepared.
Only a few mothers felt they had an easy time or had positive
memories of the confinement.   In view of the fact that many
mothers reported that they were extremely anxious during pregnancy
and apprehensive about giving birth, it is interesting to note
that several studies have indicated that there is a relationship
between high anxiety levels during pregnancy and difficulties
during delivery (for a review of these studies see McDonald, 1968).
Some of the mothers' graphic descriptions of the birth are recorded
below.
    'The day I knew I was having it I broke out in a sweat.   I was
    that terrified of what was going to happen to me.   I remember
    shouting 'get it out, kill it or something.'   It was that
    agonising, I didn't know what to expect.   They were all giving
    me different instructions and I was shouting and swearing.'
    'They kept making the drip go faster and faster.   It was
    horrible.   I think in the end I kept passing out it was so
    painful.   I don't remember him actually being born.   They
    tied my legs up.   I can't stand that.   I hate being restric-
    ted and I go all panicky.   They had to use forceps as well and
    that didn't help any.   They kept me drugged but I was a
    nervous wreck by the end of it all and I was quite badly torn.'
    'It was terrible.   I've never been so frightened in my life.
    I can remember screaming hysterically before the anaesthetic
    was given to me.'
    'I was told I was the worst patient the hospital had ever had
    because I made so much fuss.   I was accidentally taken to the
    wrong hospital when I went into labour so I had to get up and
    be moved to the right hospital.   I felt the birth was all for
    nothing at first and I just didn't care.'
While the physical care of pregnant women in this country is of

a very high standard, much less professional attention has been
paid to their emotional needs and to helping them establish mutually
satisfying relationships with their babies.   It is only in recent
years that research by ethologists and developmental psychologists
has drawn attention to the fact that some common obstetric and newborn intensive care practices may seriously impede maternal-child
bonding, thus increasing the risk of rejection, neglect and battering.   Gradually awareness is increasing that 'mothering does not
always come naturally - it requires the stimulus of infant behaviour
and the opportunity for early interaction' (Rutter, 1974).   Con-.
siderable importance is now being attached to the nature of the
initial contact between mothers and babies.   For example, Macfarlane and his colleagues (1974) are studying the way mothers greet
and respond to their babies immediately after the delivery as it is
thought that such factors may prove useful indicators of the
quality of future mothering behaviour.   Discussions with our
mothers about their initial reactions and responses to their babies
proved very revealing.

TABLE 4.1 Mother's initial feelings for the baby (N = 23)

Very loving/motherly/accepting	2
Fairly loving/motherly/accepting	2
Ambivalent	5
Neutral/no intense feelings	2
Fairly rejecting/unsure	3
Openly rejecting/not loving/not motherly	9

   Only four mothers recalled experiencing immediate, positive
feelings towards their babies.   A few described having a very
mixed reaction comprised of feelings of warmth and attachment
together with uncertainty and fear.   Two mothers could not recall
having any intense feelings for their babies at first.   Half of
the mothers said that their initial reactions were negative and
that in the main they felt detached, cold, unsure and awkward with
their babies and in a few instances openly hostile.   Some of
these mothers were especially disappointed by the sex of the baby
or somewhat revolted by its appearance.   Some of the comments
made by the different mothers appear below.
   'When they brought him to me he was bright red and screaming.
   He looked really horrible and I felt awful.   I think things
   got off to a bad start after that.   I used to say to my
   husband that I didn't really like him.'
   'I was that disappointed and I felt so let down.   I wanted a
   boy so much.   She just looked like a round ball with no eyes.'
   'I wouldn't hold the baby till the girl in the next bed had
   examined him and told me that he really was all right.   Even
   when he was so tiny he was very active and didn't seem like a
   normal baby.'

'From the beginning he never felt my baby.   I wanted a girl so
I could give her all the love and affection I never had.   I
kept saying I didn't really feel anything for him but nobody
really listens.'
'When I heard there was something wrong with him and they took
him away I felt awful.   I thought it was because I hadn't
wanted him.'
'Right from the start he was wilful and wicked and would never
sleep or eat properly.'
While it is recognised that all this information is retrospective and obtained from the mothers after referral for suspected
abuse, it seems likely that at least half of the mothers experienced
some difficulties in claiming and relating to their babies in the
early stages, which might have been picked up by perceptive hospital staff.   Several mothers remarked to us that the atmosphere of
enforced cheerfulness in hospital was not conducive to expressing
or discussing their anxieties and negative feelings nor was there
much opportunity for this.   One mother reflected on her abortive
attempt to get some support and understanding as follows:
'I confided to the Sister that I felt awkward and did not
really know how to do things for the baby but all she replied
was, "you'll soon know what to do by instinct."   What is all
this instinct, I'd like to know and where does it come from?'
'I used to look at myself and wonder whether I was abnormal
because I didn't feel it.   I now think you have to work at
mother love.   It doesn't just come like the books say.'

Adoption plans

While reflecting on the mothers' early reactions to their babies it
is relevant to note that adoption was seriously considered in only
four cases.   In two of these, the children were thought to be unsuitable for adoption on medical grounds and the mothers' plans
were thwarted.   In the third case, the mother decided to keep her
baby to oppose her parents who were pressing for adoption and the
other mother withdrew her baby from the adoption agency's residential nursery when he was just over two months old and placed him
with a daily-minder.
The attitudes of these four mothers towards their children
remained consistently rejecting or extremely ambivalent up to the
time of referral.

Condition of the children at birth and developmental history

The more we discover about the reciprocal influences of the mother
on the child's behaviour, and of the child on maternal behaviour,
the harder it is to untangle whether factors in the parents or
factors in the child contribute most to abuse.   For many years
infants tended to be regarded as passive beings and researchers
concentrated on looking at how a mother's attitude to child-rearing and her actual maternal behaviour shaped the behaviour of the
infant.   However, during the past decade the role of the infant

in patterning the mother's behaviour has received increasing attention and researchers such as Richards (1972, 1974a) and his
colleagues have demonstrated that neo-natal behaviour can exert
considerable influence on the mother's behaviour.

In this context it is interesting to note that several researchers (Milowe and Lourie, 1964; Johnson and Morse, 1968a) in the
field of abuse, have suspected that in some cases, certain temperamental characteristics or physical defects in the child can act as
a factor precipitating abuse, particularly those which lead to lack
of responsiveness or atypically difficult behaviour, creating frustration in the parents. With this in mind, we reviewed all available information on the condition of the children at birth and
their subsequent development in the hope of throwing further light
on the kind of child who is at risk of abuse. In particular we
were interested to see whether we could pick out a group of children with persistent problems from birth up to the time of
referral. However, our attempts to trace systematically the
children's progress and verify the mothers' reports of problems
were frequently hampered by the lack of detailed information available from official records. Hence, we were often forced to rely
entirely on the mothers' reports of problems but recognise the
difficulties inherent in giving credence to parental reports on
the child's behaviour prior to the occurrence of abuse.

A table giving details of the children's condition at birth and
subsequent problems they presented appears below.

The neo-natal period

Birthweights were obtained for all the children and three (12 per
cent of the sample, cases A, L, X in Table 4.2) were reported to
have weighed less than 2,500gms. During the period in which our
children were born 6.6 per cent of the total live births in England
and Wales were premature (DHSS, 1974c). No breakdown of statistics relating prematurity to social class was available for this
period but the incidence of low birth weight is known to be nega-
tively related to social class (Drillien, 1964; Crosse, 1971).
It seems likely that our figure of 12 per cent is only marginally
higher than the expected frequency when social class is taken into
account, as there was a trend for our sample to be skewed towards
the lower end of the social class distribution (albeit a statistically non-significant trend). This suggests that prematurity
as a 'cause' of battering is not of prime significance as far as
our study is concerned.

Several researchers have drawn attention to the number of low
birth weight babies in their samples (Simons et al., 1966; Elmer,
1967a; Skinner and Castle, 1969; Klein and Stern, 1971; Castle
and Kerr, 1972; Smith and Hanson, 1974b and Oliver et al., 1974)
and it has been suggested that these babies are particularly at
risk from battering. One reason sometimes given is the difficulty
in bonding following early separation (Klaus and Kennell, 1970;
Klein and Stern, 1971). The second reason is associated with
possible feeding and sleeping difficulties in the premature baby.
However, Smith and Hanson (1974b) point out that many low birth

TABLE 4.2 Details from medical records of the children's condition at birth and any feeding, sleeping or crying problems prior to referral reported by mothers (N = 25)

Case	Child's age at referral (months)	Child's condition at birth	Neo-natal period	Problems 0-3 mths	3 mths-1 year	1-2 years	3 years +
A	1	Birthweight less than 2,500 gms (a twin)	Received special care for 1 mth and detained in hospital after mother was discharged	Case referred when baby 1 mth old			
B	1	Normal, healthy	Uneventful	Severe sleeping and crying, moderate feeding			
C	2	Normal, healthy	Uneventful	Severe sleeping and crying			
D	2	Normal, healthy	Uneventful	Severe crying, moderate feeding			
E	7	Jaundiced	Uneventful	Severe feeding and crying	Severe feeding (*) and crying		
F	7	N.I.	N.I.	N.I.	N.I.		
G	8	Neo-natal illness recorded, described as premature though birthweight 6lbs 13oz	Child received special care after birth, and separated from mother for 1 day	Severe feeding (*) and crying, mild sleeping	Severe feeding (*), moderate sleeping and crying		

Case	Child's age at referral (months)	Child's condition at birth	Neo-natal period	Problems 0-3 mths	3 mths-1 year	1-2 years	3 years +
H	8	Kidney infection recorded. Slow to gain weight	Child received medication and detained in hospital for 15 days with mother till started to gain weight	Moderate feeding (*)	Moderate feeding, mild sleeping		
I	9	Normal, healthy	Uneventful	N.I.	Mild feeding		
J	9	Respiratory difficulties and aspiration pneumonitis	Received special care and in incubator for a while after birth. Baby detained in hospital 2 weeks after mother was discharged	None reported	None reported		
K	10	Normal, healthy	Uneventful	None reported	None reported		
L	11	Birthweight less than 2500 gms. Developed asymptomatic hypoglycaemia and feeding difficulties	Received special care. Required hourly feeding at first. Child separated from mother for 4 days, then detained in hospital for 1 week after mother was discharged	None reported, though difficulties noted in offical records	None reported		

Case	Age	Condition at birth	Early history				
M	12	Normal, healthy	Uneventful	N.I.	N.I. Moderate sleeping		
N	14	Normal, healthy	Child with mother, then discharged from hospital to residential nursery and remained there several weeks	None reported			
O	14	Congenital syphilis recorded	Child treated for congenital syphilis	Child away from home	Child away from home		
P	15	Normal, healthy	Uneventful	None reported	None reported	Mild sleeping	
Q	22	Normal, healthy	Uneventful	N.I.	N.I.	N.I.	
R	27	Normal, healthy	Uneventful	None reported	Severe sleeping and crying	Severe sleeping and crying	Severe sleeping and crying
S	28	Normal, healthy	Uneventful	None reported	Moderate feeding	None reported	None reported
T	31	'Foetal distress' recorded. Described as in 'poor condition at birth'	Child received special care and kept in incubator. Separated from mother for 5 days	Severe feeding (*), sleeping (*) and crying (*)	Severe feeding, sleeping and crying	Severe feeding, sleeping and crying	Severe feeding (*), sleeping and crying
U	32	Normal, healthy	Uneventful	None reported	None reported	Mild feeding and sleeping	Moderate feeding and sleeping
V	33	Normal, healthy	Uneventful	None reported	None reported	None reported	None reported

Case	Child's age at referral (months)	Child's condition at birth	Neo-natal period	Problems 0-3 mths	3 mths-1 year	1-2 years	3 years +
W	34	'Cerebral irritation' recorded at birth	Child put on pheno-barbitone at birth for hyper-activity until 3 weeks old, but discharged from hospital with mother	Moderate sleeping	Mild sleeping (*). Feeding problems also noted in official records	Mild feeding (*). Sleeping (*) and crying	Moderate sleeping (*), mild feeding (*) and crying
X	38	Birthweight less than 2,500 gms and neo-natal illness recorded	Received special care after birth and separated from mother for 2 days	N.I.	N.I.	N.I.	Moderate feeding, mild sleeping and crying
Y	41	Feeding difficulties recorded. Also suspicion of bilateral sub-dural haematoma	Child vomiting all feeds 2 days after birth. Child detained in hospital 4 days after mother discharged	Severe feeding (*). Sleeping and crying	Severe feeding (*) and crying (*)	Severe feeding (*)	Moderate feeding, sleeping and crying

Key: N.I. = No information from mother
(*) = Problems confirmed in official records

weight babies in his own and other series may be simply explained
as reflecting those maternal characteristics that predispose to
delivery of low birth weight babies, such as low social class,
youthful and single status, and rejecting attitudes during pregnancy (Drillien, 1964, Crosse, 1971) which are also prevalent in
the samples studied.

It is noteworthy that in addition to the three low birthweight
children in our sample, medical records revealed that eight children (cases E, G, H, J, O, T, W, Y in Table 4.2) suffered neo-natal
problems of varying severity.   Seven of these eleven vulnerable
babies required special care and were separated from their mothers.
Four were separated for a period varying from one day to one week,
and three between one week and one month, being detained in hospital after their mothers were discharged.   Although Smith and
Hanson (1974b) are somewhat sceptical of the prophylactic value
of increased or improved maternal child contact after confinement,
it seems that the difficulties of adjustment to their babies
experienced by some of the 'unwilling' mothers in our sample may
well have been exacerbated by the fact that their babies were separated from them at a crucial stage.   The work of Seashore and
her colleagues (1973) not only indicates that denial of early
mother-child interaction has a negative effect on maternal self-
confidence but also that mothers who have low self-confidence
initially are most vulnerable to these effects.

It is interesting that Richards (1974b) reports clear indications of the effects of a 'psychological' separation which can
occur even when the mother and child are in physical proximity.
This happens when the infant's condition does not allow it to play
a full role in the reciprocal interchanges with the mother.   We
can only speculate whether this kind of 'psychological' separation
occurred in our cases, but we do have evidence that a number of
babies suffered neo-natal problems which undoubtedly affected
their responses.

Problems presented by the children

With reference to Table 4.2 it can be seen that nine babies (cases
B, C, D, E, G, H, T, W, Y) were reported to have presented problems in the first three months of life.   Three were babies who
were apparently normal and healthy at birth but who were referred
with serious injuries at a very early stage, and six were babies
who suffered neo-natal problems.   These six babies (cases E, G,
H, T, W, Y) continued to present problems during the period of
three months to one year and an additional four children (cases I,
N, R, S) were reported to have developed problems.

When we come to look at problems in the one- to two-year
period, it should be remembered that only twelve children fell
into this age range.   Four children (cases R, T, W, Y) continued
to present difficulties and the two others (cases P and U) developed problems for the first time.

Six (cases R, T, U, W, X, Y) of the eight children who fell
into the two to four years age range were reported to have presented problems prior to referral.   It can be seen from the table

that three (cases T, W, Y) of these children were reported by
their mothers to have presented problems from birth onwards and
official records confirm the existence of problems.   In view of
the rearing difficulties experienced by the parents of this particular group of children we were puzzled how the children had
reached the older age range without apparently being abused.
However, further enquiries revealed that one child had received
serious inflicted injuries and the other two had histories of
'accidents' and rough handling, prior to referral.

When considering the mothers' reports of problems it is virtually
impossible to evaluate to what extent some of the babies' initial
difficulties contributed to adverse mother-child relationships and
to what extent their subsequent difficulties resulted from or were
exacerbated by maternal attitudes and behaviour.   We suspect that
in some instances the existence of problems may have been denied
by mothers who were either totally unforthcoming on this subject
or tended to idealise the situation.   Whereas in others, we feel
that problems may have been exaggerated merely reflecting the
mother's perception of the child with little relationship to objective reality.   Gregg and Elmer (1969) report that when they
assessed the behavioural characteristics of thirty abused children
and eighty-three children thought to have sustained accidental
injuries, using a modified version of the Thomas, Chess and Birch
method, no differences in mood or activity level were found between
the abused and non-abused children.   In fact, the abused children
were more easily distracted and it was thought that they had been
easier babies to look after.   However, these findings were at
variance with the opinions of the mothers of the abused children,
most of whom saw their children as predominantly negative.   Smith
and Hanson (1974b) note that significantly more mothers of
battered children than control mothers considered the child difficult.   Yet, observations of the battered children did not confirm
that they were harder to manage than the controls.   They were
described as being lethargic in some respects rather than hyperactive and after being some time in hospital were no more irritable
than the controls.

From our discussions with the mothers of the children in the
younger age ranges it seems that feeding difficulties and continual
crying caused them most distress and made their patience wear thin.
In one case, even before the mother was discharged from hospital
with her baby, it was noted on the hospital records that the
baby's continual crying angered her and in her own words, 'I can't
stand it, it goes right through me.   She only cries to annoy me.'
Another mother when recalling the problems she had experienced
with her baby said, 'he was an incredibly difficult baby from the
beginning.   He just cried and cried all the time and we practically had to force feed him.   You could do nothing with him, you
really couldn't and it made me feel so helpless.   I did everything by the book for him and stuck to a routine so if he woke
early, I didn't feed him.   When he wouldn't take his food I used
to take the teat off his bottle and pour the milk down him and
occasionally I hit him with the bottle.   My husband would say,
"you are silly, because you're only making more mess for yourself",
but at least it relieved my feelings.'

It is interesting that Smith and Hanson (1974) also report that crying, clinging and whining behaviour were severe problems for significantly more mothers of battered children than control mothers and may have precipitated battering.   It seems that abusive parents have particular difficulties in tolerating and responding to a child when it is crying or in a general state of misery and our own direct observations bear this out.   It has also been noted in the literature (Steele and Pollock, 1968; Okell, 1972) that battering mothers often express fears of spoiling their babies, to the point where picking up and cuddling a tiny baby is avoided, lest the child get the better of them.   Bearing these points in mind, the findings of a study by Bell and Ainsworth (1972) throw new light on persistent crying problems, which may have particular relevance to cases of abuse.   They demonstrated that infants whose mothers are promptly responsive to crying, cry less by the end of the first year than infants whose mothers are slow to respond.   Close physical contact is the most frequent maternal intervention and the most effective in terminating crying. They conclude that the development of non-crying modes of communication is associated with maternal responsiveness to infant signals.

Evidence of illness, retardation and physical defects in the children prior to referral

As could be expected, some children were reported to have suffered illness of an episodic nature prior to referral.   However, as far as we know, none of the children suffered chronic illness.

Only one child (case X) was noted to be uniformly retarded in all his functioning prior to referral.   He had been referred to a special assessment clinic where he was described as 'a case of minimal cerebral damage coupled with gross deprivation'.   Two other children (cases S and T) were described in health visitors' records as being retarded in some areas of development.

None of the children in the sample was noted to have major congenital anomalies, but six (cases E, G, J, M, T, X) had minor physical defects which were giving rise to anxiety in the parents in some cases.   Another child had a history of convulsions of unknown aetiology.   Findings on this topic vary from study to study.   For example, Gregg and Elmer (1969) report that none of their thirty abused children had physical defects which should affect the quality of 'mothering', whereas in two recent British studies, Smith and Hanson (1974) and Oliver et al. (1974), report a considerably higher prevllence of serious congenital defects amongst battered children than in the population at large.

History of failure to thrive

Records revealed that five (cases E, S, T, X, Y) children in the sample had a history of not thriving well.   At the time of referral three (cases E, T, X) continued to demonstrate failure to thrive as indicated by height and weight below the third

percentile.   A number of researchers, including Elmer and Gregg
(1967), Koel (1969), Martin (1972) and Smith and Hanson (1974),
report cases of coexisting failure to thrive and trauma.   It has
been suggested that growth and development, particularly in
infancy, are sensitive indicators of the quality of mothering.
As far as we know none of the five children in our sample had been
medically investigated to establish whether there was an organic
cause of growth failure, but it seems likely that impaired growth
was related to affective and sensory deprivation.   It was
noticeable that two of the three children who demonstrated failure
to thrive on referral began to thrive better as soon as they were
separated from their parents.

History of neglect

Two children (cases L and S) had a history suggesting mild neglect
(e.g. one had persistent cradle cap and severe nappy rash) and two
(cases N and Y) of severe neglect (e.g. one had been hospitalised
because of an infection, dehydration and neglect).   At the time
of referral four children showed some signs of neglect (cases B,
F, S, L) and one (case M) was in an extremely neglected condition
with head lice, open sores and filthy, inadequate clothing.   This
finding is worthy of note, because although most children in the
sample had received adequate or good physical care, it is apparent
from our study and that of Smith and Hanson (1974) that abuse
and neglect clearly overlap in some cases.

2 THE NATURE OF PARENT-CHILD INTERACTION IN THE FIRST THREE MONTHS
OF TREATMENT

This section is based on workers' assessments of parent-child
interaction in the first three months of treatment and how the
parents appeared to experience their roles as parents.   When
approaching this vital topic we drew heavily on the studies conducted during the 1960s by researchers such as Morris and Gould
(1963), Young (1964), Nurse (1964), Galdston (1966), Elmer (1967a),
Johnson and Morse (1968a), Steele and Pollock (1968) and Melnick
and Hurley (1969).   In brief, their findings suggest that abusing
parents lack appropriate knowledge of child-rearing, and that
their attitudes, expectations and child-rearing techniques set
them apart from non-abusive parents.   The abusive parents imple-
ment culturally accepted norms for rearing children with an
exaggerated intensity and at an inappropriately early age.
    In our study we have attempted to examine further some of the
qualitative differences in patterns of parenting and to enumerate
their occurrence more precisely.   These include, for example, the
abusive parents' basic lack of empathy and inability to respond
to their children's emotional needs, their rigid expectations and
demand for premature high performance, their distorted perception
of the child and role reversal in the parent-child relationship.
Such topics will be discussed in detail later in this chapter.
    In this section it should be noted that the size of the total

sample is reduced to twenty-four as one child died of its injuries
within hours of referral.   Also the size of the sample varied
from item to item for the following reasons:
1 Six children were away from home throughout this period which
meant that restricted parent-child interaction in unfamiliar surroundings was all that could be observed.   Thus, many items could
not be coded but attempts were made to assess the parents' basic
attitudes towards the child, together with the more enduring
features of parent-child interaction regardless of the setting.
2 Ten children were away from home for part of this period.   In
these cases attempts were made to rate the majority of items where
it was felt that a realistic assessment of parent-child interaction
could be made.
3 As the age of the children ranged from one month to four years
a few items were not applicable to the very young children and
could not be coded.
   All the items, where appropriate, were coded separately for
mother and father, but typically direct information from the
fathers was limited and workers had less opportunity for observing
the fathers' interaction with their children than they had for
mothers.   We were also aware of the dangers of relying solely on
the mothers' reports of the fathers' relationship with the child
as this seemed an area which was wide open to distortion.   Thus,
some items relating to the fathers have been omitted owing to insufficient reliable data.

TABLE 4.3 Parents' acceptance/rejection of the battered child

	Father (N = 22)	Mother (N = 24)
Warmly accepting	9	2
Fairly accepting	3	3
Ambivalent/Conditional acceptance	6	12
Fairly rejecting	4	3
Harshly rejecting	0	4

Although it seemed to us that considerably more fathers than
mothers had a positive attitude towards the child and none was
harshly rejecting, it is necessary to re-emphasise that workers
had much less contact with fathers and fewer opportunities to
observe them interacting with their children.   Also the fair
degree of attachment which many fathers felt for their children
did not preclude feelings of jealousy when mothers were attentive
to the children instead of them.
   Half the mothers revealed strongly ambivalent feelings towards
the child and their acceptance was clearly conditional upon the
child's being responsive and rewarding.   These were mothers who,
while often stressing their love and affection for their children,
were overwhelmed by their dependency demands.   As Johnson and
Morse (1968b) observed, 'the child was seen more often as a

burden and a source of irritation than as a source of satisfaction.'   One mother when speaking about the child, commented
grimly to her worker, 'Not that I wish he wasn't here.   I
wouldn't be without him, but I don't want another baby, at least
not now.   I wouldn't like to go through all this again.'

The four mothers who were harshly rejecting had all rejected
their babies at birth.   Two of these children were still very
young but the other two were in the older age range and had consistently aroused strong negative feelings, verging on hatred, in
their mothers.   In one case the mother said, 'From the minute
she wakes up everything about her irritates and annoys me.   I
can't bear her near me.   She has never felt my baby.'   In the
other case the worker reported that the child was 'anathema to the
mother'.   Generally, the mothers were slow to praise but quick to
criticise the child's efforts and abilities, often seeming
threatened by the child's childishness.   Four children were constantly ridiculed and disparaged by their mothers even in the
presence of the workers.

Meeting of the child's dependency needs

It was apparent that many of the parents had severely frustrated
dependency needs and turned to their children for most of their
emotional gratification with an underlying conviction that their
children should quickly respond to their needs and moods and
should initiate the love in the relationship.   This has been
described as a reversal of the dependency role, which is closely
linked with the parents' high expectations and distorted perception of the child (Morris and Gould, 1963).   Most mothers seemed
incapable of sustained sensitive, emotional interaction with their
children and had a low level of empathy, marked by an inability
to tune into the child's needs for warmth, comfort and reassurance.
A few parents showed an intellectual awareness of the child's
needs but were quite unable to respond to them in practice.   As
Steele (1966) observed, 'the parents are predominantly insensitive
to the ebb and flow of the infant's needs.'

Several of the very insensitive mothers revealed strange attitudes to the child's emotional needs and in the main ignored
them.   One mother told the worker that she had deliberately not
responded in the hope the child would grow up detached and self-
sufficient.   'I thought that if she could not be hurt by me, then
she could not be hurt by anyone.   You know I loved my parents but
I never felt I got anything back.   I suppose with Sally being the
first one, I didn't want to show her too much love in case she
would reject me.   It's been different with the other two, I've
dared to give them a bit more.'

In six cases there was evidence that the child was often shut
away on his own for long periods of time.   Undoubtedly this
action was used by the mothers as a safety valve when they could
no longer stand their children's demands.   In the words of one
mother, 'It was the only way out of an unmanageable situation.
When I started to shut her away in the bedroom it was as though
she didn't exist.   She would come out for meals or to have her

53   Chapter 4

clothes changed but began to expect nothing more than to play with her toys on her own.'

TABLE 4.4 Mothers' expectations of the physical developmental and emotional behavioural attributes of the battered child in relation to his age and developmental level (N = 23)

| | Emotional | | | | | | |
	Very high	Fairly high	Average	Low	Very low	N.I.	Total
Very high	4					1	5
Fairly high	3	5	2				10
Average		2	3				5
Low		1		1			2
Very low							
N.I.	1						1
Total	8	8	5	1		1	23

(Physical)

A striking finding is that the majority of mothers had high expectations of the child's physical or emotional behaviour or both. It can be seen from Table 4.4 that nine mothers had unrealistically high expectations of either the child's physical or emotional behaviour or both, and similarly a further ten mothers had fairly high expectations. Although other researchers such as Johnson and Morse (1968b) and Steele and Pollock (1968) have referred to the high expectations of abusive parents, it appears that we have made the first attempt to document this important component of parental attitudes more precisely. Finding ways of modifying these extreme expectations and reducing the unrealistic investment in the child proved to be one of the most difficult treatment tasks.

Many of the mothers were desperately keen for their children to be advanced in all respects. They appeared to have little idea of normal child development and expected a high level of physical performance and an ability to anticipate and respond to their own moods and needs and to obey orders far beyond the child's capabilities. For example, one mother was very frustrated that her child was not walking at eight months and was forever forcing him on to his feet. She also became infuriated when the child continued to mess his food in spite of orders to the contrary and would make him go without, commenting, 'I believe in table manners and he's got to learn now. I won't let him eat and watch television.' She also expected the child to repeat words after her and remarked exasperatedly to the worker, 'he is such a twit, he says Mama but never at the right time.'

TABLE 4.5 Mother's perception of the battered child (N = 21)

Described child very differently from the way worker sees him	2
Describes child somewhat differently from the way worker sees him	9
Describes child more or less as the worker sees him	10

An attempt was made to assess the parent's perception of the child as it has been noted in the literature that abusive parents appear defective in their capacity to test the reality of the child, typically having a specific fantasy about the child or misperceiving him as in some way 'bad'. It is thought that these misperceptions are particularly extreme at the time abuse occurs. However, the nature of the psychological mechanisms underlying the parents' distorted perception of the child is the subject of debate amongst researchers such as Kaufman (1962), Galdston (1969) and Steele (1970).

Whilst recognising that all parents at times project both positive and negative feelings onto their children or attribute certain qualities to them, we concluded from our observations of parent-child interaction, that nine mothers consistently perceived the child in a somewhat distorted way and two in a very distorted way. With the exception of one mother who idealised her baby, constantly emphasising what a good, perfect baby he was, these mothers were frequently noted to ascribe bad behaviour to their children unjustifiably and to misconstrue their children's moods, particularly misery, which they often interpreted as 'temper'. Similarly Galdston (1971) has referred to the inconsistencies, exaggeration and inappropriateness of the mother's complaints about the child and he comments, 'as their attention turned to their children the view of the child as a saint or a sinner emerged.'

All our mothers whose perception of the child was distorted also had high or unrealistically high expectations of their children, attributing almost adult feelings and reactions to them in a disconcerting way. In one case in which the mother stated that she thought it was time for her child to mix with other children as he needed preparing for school, the worker recorded that she had to remind herself that the child in question was less than a year old!

Both the mothers whose perception of the child was thought to be very distorted were harshly rejecting and projected all their negative feelings on to the child. It seemed that they had got stuck in such a negative pattern of interaction with the child that they could not see anything he did in a positive light. In one case the worker commented, 'For the mother this child seems to symbolise all that is distasteful and that has been forced upon her in life. The child also embodies all her father's hated aspects for the mother. The mother often refers to the child as wild and wilful with wicked intentions.' In the other case the mother described the child as 'strange and different from the others and deliberately out to get me.'   In fact, both these children were showing signs of regression and disturbance but were extremely passive, compliant and obedient.

TABLE 4.6   The parents' physical handling of the child

	Father (N = 20)	Mother (N = 24)
Very warm, gentle handling, moulds to child, gives plenty of cuddling	4	2
Fairly warm, gentle handling of child, gives some cuddling	9	4
Swings between very warm and very distant handling	3	4
Fairly distant, mechanical handling, lacks tenderness, little cuddling	2	9
Very distant, rough, mechanical handling of child, no tenderness, avoids physical contact	2	5

During the relatively limited periods of time the fathers were observed interacting with their children by the workers, their physical handling was noted to be generally warmer and more gentle than that of the mothers.   However, in several cases workers had reservations about whether this would have been sustained if the fathers had been with the children in their presence for longer periods.   In addition, it is necessary to point out that in contrast to the mothers, few fathers had extensive contact with their children or were regularly involved in caretaking activities.

A few parents were noted to be capable of a warm physical response at times when the child was not being demanding or when they were anxious to make reparation to the child, whereas at others, they were cold, distant and lacking in tenderness.   For example, one worker commented, 'the mother's handling of the child varies greatly.   At times she clings on to the child, cuddling him for long periods, almost stifling him with her need to love.   At other times, especially during caretaking activities, her handling is distant and mechanical.   Bottle feeding is akin to pouring water down a drain.'   We noted that feeding time was particularly difficult for many parents who frequently turned the situation into a battle of wills.

A number of mothers were described as having 'no sense of timing in their approach to their children, handling them in an unsure, abrupt fashion with little tenderness.'   A few interacted with their children in a teasing fashion, forever tweaking

or pulling at them, tossing them up and down and tickling them
excessively.   One worker commented, 'the child is subjected to a
constant unphased barrage of stimulation by both parents', while
another observed, 'Mrs X just has not got the motherly touch and
Bill's responses dry up when he sees her.'   Some of the very
cold mothers were noted to treat their children like objects,
avoiding physical contact wherever possible.   Cold, insensitive
handling was frequently accompanied by hostile, negative verbal
interaction with the child.   For example, in one case the worker
commented that the child was subjected to 'verbal battering' and in
another, the mother was described as 'barking at the child'.

Incidents of rough handling were observed by the workers in over
half the cases.   These ranged from relatively minor examples of
clumsy parenting which caused temporary discomfort to the child,
to more extreme actions, in one case with persecutory connotations.
At such times it was not difficult for workers to imagine how
injuries might have occurred.   In a few cases the parents'
actions appeared unintentional in that their normal awkward or
clumsy child care was exaggerated by impatience into yanking,
pulling and slapping.   The extent to which such practices occur
in the general population is not as far as is known possible to
gauge, but they are probably not uncommon.   In some families the
children were pawns in marital conflict.   One worker related how
the parents played sinister games with their baby, tossing her
from one to the other until she was screaming and gasping for
breath.

Assessment of mothercraft, i.e. the mother's ability to cater for
the child's physical needs (N = 22)

Two mothers were very neglectful and inadequate at physical caretaking.   One of these cases was described by the worker as
follows, 'Child frequently in filthy, neglected state and unsuit-
ably clothed. .This mother provides really haphazard child care
with absolutely no routine.   Child got up, washed and fed merely
when mother feels like it.   Frequently left in dirty nappies for
long periods "to teach him".   The only bedding in the cot is a
damp, filthy blanket.'   Five mothers were very inconsistent and
the standard of physical care they provided fluctuated considerably according to their mood.   At times they were neglectful,
leaving their children cold, unchanged, hungry and unstimulated
and at others were relatively efficient caretakers.   Of the remaining mothers, nine were assessed as good or adequate at physical
caretaking and six as obsessional.   The latter group set themselves unrealistically high standards and were plagued by feelings
of failure and inadequacy because they were unable to live up to
their image of the 'ideal mother'.   They laid tremendous emphasis
on neatness, cleanliness and routine, but felt that with young
children around 'they could never get straight'.   Workers observed
that there was considerable impatience behind their performance of
mothering tasks coupled with rigid expectations.   One mother was
described as 'servicing the child with mechanical efficiency in a
self-centred way'.   Several of these mothers could not refrain

from intervening when the child was attempting to feed or dress
himself, in order to avoid a mess being made or to control and
speed the process up.   For example, one mother even made her child
eat her meals standing up to avoid wasting time.   Another of these
obsessional mothers was morbidly anxious about her child's health,
always forcing medicine down him, overfeeding and overdressing him.

Mother's protective behaviour towards the child (N = 18)

Only two mothers were assessed as showing average, normal concern
about the child's safety, whereas the other mothers verged on the
neglectful or over-protective.
     Ten mothers were assessed as being fairly poor at monitoring
the child's environment.   They tended to 'switch off their attention' from the children, leaving them to their own devices for
quite long periods of time and were slow to anticipate potential
dangers.   There was also evidence that five of these mothers left
their children alone and unsupervised in the home on occasions.
Paradoxically, several of the mothers in this group were described
as being very anxious about their children's safety in the
abstract, making frequent references to their fear of environmental hazards and accidents.   It is interesting that Smith and
Hanson (1975) report that the mothers of the battered children in
their study were relatively careless over their whereabouts or
well-being.
     Five mothers were assessed as being fairly over-protective in
the sense that they were inappropriately restrictive of their
children's freedom to explore, etc. in relation to their age and
developmental level and rather over-concerned with external
dangers.   Their restrictive actions seemed to be another dimension of their powerfully controlling relationship with their
children.   In addition, one mother was assessed as over-protective to the point of smothering the child.   She had totally
unrealistic fears about his safety and would not even permit him
to crawl about the living room in case he hurt himself.

TABLE 4.7   Mother's attitude to child's need to play (N = 18)

Facilitates and is sensitive to child's need to play	6
Shows little interest	5
Interferes with play activity	5
Discourages child from playing	2

     Six mothers were noted to have a constructive attitude to their
childrens' need to play.   They made the best of cramped space to
enable their children to pursue their activities, providing them
with an adequate selection of age-appropriate toys or making
imaginative use of other objects as toys.   Five mothers showed
little interest in their children's play activity.   These children were free to make use of whatever toys were available but
received no stimulation or encouragement.

In two cases mothers were observed actively to discourage their
children from playing, restricting their movements and providing
very few toys.   In the other five cases, the mothers constantly
interfered with or 'programmed' their children's play.   Several
of these mothers were noted to be very childlike themselves and
would often interrupt the child's activities to satisfy their own
needs for play.   In the words of one worker, 'This leads to a
hectic interchange between mother and child.   First she frustrates
him, then pushes him to uncontrollable levels of excitement, and
herself becomes childish and exuberant.'

Parental attitudes to discipline

Cultural and class-related differences in parental attitudes to
discipline and use of physical punishment have been extensively
documented by researchers (e.g. Sears, Maccoby and Levin (1957);
Newson (1963), (1968); Erlanger (1973).   Since child abuse is
sometimes hard to distinguish from harsh discipline, the attitudes
to discipline of parents suspected of abuse and the extent to
which physical punishment is used by them in child-rearing is of
particular interest.   With one or two exceptions, researchers
have tended to make only general references to this topic rather
than detailed observations.   According to writers such as Steele
and Pollock (1968), Wasserman (1967) and Johnson and Morse (1968b),
abusive parents tend to be 'moralistic' in their views on parental
authority and discipline.   Indeed, one of the main differences
noted between non-abusive and abusive parents is that the latter
expect exemplary behaviour from their children early in infancy
and feel justified in implementing disciplinary measures with
exaggerated intensity and at an inappropriately early age.   Elmer
(1967a) in a study of abusive and non-abusive families, reports
that although there was no difference in the frequency of punishment between the two groups, 'the non-abusive families tended to
use a few types of punishment consistently, while some abusive
families used a broad range, which suggests they were desperately
trying to find some way of managing their children.'   Young (1964)
also found that all of the abusive families were inconsistent in
disciplining the children and that punishment and power were dominant family themes.   In Smith's and Hanson's (1975) study both
the mothers and fathers of the battered children were found to
use physical punishment far more than to be expected for their
age and class.   Mothers were also characterised by being punitive
on other indices; in their tendency to use love-withdrawl as a
sanction against misbehaviour, in their use of material rewards
(pacifiers) and in their demands for obedience.
    It was apparent from our discussions with the mothers that
great emphasis was laid on discipline and control even with very
young children.   In practice they mainly tended to fall into two
groups, either being consistently strict and controlling or vacil-
lating between indulgence and strictness.
    Twelve mothers were observed to use physical punishment but
this may well be an under-estimate of its actual use as mothers
were likely to be more restrained in the worker's presence.   In

two cases, mothers made use of mild physical punishment only, for example, lightly smacking the child's hand by way of restraint. In five cases mothers were noted to lash out impulsively at the child with varying degrees of severity.   There was little build-up to these incidents and little apparent provocation from the children.   In some instances they were hit for behaviour that had previously been ignored or regarded as amusing.   In this group it seems that physical punishment was used 'more as an ex-pression of agitation rather than as purposeful discipline' (Johnson and Morse, 1968b).   In the remaining five cases, mothers were observed to use relatively severe physical punishment and moreover inappropriate for the child's age.   In particular, this punitively strict group of mothers exhibited the 'sense of right-eousness' described by Steele and Pollock (1968).   Workers' des-criptions of two of these cases appear below.

'The mother frequently smacks, slaps, pushes and yanks at both children when they arouse the slightest displeasure in her. With the battered child this goes well beyond the most generous norm verging on and at times including sadistic emotional and physical cruelty.   In her own words, "they never give any trouble, they dare not."'

'When the baby ignores the mother's commands to leave some-thing alone, a flash of fury goes across her face.   She resorts to dragging the child bodily into the middle of the room, pulling on her arms and slapping her.   On one such occasion the baby babbled at the mother, who became further insensed and gave her a good shaking, shouting, "you've got to frighten her out of it, she's got to learn."'

Our general impression was that few couples were united in their approach to matters of discipline and control and that, in the main, the fathers were less strict than the mothers.   This re-sulted in considerable conflict over discipline in a number of families.   On the one hand fathers would admonish their wives for being too strict with the child and undermine their discipli-nary efforts, and on the other would criticise them for not con-trolling the children enough if they happened to be irritating them or interfering with their own activities.   A common complaint voiced by the mothers was that their husbands were passive and in-effectual over disciplinary matters.

Conclusion

Our detailed analysis of the parents' interaction with the battered child, whilst confirming and augmenting many of the find-ings of previous researchers, suggests that it is very misleading to make global statements about battering parents' relationships with their children.   Even in our small sample there was con-siderable variation in the parents' attitude towards and handling of their children and no parents were rated at the negative extreme of every item.   As in Smith's aɪ.d Hanson's (1975) study, the mothers' inconsistency and unreasonableness in child manage-ment was a striking feature of many cases and this may reflect the role confusion they experience when faced with parenthood.

3 WORKERS' IMPRESSIONS OF THE BATTERED CHILD AND SIBLINGS
DURING THE FIRST THREE MONTHS OF TREATMENT

Clinical observations of abused children by researchers such as
Morris et al. (1964), Galdston (1966, 1969, 1971, 1973), Ounsted
et al. (1974) and Oliver (1974), suggest that many of the children
are considerably damaged emotionally as well as physically, by
the time they come to professional attention.   We observed in
our children some disturbing characteristics similar to, though
not always as extreme as those previously reported, which left us
deeply concerned about the children's future wellbeing.

Although over half the children were considered to be attrac-
tive and good looking, many of them were described as 'appealing
but pathetic' and evoked protective feelings in the workers.
Frequent references were made to their pallor and the fact that
they looked older than their years.   Another striking characteristic of the children was their expression of wariness although
none displayed the 'frozen watchfulness' described by Ounsted et
al. (1974).

The remaining children, who tended to irritate and evoke predominantly negative reactions in the workers were either unattrac-
tive, rather gross, podgy, inert children, lacking animation, or
hyperactive, aggressive, provocative children, who constantly
sought to be the centre of attention.

Although we took account of the children's recent negative
experiences such as pain and separation from their parents, which
seemed to have a particularly traumatic effect on the children
aged between twelve and twenty-four months, only three children
could be described as predominantly happy, contented and emotionally well-adjusted.   The rest of the children tended to be either
depressed, withdrawn, unresponsive, passive and apathetic or
anxious, tense, constantly on the alert and attention seeking.
Three children were showing recognised signs of disturbance such
as rocking or monotonous head-banging.   It is interesting to note
in this context that Green (1968) postulates that early physical
abuse which occurs in a matrix of overall rejection and stimulus
deprivation, may enhance the development of pain-dependant
behaviour in general.   Some descriptions of the children and
their characteristic modes of response appear below.

'Initially, a very sick baby but quickly responded to love and
affection.   A very good looking child with blonde curls, blue
eyes, a ready smile and happy disposition.   He quickly became
the favourite of the hospital ward.'

'A solemn, wistful, wary, angelic looking little boy, under
weight for his age, pale, drawn, dejected and depressed.   He
kept away from the other children and was always the onlooker
or the outsider, tending to play neatly on his own in a
corner.'

'A pale, dark haired, little boy with an anxious watchful expression of a little old man.   He was usually withdrawn and
depressed and seemed to have a resigned acceptance of anything
that was done to him.   However, he would respond to attention
and encouragement with an appealing grin and infectious
chuckle.'

'A rather strange child in appearance.   Her manner was deliberately stupid at times as though she was playing the fool.
There was something pathetic and appealing about her and what
felt like a potential maelstrom hidden beneath the compliant
exterior.   Her predominant mood seemed to be depression which
was marked by an anxious activity that verged on the desperate.'
'The baby had an old, wary, egg-headed sort of look, rather
like a pale, old-fashioned baby doll.   She was very lively and
constantly on the alert, frequently looking to her mother to
gauge her reaction.   She was very advanced in several areas of
her development, almost as though she was keeping pace with her
mother's high expectations and was quick to repeat antics that
were met with her approval.   She did a greal deal of smiling
and looking to adults for a response.'
'An anxious, restless, little boy, aggressive towards other
children, attention seeking, provocative and controlling.   He
was constantly darting around and often sweating profusely
from manic, energetic activity.   Altogether an exhausting and
infuriating child.'

An important diagnostic observation was that although a number
of children were rather constricted in their movements and
appeared unsure and wary of their parents, none actively turned
away from them or manifested extreme fear as reported by Morris
et al. (1964), Galdston (1966) and Oliver (1974).   For example,
a child who had received multiple fractures and had obviously
been battered on several different occasions was delighted to see
her parents and clung to them whenever they visited.   This
absence of marked fear may have been because many of the seriously
injured children, who were in the younger age range, simply did
not understand or retain the fact that it was their parents who
had assaulted them.   Also, the parents were presumably an important source of security for those children who had been placed in
strange, new surroundings, even if they had maltreated them
previously.

We were interested to note the children's response to parental
discipline, where appropriate.   It has been suggested that some
incidents of abuse occur when parents whose standards for miscon-
duct are particularly severe, become infuriated when their children actively disobey them or are unable to respond to their
orders (Gil, 1970).

We observed that some children were instantly obedient and
submissive to restrictions imposed on them to the point where, in
a few cases, their behaviour was almost totally controlled by
their parents.   An extreme example appears below.

'The child was completely oppressed by her mother and often
appeared as though all her spontaneity had been crushed to the
point where it was an effort for her to continue to breathe.
However, she remained alert to the need to jump in response to
her mother's orders.'

Other children tended to respond in a very inconsistent manner
to parental discipline and appeared bewildered and confused by
the conflicting cues they received.   One worker commented on
such a child as follows:

'Bill appears utterly confused about what is expected of him.

Sometimes he acts like an exuberant little clown and can be
quite defiant, whereas at others he is extremely acquiescent and
gives almost programmed, automatic responses to his mother's
orders.'

Two of the older hyperactive children were particularly provocative with their mothers and constantly tested them out to the
limits of their endurance.   They were both described as anxious
children and it seemed to the workers as though they gained some
relief from feared, unpredictable pain, by controlling the situation and provoking their mothers into hitting them.

Several writers, for example Davoren (1968) and Martin (1972),
have noted that some abused children seem able to act in a therapeutic way towards their anxious and angry parents, or other caretakers, from a remarkably early age.   We saw no striking examples
of this precocious solicitousness among the battered children
although many of them seemed to be extremely perceptive of their
parents' moods.   For example, one baby seemed to sense when his
mother was overwrought and on such occasions would endure very
awkward, rough handling with marked passivity, whereas at other
times he would protest violently, wriggling and crying.   This
sensitivity to the mother's mood did not necessarily work to the
child's advantage.   In another case, the mother told her worker
that whenever she felt weepy and depressed, her baby started to
cry and grizzle the minute she approached his cot.   This merely
exacerbated her mood and she quickly became irritated with him.

Workers' assessment of the battered child's development

In common with the findings of other researchers (Martin, 1972;
Smith and Hanson, 1974) language retardation was a striking feature
in a number of our children.   Of the twelve children aged twelve
months or over, two were showing no evidence of speech and the
speech of nine children was retarded.   The older children tended
to cling to baby-talk and their articulation was slurred and unin-
telligible.

Eight children appeared to the workers to be retarded in other
areas of their development.   Six were children who had no injuries
or minor injuries on referral and two had serious injuries, in one
case, including a head injury.   In several of these cases the
child's slow development had been noted in official records prior
to referral, or was noted when the child was medically examined at
the time of referral.   The developmental picture in these children suggested inadequate stimulation.   In some cases inhibited
mobility seemed to be the consequence of parents restricting the
children's exploratory behaviour, refusing to allow them to initiate activity or confining them to their cots for long periods.
A few typical examples appear below:
   'The baby, aged seven months, was strikingly inert, not in a
   lethargic way but more as though he was afraid to move.   He
   rarely played and seemed very intimidated by his mother.'
   'The child, aged eleven months, was particularly retarded in
   his motor development.   He had only recently learnt to sit up
   without support and could barely move himself around on his

bottom so that he became extremely frustrated when insufficiently mobile to reach for toys. He seemed to have spent
most of his life confined to his cot or pram.'
'The child, aged twenty-eight months, was generally constricted
in her movements and occasionally seemed to be immobilised
through tension and fear.'

Workers' observations on the battered child's siblings

The parents' interaction with the other children in the family
was assessed in a similar manner to their interaction with the
battered child.   However, as there were only twelve families in
which the battered child had one or more siblings it is not possible to draw detailed conclusions from our findings.   It will be
recalled that ten of the families contained siblings under four
and three had three children under four.   Hence, in addition to
the battered child there was a considerable number of other vulnerable young children in the families referred to us.

Although some researchers, for example Woolley and Evans (1955),
Merrill (1962) and Nurse (1964), have observed that often only one
child in a family is singled out for abuse, the findings of
Skinner and Castle (1969), Oliver (1974) and Smith and Hanson
(1974) reveal a high incidence of abuse to one or more siblings
of the presenting children.

In our sample there were only two families in which siblings
had a recorded history of injury thought to be the result of abuse,
but in our view this is likely to be an under-estimate of the
incidence of actual abuse of siblings.

Although there were indications in some cases that the siblings
tended to be treated by their parents in a warmer, more accepting,
empathetic manner than the battered child, the differences were
slight and their handling left a lot to be desired.   They, like
the battered children, were expected to fulfil a complex of parental needs and in the main appeared to fare little better
emotionally.

Whilst there was evidence that some parents were better able to
respond to their children at some stages of development rather
than others, our overall impression was that the parents' ability
to nurture or 'mother' young children in general was impaired.

Battered children are often referred to as scapegoated children
and we felt that this concept warranted careful examination.   In
the twelve families with more than one child, there was no case in
which the battered child could be described as the scapegoat for
the family as a whole.   However, in six cases, the battered
child, rather than any of the other children, appeared to have a
special pathological meaning to one of the parents and was the
focus of all his negative projections.   In another case, there
was an interesting example of displacement of a mother's aggression and frustration towards an extremely disturbed, provocative
and uncontrolled toddler, who was the obvious target for abuse,
on to a tiny, relatively placid baby.   The displacement theory
was strengthened by the fact that most of the father's attention in
the home was directed at the baby and the mother resented this.

In several cases the siblings were clearly being used by their parents to act out their marital conflicts, resulting in fierce sibling rivalry amongst those children who were old enough to be aware of the feelings of rivalry they evoked in their parents.

The effects of parental violence on the siblings of the abused child, regardless of whether they have been abused themselves, is to date a neglected area of study.   However, it is a sobering thought that, as many of our families were living in cramped conditions, some siblings probably witnessed incidents of battering.
It seemed to us that whereas some of the siblings were anxious and uncertain about what might happen to them, others had learnt over the years how to recognise danger signals, keep out of the way and avoid provoking their parents.   There was one striking case in which a young sibling frequently acted to meet the mother's needs so that if the mother was upset, the child would immediately go and comfort her.

We would agree with Court (1973) that the role of fear in the lives of children from abusive families and its repercussions in later life, warrants further study and that careful attention should be paid not only to the mental health of the battered child, but also to that of the siblings.

Chapter 5

THE PARENTS

CHILDHOOD AND BACKGROUND

At the time our study began, there was general agreement in the
literature on child abuse that parents of abused children were
themselves the victims of physical/emotional abuse or neglect
during their childhood. Emotional abuse was felt to be of particular importance, and was described in terms of experiences of
rejection, hostility, emotional coldness and 'emotional loss'
during childhood, with little opportunity for positive identification with parental figures (Spinetta and Rigler, 1972).   In
their study of abusing parents, Steele and Pollock (1968) reported
that although actual physical abuse or neglect was not experienced
by all their parents, 'all had experienced however a sense of
intensive pervasive, continuous demand from their parents ... expectations of good submissive behaviour, prompt obedience, never
making mistakes, sympathetic comforting of parental distress and
showing approval and help for parental actions.'   Love was
either withheld completely or given to them conditionally upon
their meeting parental needs.   In addition, they were constantly
criticised, often harshly disciplined, and some were over-protected and infantalized, seriously restricting their freedom to
mature and develop as individuals of worth in their own right.
In their childhoods there was an absence of any sense of being
cared for and cared about as individuals with needs of their own.
Steele and Pollock describe this as lack of 'basic mothering' and
maintain that it is the most important factor in the genesis of
child abuse.
   Information regarding the background of the parents in our
study was gleaned from informal discussions with them during the
course of treatment.   Many of the parents were initially reluctant to divulge this information, particularly if it was of an
adverse nature.   It was often through contradiction, retraction
of chance negative remarks and descriptions of their emotional
states during childhood, that we were able to get behind the
facade of 'normality' and 'happiness' presented by them.   In
certain instances this occurred quite late in treatment.   One
mother, for example, who initially spoke in glowing terms about

her own mother, later described an incident when she disagreed
with her.   She said that she was dragged across the room, the
buttons torn off her jumper and was then given a good thrashing.
In this 'normal' household the word 'No' was forbidden.   At the
age of fourteen years, this mother developed migraines.

The tendency to present a normal picture and idealise their
parents confirms the findings of Oliver et al. (1974).   He found
that many of the parents in his sample were convincing in their
descriptions of a favourable home life.   However, upon checking
old records on the family and other sources, he discovered very
contradictory and negative information on their backgrounds.   We
did not have access to the past records of our parents, and were
therefore unable to check information given to us by them.   It
must also be remembered that retrospective information is prone
to subjective inaccuracy and this may lead to distortion by some
parents who were openly negative about their parents and their
upbringing.   However, as noted by Ryle (1967), 'the adult's re-
collection of his childhood is quite possibly of greater relevance
to his emotional health than the objective reality to which he is
exposed.'   The need to distort towards the normal is as significant as the exaggeration of abnormal experiences.   It indicates
how these parents have coped with their backgrounds and the way
this has affected their present-day lives.   There is evidence to
suggest that they repeat their childhood experiences with their
marital partners and with their own children (Kempe, 1968;   Oliver
and Taylor, 1971;   Oliver and Cox, 1973 and Oliver et al., 1974).

BACKGROUND OF THE FATHERS
Social class of family of origin

An attempt was made to ascertain the social class of the fathers'
family of origin, but this information was not readily available.
However, the indications are that most of the fathers came from
families in social class III and below, living in urban areas.

Economic conditions

Harsh, depriving economic conditions were described in over half
the cases, though this did not necessarily indicate poverty.   In
some instances, large families and stringent standards of the
paternal grandparents may have contributed to the atmosphere of
scarcity in the home.

Family composition and status

All nineteen fathers about whom we obtained information were legitimate.   All had siblings (Mean = 3.00 siblings) and twelve were
from families of four or more children.   The average family size
was four children.   There was no set pattern with regard to
ordinal position and very little information regarding relationship with siblings during childhood.

Education of fathers

We obtained very scant information about the fathers' primary and
secondary education, but there was no evidence to suggest that any
of the fathers were educationally sub-normal or attended special
schools, though a few attended local authority boarding schools.
Most of the fathers left school at fifteen or below, but most had
some form of further training, mainly in the form of apprentice-
ships.

Pattern of care

During the 0-16-year period, thirteen fathers were cared for by
both natural parents.   Seven fathers were cared for by one parent
alone, usually the paternal grandmother, owing to death or separation from the paternal grandfathers.   A few of these fathers had
a number of different caretakers, but only two received care from
outside the nuclear family.   For example, one father was initially
cared for by his mother alone after the death of the paternal
grandfather when he was a year old.   He was the youngest of five
children, and the favourite of his mother.   However, at the age
of five years, he and his siblings were transferred to the care of
an aunt and uncle.   The father felt alienated from his siblings
and had a poor relationship with his caretakers, constantly running
away from them.   He was received into care during adolescence
after having returned to the care of his mother for a short while.

Quality of care/physical abuse and neglect

As these were emotionally charged topics, we did not specifically
ask the fathers about their experiences of abuse and neglect during
childhood, and therefore this information may not represent a true
estimate.   Only two fathers spontaneously described experiences
of physical abuse towards themselves and their siblings during
childhood.   In these two cases, the paternal grandfathers were
described as constantly drunk, lashing out at their wives and
children.   In only one case was there definite evidence of
neglect.   It is of interest that the abuse and neglect cases described above also suffered depriving economic conditions during
childhood.

Feeling and emotional states during childhood and adolescence

Feelings of being rejected, abandoned and isolated were commonly
expressed by the fathers together with feelings of being disapproved
of and belittled.   Many were left feeling lonely and worthless,
with bottled up anger and aggression which emerged in five cases
either in temper tantrums, 'panic states', or outbursts of aggression during childhood and adolescence.   One father reported that
he nearly knocked out the paternal grandfather when he was sixteen
years of age.   Another coped with his cooped-up anger and rebellion

during adolescence by opting out in day-dreams and showing marked
schizoid tendencies.   He felt abandoned by his parents, ineffectual and inadequate because of their disregard of him.

Twelve fathers either expressed hostility towards or remoteness
from their paternal grandfathers and of these, six were also rated
by workers as being over-identified with their paternal grandmothers.   In one case, for instance, the father described the
paternal grandfather as 'a right old bugger ... always drinking ...
he and Mum had a cat and dog life, always fighting ... Mum was
always leaving home ... twice round the block and back again.'
This father also described the paternal grandfather hitting him
with the flex of an iron and being 'free with his fists'.   Another
father said of the paternal grandfather, 'you wouldn't think you
could hate someone so much ... he's just an old coward'.   In these
two cases, and a third in which the paternal grandfather was a
strict disciplinarian, the fathers engaged in minor criminal activities during adolescence.   These fathers sided with the paternal
grandmothers against their own fathers, and it seemed that the
paternal grandmothers looked towards their sons to compensate for
their poor marital relationships.

Over-identification with paternal grandmothers also occurred in
cases where the paternal grandfathers were absent from the household.   Fathers were smothered by the paternal grandmothers and
were not permitted to break away.   They were left with feelings of
hostile dependency towards their mothers, isolated from their
peers, unable to relate to them and form relationships outside the
home.   One father strongly identified with the paternal grandmother, said that he felt 'sucked dry' by her, and had considerable
difficulty in breaking away from her in later adolescence.   During
adolescence some of them had to assume the breadwinning role in the
families, or assume the caring role towards their siblings (Morris
and Gould, 1963).

It would appear that only one father was assessed at a Child
Guidance Clinic during adolescence for persistent truanting.   The
same father was on tranquillizers to 'calm me down' while in the
army, as he was prone to violent outbursts.

BACKGROUND OF THE MOTHERS

Information regarding the background of the mothers is more complete
than that obtained for the fathers, and a grimmer picture emerges
regarding their childhoods.

Social class of family of origin

It was difficult to classify the social class in some cases where
families lived abroad.   However, only four families were classified as being in social class II, and twelve in social class III
and below, with over half of these families living in urban areas.

Economic conditions

In nine cases, there were reports of harsh, depriving, economic
conditions during the mothers' childhoods.   Interestingly, six of
these mothers were from families in social class II or III.   As
with the fathers, it seemed that sometimes the harsh and stringent
standards of the parents, particularly the maternal grandmothers,
rather than acute shortage of finances, created an atmosphere of
scarcity in the home.   Lights had to be switched off at a specific time in order to save electricity, clothes, often second-hand,
had to be kept spotless and worn for years.

Family composition and status

Twenty-two mothers were legitimate, two were illegitimate and one
was adopted.   Five of the mothers were only children and the rest
had siblings (Mean = 3.2 siblings).   Thirteen mothers were from
families of four or more children, and the average family size was
four children.   There was no set pattern with regard to ordinal
position.   It would seem that the size of the family contributed
to competitiveness between siblings in a few cases of families with
five or more children.   One mother, the youngest in a family of
seven, said that she 'always felt left out', and was rated as being
both rivalrous towards and 'paranoid' about her siblings.   Her
brothers were overbearing and strict with her and she remembers an
occasion when one of them knocked her teeth out when she failed to
do her mathematics homework.   She attempted to gain the attention
of her parents by assuming the role of 'clown and joker' in the
family, but felt that she was ignored by them.   A few mothers
also reported feelings of being 'sandwiched in' and fierce jealousy
towards their youngest 'favoured' siblings.

Education of mothers

Ten mothers stayed on at school till the age of sixteen years or
over.   Half left at fifteen or under.   Whereas in their study of
battering parents, Smith and Hanson (1975) found that compared
with their controls a significant proportion of the battering
mothers attended special schools, there was no evidence to suggest
that any of our mothers were educationally sub-normal or attended
special schools.   A few attended private or local authority
boarding schools, where rules were rigid and discipline was strict.
It would appear that most mothers were of average intelligence and
had some form of further training.   This ranged from civil
service to hairdressing.

Pattern of care

By the time they had reached sixteen years of age, fourteen mothers
were no longer receiving care from both their natural parents.
Ten of these fourteen were deprived of this care even during their

first year of life.   Ten mothers experienced a disrupted pattern
of care through the death of one or both maternal grandparents, or
the separation of the maternal grandparents during childhood.
Another four mothers experienced a disturbed pattern of care,
mainly because maternal grandmothers were unmarried and unable to
cope on their own.   During the 0-1-year period, four mothers had
one or more changes in caretakers and during the 2-5-year period,
eight mothers had one or more changes in caretakers.   During the
6-16-year period, four mothers experienced one change, while five
experienced more than one change in caretaker.   It was our impression that patterns of separation and reunion with the maternal
grandparents/substitutes, especially during the 6-16-year period,
occurred to suit the needs of the caretakers rather than those of
the children.   A few mothers went into and came out of care, a few
were sent to boarding schools, one mother remarking that at the
request of her parents, she was allowed home only once a year.

The description of one mother as a 'broken-up and traumatic
child', would appear to fit many of our mothers.   This mother
spent the first four years of her life with both maternal grandparents, was then received into care for six months when the
maternal grandmother was ill and the maternal grandfather deserted.
Up to the age of eleven years she was cared for by the maternal
grandmother alone, who was frequently ill during this time and then
died.   The mother spent the next four years in a Children's Home
and then went to live with the maternal grandfather and her step-
mother, but had a poor relationship with them.   They separated and
the maternal grandfather blamed the mother for this, and she left
home to live on her own.

Thus, broken homes during childhood, with the lack of a constant
caring figure and mixed patterns of care, were experienced by over
half the mothers in our sample.

Quality of care/physical abuse and neglect

Of a sample of sixteen, nine mothers said that they had been physically abused by their parents as children.   One mother said that
the maternal grandfather often used physical punishment and beat
and bruised her, especially in later childhood.   Another mother
described how she was timed by her aunt over the performance of
tasks.   She was beaten if she was unable to complete these tasks
in the allocated time.   There was no evidence to suggest neglect
of the mothers.   It is of interest that in six cases where abuse
to mothers was reported, economic conditions were also described
as harsh and depriving.

Feelings and emotional states during childhood and adolescence

Feelings most commonly expressed by the mothers were of abandonment,
isolation, emptiness and unhappiness.   One mother, nicknamed 'doll'
by her parents, perceived this as meaning that she was 'stuffed-up'
and 'lifeless', a nonentity in their eyes.   She used to write
letters to nobody and post them through vents.   Another mother,

who spent the majority of her childhood in care, said that she felt 'unwanted and different from other people who had homes'.   Another felt generally 'unloved and uncared for'.   The mothers coped with these feelings in a number of ways.   A few developed psychosomatic symptoms during early adolescence, for example, migraines and phobias - 'I hated eating and drinking in front of people.'   A few developed other neurotic and psychotic symptoms such as anxiety states, hallucinatory states and depression.   One mother is des- cribed as 'prone to depression and anxiety all her life, and bottled up feelings of aggression'.   A few mothers identified with their aggressors, blamed themselves and said of the strict discipline they had received, 'it was good for me'.   A few rebelled against their parental figures, 'Everything I've decided to do has been because it was the very thing they didn't want me to do.'   'She developed an assertive, stubborn side and battled her way through.... She was a terror, couldn't settle and had a foster home breakdown.'   A few mothers expressed bottled up frustration and aggression in the form of temper tantrums and bouts of aggression, 'she went blue with rage'.   Adolescence was characterised either by stormy conflict with parents/caretakers, and a gay abandoned social life, or social isolation and withdrawal.

From comments made by the mothers, thirteen (52 per cent) were rated as having experienced a strict/rigid upbringing or being generally negative about their upbringing.   Five mothers perceived the paternal grandmothers as possessive and over-protective, though at the same time idealising them.   Smith and Hanson (1975) repor- ted that 39 per cent of their battering mothers had an impaired relationship with their parents during childhood.   Descriptions from a number of different cases will perhaps best illustrate these attitudes, with quotes from the workers or from the mothers themselves.

'One mother was 'caught-up' in a web of deceptive relationships, especially with her step-mother, who was excessively restrictive and created ridiculous rules in the home.   She described her step-mother as "evil", always intervening and deprecating, but able to be bought off with expensive gifts.   There wasn't an ounce of mothering in her.   The maternal grandfather was weak and ineffectual, dominated by his wife, and sexually attracted to his daughter during her adolescence.'

'The maternal grandfather was rigid, belligerent and uncaring, and seemed to let his own oedipal fancies run away with him, accusing the mother of being "depraved".   The maternal grand- mother was described as "cold and lacking in empathy", not liking children and "never cuddled us".   On one occasion the maternal grandfather told the mother and the maternal grand- mother, after chucking them out of the house, "if I ever see you in the street, I'll throw you under a bus."'

'The mother was often left to her own devices, yet also smothered by the paternal grandmother and made to feel respon- sible for her.   She had a convent education and was terrified by the nuns into constant obedience.   Both parents sought mother's sympathy and she was torn between them, though paternal grandfather was often "drunk and truculent".'

'Maternal grandmother threw maternal grandfather out of the

house when mother was nine years old.   Maternal grandmother was strict and possessive and the mother was a "victim of infanta- lism".   At the age of fourteen years, she was still taken to school by the maternal grandmother."

There seemed to be little room for normal growth and development for most of the mothers.   Some were caught in 'double-bind' situa- tions with their parents, from which there was no escape.   Others were bound in a neurotic tie to their maternal grandmothers so that a hostile/dependant relationship developed.   Parents sought emo- tional gratification from their children, creating 'role reversals', and in a few cases, the children were expected to take responsibil- ity for 'mothering' the family.   In a few cases, maternal grand- fathers were sexually aroused when their daughters reached puberty and became aggressively possessive of them.   In addition, constant denigration, harsh discipline and rigid standards denied them the opportunity to experiment and develop as individuals in their own right.   Smith and Hanson (1975) report that a significant propor- tion of their battering mothers described their own mothers and fathers as unreasonable in their discipline.   A smaller but never- theless significant proportion described their parents as harsh and rejecting.

It is of interest that eight mothers became pregnant during adolescence, and five of these mothers were under the age of seven- teen at the time.   Only one of these eight mothers was married at the time of conception.   It seems fair to assume that they were motivated either consciously or unconsciously by the need to separate from their parents.   In a few cases, the choice of partners much older than themselves suggests a search for a 'loving father figure'.

Although a few of the mothers experienced neurotic/psychotic symptoms during childhood and adolescence, it would appear that they did not receive special psychiatric treatment.   Smith and Hanson (1975) found in their sample that a significant proportion of their mothers suffered two or more neurotic symptoms during childhood, and some felt emotionally handicapped as a result of these symptoms.

Psycho/physical characteristics of the grandparents

Oliver and Taylor (1971) and Oliver and Cox (1973) described a history of pathology with 'mental illness, profound disturbances of personality and degree of subnormal intelligence' in families of abusing parents running through a number of past generations. In addition, there was evidence from past records, of physical and emotional abuse and neglect to children in the family pedigrees, these families being known to various social agencies.   Similarly, Smith and Hanson (1975) found that quite a high proportion of the parents in their sample had close relations with a history of 'nerves' or hospital admission for psychiatric illness.

We were unable to obtain a great deal of information about the characteristics of the grandparents in our study and our findings are based on a very reduced sample.   Anti-social behaviour in the form of drunkeness, aggression and minor criminal activity was

described among a few of the grandfathers.   Serious mental health
problems in the form of clinical depression and bizarre, obsessive
and phobic behaviour was described among a few grandmothers.   This
was sometimes combined with serious incapacitating physical ill-
health.   Certainly, these features seemed to contribute to conflict
and tension in the home, and in a few cases, may have led to the
break up of families.

CONCLUSION

The parents in our study were mostly from families in social class
III and below, living in urban areas.   The average family size
was four children.   Harsh, depriving economic conditions were experienced by just less than half the parents, but there was little
indication of poverty or neglect of the children.   Less than half
the mothers and a few of the fathers were physically abused during
childhood, but these figures may be an under-estimate.   There
appeared to be no evidence of subnormal intelligence among the
parents in our sample.   There are indications that many of them
suffered severe emotional problems during childhood, though they
did not receive psychiatric help for these problems.

    In our assessment, only one father of a sample of seventeen, and
one mother, of a sample of twenty-five, appeared to have experienced a childhood free from physical or emotional abuse.   Neither of
these parents was implicated in injuring their children.   This is
of interest in view of the findings of Oliver et al. (1974).   In
their sample of thirty-four abusing families, they found that compared with the non-involved partner 'implicated parent figures
were more likely to have been subjected to physical or mental abuse
or neglect in their childhoods.'

    The most predominant feature in the background of the parents
in Oliver's sample was that 58.2 per cent were known to have
suffered 'severe or prolonged mental abuse during childhood'.   All
the 'implicated' parents were in this group.   In our sample, 80
per cent of the parents would appear to have suffered various
degrees of emotional abuse during childhood.

    In the first instance, it would appear that caring was severely
disrupted for many of our parents.   Loss of parents during childhood is thought to be significantly higher than normal among
'problem' groups such as delinquents, adult criminals and mentally
ill adults (Brown and Epps, 1966).

    Table 5.1 compares our sample with a sample of 546 women pris-
oners (average age thirty-one years) and census controls (Brown,
1968).

    It would appear that in relation to loss of either or both
parents our figures are comparable to those of Brown, and twice as
high as his census controls.   However, the mothers in our sample
would seem to have suffered the loss of both parents to a substan-
tially higher degree than both Brown's women prisoners and the
census controls.   In addition, 24 per cent of our mothers and
10 per cent of our fathers suffered a loss of a parental figure
owing to separation of their parents during childhood.

TABLE 5.1 Loss of parents due to death during childhood before
age 15 years

	Brown's figures (N = 546 women prisoners)	Census controls	Our sample (N = 25 (m) N = 21 (f)	
			M	F
Loss of either or both parents before 15 years	25.6%	11%	24%	23%
Loss of both parents before 15 years	2.6%	1.2%	8%	-

Disruption of care during sensitive early months and years of
life, seems to have played a significant part in the lives of our
parents.   It would appear however that the quality of care before,
during and after separation or loss, whether by substitute or
natural parents, was equally important in determining their development (Rutter, 1974).   Together with loss of parents, mixed
patterns of care with inadequate substitutes and several changes
of caretaker would suggest that in many cases a constant caring
environment during childhood was lacking.   The picture also
emerges from the information on the backgrounds of both mothers
and fathers, but especially the mothers, that they experienced
themselves as children who were rejected, denigrated, greatly restricted and sometimes stifled by their parents.   Children were
often used by their parents and caretakers to satisfy their own
unmet emotional needs, and beings on to whom feelings of frustration and aggression could be projected or displaced.   At any rate,
it would appear that most of our parents were emotionally undernourished as children and had poor role models in their caretakers.
It would be surprising if their experiences as children did not
seriously affect their ability to assume their roles as marital
partners and parents in adulthood.

SOCIAL SITUATION AT TIME OF REFERRAL
Employment

At the time of referral, twenty-one of the fathers were in regular
employment and four were not working.   Those unemployed were all
only temporarily out of work and there were none with serious long-
term histories of unemployment.   Four fathers were self-employed.
Statistical comparisons with the general population on unemployment
and self-employment are not possible because the national figures
include both employers and self-employed and because our sample is
too small.
Over half the fathers were dissatisfied with their job at this
time, either because conditions and pay were poor, or because they
were discontented with the type of work.   A few had made several
job changes in the previous year.   Half the fathers were working
fifty hours or more a week and a few worked seventy or more.   This
meant that their wives and children saw little of them and over

half the mothers complained of isolation and lack of support from
their husbands.   A typical example is the case of a seriously
injured child whose father worked as much overtime as possible in
the evenings and at week-ends 'to make a better life for us all'.
His wife, consequently alone a great deal with the child, suffered
feelings of loneliness and despair which she could not share since
she theoretically approved of her husband's desire for betterment.
After a time in treatment, this husband commented to his social
worker that in retrospect he felt he had been continuing to work
such long hours to avoid the dawning realisation of his wife's
state of mind.   'I'm as much involved as she is really.   I just
closed my eyes and went on working.'   We feel that in some of our
families the fathers' long hours of working helped contribute to
the situational stress leading to the child's injury.

Only four of the mothers worked full-time out of the home at the
time of referral; one had a part-time job and two did some work
in the home.   Half the non-working mothers were anxious to find a
job; feelings of frustration at the home-based role of mother and
housewife were common.   'I'd like to prove I could do something
of my own.   It's always the same at home.   I feel like a change
and seeing some new faces.'   Clearly many of the mothers did not
find bringing up small children on their own a satisfying or sufficient activity, and suffered from feelings of futility, frustration and identity loss.   This feeling is of course common to many
young mothers in the general population and is exacerbated by
marital disharmony, unwilling parenthood and inadequate housing,
factors which were true of many of our parents.

Finances

Table 5.2 shows net family income at the time of referral.

TABLE 5.2   Net income per week (N = 25)

Net income per week (including both parents' earnings, where applicable)	Number of families
£0-£15	4 (3 on Social Security)
£15-£20	1
£21-£25	10
£26-£35	2
£36-£40	4
Over £40	1
Unknown	3

Comparisons with national figures are bound to be rather unprom-
ising since our sample is so small, social class and the amount of
over-time worked both affect income generally.   National figures

are for gross wages and ours are for net wages.   However, Tables
5.3 and 5.4 give some idea of a comparison between our figures and
those from the Annual Abstract of the Greater London Statistics
(1970).

TABLE 5.3   Average weekly wage

1970	National £26.2 (gross)	Greater London £26.9 (gross)	Our sample £27.4 (net

TABLE 5.4   Median weekly wage

1970	National £25.6 (gross)	Greater London £27.2 (gross)	Our sample £25 (net)

The year 1970 was taken for comparison since 70 per cent of our
working fathers were referred in that year.
    Although few of the families were at all affluent, severe
poverty was not a major factor, and the low incomes from Social
Security were only temporary.   Since in the majority of our
families there were two parents and one or few children, one would
not expect to find much evidence of severe poverty, as the main
groups affected are large families, single-parent families and the
old.
    However, the majority of the parents, like most parents, had a
family income of between £20 and £30 a week, and in an area of
acute housing shortage and high rents, money was a major problem
for many of them.   In at least a third of the cases financial
worry can be seen to have helped contribute to the general stress
in the home; in nearly half the sample there was a history of
debts, usually rent arrears.

Accommodation

Tables 5.5, 5.6 and 5.7 show information about our families' accommodation, compared with the picture for the three boroughs as a
whole (Greater London Census, 1971.   See Census Notes 3.8.1 for
definition of sharing.   See Census Notes 3.1.5 for definition of
rooms).   The material was obtained by reducing the borough figures
to a total of twenty-five.   The numbers for each borough were
weighted according to the number of cases to produce a proportional
figure.   No statistical analysis could be applied owing to the
small number, however it would appear that our sample did not
differ statistically from what would be expected.

TABLE 5.5   Tenure of accommodation (N = 25)

	Owner occupied	Council rented	Privately rented
Boroughs	3	4	18
Our sample	1	4	20

TABLE 5.6   Kind of accommodation (N = 25)

	Non-sharing	Sharing
Boroughs	22	3
Our sample	11	14

$x^2 = 8.91$ $p < 0.01$

For statistical analysis, owing to the small size of the sample, shared and non-shared accommodation were added together and the figures were divided into below 1.0 person per room and above 1.0 person per room.

TABLE 5.7   Persons per room (N = 25)

	Below 1.0 person per room	Above 1.0 person per room
Boroughs	22	3
Our sample	8	17

x^2 test for independent samples was applied, resulting in $x^2 = 14.0$, $p < 0.001$

It can therefore be seen that the housing conditions of our families were significantly worse than those of the general population in the area, which was sub-standard, in particular, as can be seen from the above tables as regards the number of people per room and the sharing of facilities.

The privately rented accommodation in which the majority of our families were living was generally of a very low standard, with relatively high rents.   In most cases, the social worker assessed housing as inadequate for the families' needs.   For example, in only four cases did the   child have a separate bedroom.   Smith et al. (1974) also note the importance of this factor.   Over half of our parents felt that housing was a serious problem in their lives and it was certainly another factor contributing to the situation in which the child was injured in at least half the cases.   In eleven out of fourteen cases of serious injury, housing presented a major problem.   Cramped sleeping accommodation, lack of play

space for children, inadequate and unhygienic toilet, bathroom and
kitchen facilities, difficulties with co-tenants: all the familiar
problems of urban rented accommodation were encountered by many of
the families.

We found many of the families' homes barren and unhomely in atmosphere.   Over half were described by the workers as 'uncomfortable', either because they were neglected or too clinical. Although
over half the families were lacking in domestic equipment, the
general standard of housekeeping was reasonable with only two
families being described as 'very dirty' (in both these cases a
Public Health Inspector was called in).   However, there was almost
complete absence of personal possessions and individual attempts to
personalise the home in over half the families as this description
illustrates: '... a large high ceilinged L-shaped room with quite
adequate separate kitchen and bathroom, clean and tidy and cold ...
quite lacking in life or personality ... like a rather dreary bed
and breakfast room, dutifully and unlovingly tended.'

Over half of the families had moved into their accommodation
within the past year, and most of them were anxious to move as soon
as possible.   This corresponds with the findings of Skinner and
Castle (1969) on the high level of mobility amongst battering
families, and they comment, 'there were indications that clients
changed their accommodation in an attempt to reduce stress which
stemmed from their emotional problems.' We would not wish to
attribute too much to our families' mobility in view of the inadequate housing which was so common, as the following illustrations
show:

'Poorly furnished and depressing ... parents did not really see
it as a home but more as somewhere to eat and sleep.'
'Dirtyness and messyness were very apparent ... their one room
was like an over-crowded furniture store and most of our contact was made in the kitchen which was chilly and damp ... it
must for the parents, have felt like living in a refugee camp.'
'Dark and lonely attic up unsafe, dark flight of stairs. Bathroom four floors down, kitchen two floors down. Whole house
smelly, dirty and depressing.'

Parents' interests and activities

'It's all very well for him - he's out at work all day and then
he's free in the evenings too.' In sixteen families, the father's
main activity was going to the pub and the wives resented this
freedom and source of company and reassurance.   'I'm the one who
has to stay in the evening while he's out enjoying himself with
everyone making much of him.'

Very few couples made use of baby-sitters to go out together in
the evening, and less than half the mothers seemed to have any
interests or activities at all outside the home. 'I don't seem
to feel like it any more.   I've changed completely .... I hardly
think of going out now. My husband thinks it's a shame really.'
'I try and read or watch T.V. to pass the time but it does pass
slowly.'

Many talked lovingly about their days of freedom before marriage

and children.   'I think that was the best time of my life.   I
can't believe that was me then - I used to be a real raver.'
    Other researchers have found similar patterns.   Elmer (1967a)
commented on the striking lack of activities and relationships
outside the home of her group of mothers, and Smith et al. (1974)
described the same discrepancy between the parents in the extent of
their interests.   He commented, 'it is more probable however, that
this failure (by the mothers) to participate in recreational activities is a reflection of the incompatibility between parents
themselves.'

Current relationships with extended family

In half of the families, both fathers' and mothers' parents were
either dead or living abroad, so that there could be no regular
contact.   Nevertheless, ten of these mothers and four of these
fathers appeared still emotionally dependent on their own parents.
For example, some mothers had families living overseas, whom they
had left as young girls starting out on a brave new life.   They
now felt ashamed and guilty that they had not fulfilled expectations but had produced unwanted babies, and failed to take advantage of the opportunities they had come to find.   One such mother
had deceived her parents about the age of her child and untruth-
fully told them that she was married, and was now full of guilt and
resentments towards them.   'I'm sure they know the truth really -
they always did - but why shouldn't I lead my own life? - oh, I
would feel awful if they ever found out.'   She had not seen her
parents for five years.   Another mother, who had not seen her
family since she left her homeland many years before, seemed constantly to hear the strict, unforgiving parental voices ringing in
her head, passing judgment on her life.
    In the other half of the families, who had parents living within
reasonable distance, nine of the fathers saw the paternal grandparents once a month or more often.   All of their wives experienced their in-laws as hostile towards them and all but one of the
nine themselves felt strong hostility.   'He goes to see his mother
every week, but I never go unless I have to.   She can't stand anyone her sons marry and I can't stand her either.'   Over half
these mothers described their husbands as still emotionally dependent on their parents and felt critical and jealous of their
relationship.   'I can't stand the way he still runs round her.
Can't he stand on his own feet?   He takes more notice of her still
than he does of me.   He still thinks she's the ideal of woman-
hood.'   It must, however, be remembered that information on
relationships with the extended family did not generally come from
discussions with the father or direct observations of interaction
but from conversations with the mothers.
    In seven cases only, the maternal grandparents were seen monthly
or more frequently and in most of these the mothers described mutual
hostility.   There were several examples of mothers being undermined
in the care of their children, either by open criticism or by the
maternal grandmother taking over and running her daughter's home.
The quality of this type of hostile dependency is well illustrated

by one mother, whose own mother served her a special meal of rump
steak and chips as a comfort after the child had been removed by a
Place of Safety Order.   The mother commented to her worker, 'I
really didn't like her doing that - it seemed to choke me - but of
course I had to eat it.'   Only one mother in the sample had
parents near by to whom she could easily and freely turn for
support.   Only a few of the parents had a sibling who was a positive source of friendship and support.   There were a few cases in
which fathers were hostile towards the maternal grandparents, particularly when they resented their wives' continued dependency,
although it relieved some pressure from them.   Occasionally, when
maternal grandparents had been opposed to their daughters marrying,
fathers still felt that their in-laws were trying to sabotage the
marriage.   In general, there were no cases in which fathers had a
warm or supportive relationship with the maternal grandparents.

Parents social isolation

Loneliness, distrust of neighbours, feelings of alienation from
the local community and of 'being a stranger in my own house' characterised most of the mothers in our sample, who often lived as
though trapped within their homes, viewing the outside world with
fear and anxiety.   Other workers have noted a similar degree of
social isolation among battering parents (Steele and Pollock, 1968),
(Elmer, 1967b), (Smith et al., 1974).   As Elizabeth Elmer commented, 'Along with quite overwhelming stress went a lack of emotional
support for our abusive families.   This could be seen in the embattled marital relations, in the failure of the extended family
to help the young family and in the failure of adult caretakers to
become affiliated with community groups....'
   Of the fifty mothers and fathers we knew, only ten lived in the
area in which they had grown up and still had continuous relationships with local people and services.   Over half of the remaining
forty had grown up abroad or had experienced geographically disrupted childhoods and had not had the opportunity to put down roots.
In addition, many were seriously dissatisfied with their housing
situation and hoped to move, so that they more or less hopefully
saw their present home as temporary.   In only two families was
there another adult living in the household, in both cases a grandmother.
   Several of the mothers described feeling like a stranger in the
area.   'You don't really feel you belong in a place like this ...
it's all so strange.... No, I am not a Londoner.   I hate it here.
I didn't want to come ... I hardly know a soul round here.   I
don't feel at home in this house or this area.'   The fathers
appeared less socially isolated than their wives since most worked
full-time and over half had social lives outside the homes, yet it
seemed that few had meaningful or supportive work or social
relationships.
   We were interested to see whether our parents had any person,
professional or otherwise, who could be used as a lifeline at times
of crisis.   Only four of the mothers had such a person at the time
we met them, in one case a maternal grandmother.   Some had tried

to get this kind of help and had confessed their mounting feelings
of stress to a professional person or friend, only to find that
help and understanding were withheld. As one mother vividly expressed it, 'Do you have to kill your child before anyone will
listen?'

However, it was our general impression that the parents' lack of
social and emotional resources of friendship, support and understanding was primarily a result of their own lack of trust and
self-confidence.

Several mothers fought and quarrelled with co-tenants and com-·
plained bitterly of others' lack of understanding. Workers became
accustomed to finding curtains tightly drawn in some families'
houses in the middle of the day and to being peered at through the
window before the door was opened. One mother always answered the
'phone with a tremulous and aggressive, 'Who's that there?'

Criminal histories

Information on fourteen fathers and nineteen mothers was requested
from the Criminal Records Office. In the remaining cases, a reliable check could not be made as full information on the parents
(dates of birth, maiden names where relevant) had not been obtained.

Four of the fourteen fathers (29 per cent) and none of the
mothers had been convicted of criminal offences prior to referral.
The offences were all petty, such as: 'loitering with intent',
'theft of sausages', or 'dishonestly handling a Road Fund Licence'.
Two fathers had five convictions and a third, three.   Consequently, sentences ranged from a fine of 50p to four months' imprison-
ment.

Smith et al. (1973) have drawn attention to an over-representa-
tion of criminality and recidivism amongst abusive parents and, in
respect of the fathers, our findings appear in keeping but it
should be stressed that in our sample, none of the offences could
be termed serious. In particular, it is worth stressing that none
entailed crimes of violence.

MARITAL RELATIONSHIP

At the time of referral nineteen of the twenty-five parents were
legally married; the remaining six mothers were cohabiting and
these relationships had lasted for at least a year. Twenty-two
of these fathers were the natural fathers of the battered
children.

The average age at marriage for fathers was 23.5 years and for
mothers 20.9 years. It was not possible to make a proper comparison with the general population; firstly, because social class
and age at marriage are positively correlated, and, secondly,
because of the time span. Our parents were referred over a period
of nearly four years (January 1970 to October 1973) and had been
married for lengths of time varying from one to twenty years.
However, as a rough guide, the average age at marriage in Great
Britain was 22.7 years for women and 24.7 years for men in the

years 1966-70 (Government Statistical Services 1970-72).   Therefore, bearing in mind the effects of social class, it seems that
our parents were not unusually youthful at the time they married.

TABLE 5.8   Length of marriage and/or cohabitation (N = 25)

Years	No.	%
0-1	2	8
1-2	7	28
2-3	7	28
3-4	3	12
4-5	2	8
More than 5	4	16

TABLE 5.9   Age at marriage (N = 38)

Fathers (N = 19) Ages	No.	Mothers (N = 19) Ages	No.
16	2	16	4
18	1	17	1
20	3	20	4
21	1	21	3
23	3	22	2
24	4	23	1
25	1	26	2
29	2	27	1
31	1	28	1
38	1		

    Looked at in another way, there were five mothers under the age
of twenty when they married.   This figure of approximately a quarter is lower than would be expected from a similar population, as
there has been a clear trend generally towards earlier marriage.
Only 8 per cent of all brides in England and Wales in the period
1921-5 were under twenty; by 1970 the proportion had almost quad-
rupled to 31 per cent.   This trend has been most noticeable in
the manual social groupings; the proportion of unskilled manual
workers' brides marrying before the age of twenty had risen from
21 per cent in the 1951 Census to 41 per cent in 1962 (Office of
Population Censuses and Surveys, 1968).
    Eleven (57 per cent) of the mothers were pregnant at the time
they married; five were carrying the battered child and six another
child.   A further three mothers went to live with the fathers

because of an unplanned pregnancy.   Bearing in mind the difficulties of comparison, this seems to be higher than would be expected
for a similar population.   In the years 1969-70 33 per cent of
all brides under twenty were pregnant at marriage and the proportion declined sharply with increasing age (calculations based upon
'Registrar General's Statistical Review', 1969 and 1970, Office of
Population Censuses and Surveys, 1971 and 1972).

Since the three factors most clearly associated with marital
breakdown are early marriage, low social class and pre-marital
pregnancy (Gibson, 1974), our parents seem to have had the dice
loaded fairly heavily against them when their chances for successful
marriage are viewed statistically.

Our own impressionistic information bears out this picture.
Many of the parents described relationships entered into unwilling-
ly and grudgingly because of an unwanted baby.   One father, who
was in hospital during his girl-friend's pregnancy and planning to
marry once he was home, said,'I used to lie in bed and wish I'd
never get better so I wouldn't have to face it all.'   Another
mother said, 'I wasn't very keen but there didn't seem much option.
I didn't really know him but what else could I do?'   Some parents,
whose own childhoods had been disrupted through death or the separation of their parents, spoke of their strong desire as adolescents for a 'settled family life'.   As one mother put it, 'All I
wanted was a home and husband and children - to give them what
I'd never had myself.'

Twelve of the couples had practical problems at the outset of
their marriage or cohabitation - in four cases, concerning accommodation and in eight, both accommodation and finances.   This is
not surprising since so many of the relationships arose in an
unplanned and precipitate manner.   In less than half the cases
had there been separations between the parents.   These were
generally brief and rather hopeless.   'I had to get away but I
hadn't really anywhere to go.   I knew I'd end up going back to
him.'   Very few talked of other relationships after the marriage
or cohabitation had started.   Probably most had not been together
long enough to be drawn to alternatives.   Or as one mother put it,
'All men are as bad as one another - what's the point of going to
all that bother for another one?'

Nine of the mothers described their husbands as having been
physically violent towards them at some time.   In three cases this
was serious, frequent and associated with drink;   in these families
the main lines of tension, aggression and violence flowed between
the parents rather than between parent and child.   The three
mothers involved sustained frequent injuries, such as black eyes
and broken teeth, and two of the relationships ended soon after
referral.   In the remaining six cases, the father's violent
behaviour although occasionally serious, was less frequent, was not
associated with drink, and was not the main source of stress in the
family.   Thus, although there were reports of physical violence
by fathers in 36 per cent of our families, this only seems to have
been serious in 12 per cent of the cases.   Other researchers have
also established that there is an overlap between violence to
wives and violence to children;   Scott (1974) found that twelve
out of forty-one men who had killed their children had also

assaulted their partners, and in Smith's sample (1974) 25 per cent
of the fathers had also battered their wives.   The Royal College
of Psychiatrists' Memorandum on Battered Wives (February 1974)
considers that there is an overlap, particularly with men who frequently abuse their wives.   The husbands of 'battered wives' described by Pizzey (1974) were also violent towards their children at
times, but they were men for whom physical violence, particularly
towards their wives, was a common and compulsive impulse.   In
our experience the three men who seriously and regularly injured
their wives, frequently resorted to violence in other situations.
Although there was occasional violence towards children, the disorder in the family was based primarily in the psychopathology of
the father and thus in the marital relationship rather than in the
parent/child relationship.

Many mothers talked of the effect on their lives and marital
relationship of the birth of the battered child: in thirteen cases
their first-born and in many the main reason for living together.
Over half felt that their relationship with the father had deteriorated as a result of the child's birth.   They complained of
lack of support, help and understanding in coping with the new
baby.   Far fewer fathers seem to have been involved in the physical care of their children than might have been expected (Newson,
1963).   Mothers felt the reality of being tied to the child and
resented the father's freedom.   'He has all the fun and I pay.'
'He doesn't seem to understand what it's like to be in all the
time.'   'He just went on in his own sweet way as before.'   Several
mothers, whose pregnancy had caused marriage, felt that before the
baby was born '... at least we were in it together.   When she was
born I realised that it was all down to me.   It didn't make much
difference to his life.'

Marital relationship at time of referral

When we first met the parents and were trying to offer them help
and friendship, we did not focus particularly on the marital relationship.   At that time we were more interested in the parent/
child relationship and in their experience and expectations of
being parents.   However, it soon became clear that the majority
of parents were unhappy in their marriage or cohabitation.

In eighteen cases (72 per cent) workers recorded by the end of
the first three months that the marital relationship was a major
source of tension in the family.   When talking about themselves in
the early weeks of treatment, thirteen of the mothers viewed their
relationship with their husbands as the main problem in their life.
In only two of these couples did the father appear to share this
view, and several workers who tried to talk to the fathers about
the relationship encountered denial of any difficulties or a shift
of the problem on to the mother.   'She's the one that needs help.
She's got all day to sit around and imagine things.   She has it
pretty easy.   What's she got to fuss about?'   As one worker
wrote about a father, 'He saw the relationship difficulties of the
mother as occurring within her, like some kind of flaw in her make-
up or intentions, and without reference to her social network of
which he was a vital part.'

In three couples, the mother was on the point of leaving the
father at the time of referral and in another the father was about
to leave his wife.   Three of these relationships have since ended.

Sexual relationship

We did not directly seek information about the parents' sex life,
as we had not anticipated that they would easily discuss it.
However, of the sixteen mothers who did talk about sex in the early
months of treatment, fifteen described their sexual relations as
unsatisfactory and a source of stress in the previous year.   Only
one mother talked of a satisfying sex life.   Many of the mothers
clearly felt too tired, too resentful and too oppressed by their
children to enjoy sex;   many talked of 'going off sex after the
baby was born', and feelings of being used sexually were common.
    Sleeping accommodation had its effect on sexual relationships
and very few couples had ideal arrangements.

TABLE 5.10 Sleeping arrangements (N = 25)

Together in the same bed, in own room	4
Together in same bed, children in room	12
Together in same bed with child	3
Parents not in same bed, one in child's bed	5
No information	1

    In some cases accommodation generally was very cramped, but
there were instances where parents shared bedrooms and beds with
children unnecessarily.   One mother who shared a bed with her
child, whilst her husband had a single bed, said, 'I need the boy
in my bed.   He wakes so easily and I can't be troubled then.'
This family later moved to a three-bedroomed house and continued
exactly the same sleeping arrangements as when they had only one
bedroom.   In another family, which showed clear pairing between
father and one child against mother and another child, the parents
seemed to move in and out of their own and their childrens' beds
from night to night depending on the prevailing emotional climate.
    Fear of another pregnancy also played its part in the parents'
sexual life.   At the time of referral four mothers had given birth
within the past two months and it was too early for family planning
to have been organised.   Of the remaining twenty-one, only eleven
were using satisfactory contraceptive measures (the pill, the
sheath, IUD).   Thus, ten or 47.5 per cent were either using no
contraceptives or unsafe ones (coitus interruptus or the 'safe
period').   This figure is higher than that for social classes
III, IV and V in the general population.   Bone, in a study for
the Family Planning Association (1973) found that 35 per cent of
her sample were either using no method or an unsatisfactory one.
Although there is clearly disorganisation and ignorance about

contraception in the general population, many of our parents who
were not taking any precautions displayed a good deal of ambivalence
about future conceptions.

Children as a source of marital stress

In twelve cases, workers observed marital conflict over discipline
of the children.   These patterns are discussed in chapter 4.   In
six of these families, children aroused strong feelings of rivalry
in their parents.   Sometimes, one partner was jealous of the
other's attachment to the child, sometimes one or both resented the
child's attachment to a parent and occasionally both seemed to be
fighting for the child's attention.   In at least two-thirds of our
families the marital relationship seemed particularly vulnerable
to the demands of the parental role;   emotional insecurity and a
strong need for personal power and dependency were frequently
apparent in both parents.   'Many of our parents just like other
neurotic people have demonstrated an uncanny ability to become involved with and marry people who tend to accentuate rather than
solve their problems' (Steele and Pollock, 1968).

General comments

Nearly all our information in the early months of treatment came
from the mothers, nor did we often have the opportunity to observe
the parents together.   Whilst it was clear that most of the marital relationships were unhappy and troubled, and four were at a
stage of acute crisis, it was more difficult to reach a true assessment of the emotional dynamics.   The clearest theme to emerge
from the mothers was a feeling of lack of emotional support, of
closeness, of communication, of being cared for, valued and understood as an individual.   Many of the mothers felt trapped, lonely
and out of control of their lives, resenting their husbands' lack
of achievement, apparent freedom and lack of support and understanding.   Where they needed dependency and caring, they were offered
undermining and dominance.   'It's a man's world.'   'I'm always
getting into trouble from him ... always putting my foot in it ...
I'm always in the wrong.'   'I'm dreading him coming home tonight
- he's sure to find something wrong.'   'He comes along and spoils
everything.   Everything I do he criticises.'   Resentment was
also expressed at husbands' dependency needs, in some cases very
strongly.   'I've got one baby already - I don't need two.'
   It appears that the mothers' views of their partners were not
exaggerated.   The majority of fathers were critical of their
wives' inability to cope with the home and children and were frequently undermining towards them.   'My mother brought up four of
us on £2 a week and my old man beat her up every week-end and she
didn't complain.   Why can't you manage?'   'I don't know what's
the matter with her.   Any other woman could manage one child on
her own.'
   Complicated, unsatisfactory patterns of dominance and submission
were at work in most of the couples.   Often the wives appeared

initially submissive, if not submerged; few worked or had social
lives and most were unhappy with their accommodation and lived in
great isolation.   Their resentment and bitterness towards their
husbands' apparently richer and freer lives was however often expressed by undermining and violent destructive outbursts so that
whilst denied the company and comfort they needed, they ensured
that their husbands' lives and pleasures were eroded by guilt and
bitterness.   A similar complex balance between passivity and power
has been described by other writers (Green et al., 1974, Terr,
1970).   As Blumberg (1974) observed, 'A poor husband-wife relationship in which there is a clash of aggressive and passive personalities ... can ... set the stage for child battering.'   In the
majority of cases, both parents had strong emotional needs for
security and dependence, which drew them quickly into relationships
they entered both hopefully and hopelessly.   Since they needed so
much and were able to give so little, they remained unsatisfied;
the loneliness of an untrusting marriage and the inescapable
intimacies of parenthood alienated them even further from themselves and from others.

WORKERS' IMPRESSIONS OF THE PARENTS

In writing about the families as a group, some of the richness in
their individuality is inevitably lost.   It also minimises the
heterogenous features which battering parents present when viewed
collectively (Steele, 1970).   This loss is serious when dealing
with our impressions of the parents: their appearance, predominant
moods, social functioning and psychological defences.   Yet to
write about a few of them as selected individuals would be of
little diagnostic value and would equally fail to convey the common
characteristics which were undoubtedly there when the data were
closely studied.

The mothers

At a very deep level, the mothers seemed to experience themselves
as children in a world of powerful adults.   Passivity in the
sense of feeling unable to shape their own lives and corresponding
dependence on the environment to mete out what it chose, best described the common feature in our impressions of the mothers.   A
few mothers seemed immobilised, sunk in feelings of futility.
On the other hand, a few took flight in compulsive activity,
'always struggling to get ahead of myself' as one mother put it.
Most mothers fluctuated between these two types of behaviour at
times slumped in inertia and despondency, on other occasions in an
agitated state.   Differences in appearances seemed to reflect
differences in mood and could be striking from one visit to the
next.   At the extremes, a few looked bedraggled and limp, whilst
the few who took constant trouble over their appearance looked neat
and clean rather than attractively dressed.
    It is of interest to compare our impressions with those of
Merrill (1962) who identified three main personality types amongst
abusive parents: hostile/aggressive, rigid/compulsive, and

passive/dependent.   Our parents could not be sub-grouped under
this typology as we found that the three main types were not independent.   Virtually all of our mothers showed some passive/depen-
dent features.   Less than half also exhibited rigid/compulsive
characteristics to varying degrees.   A few were of the hostile/
aggressive type but with passive characteristics and, in a couple
of cases, compulsive features as well.   It could have been that
in some cases the observed passivity was a feature of the underlying depression noted in abusive parents (Steele and Pollock,
1968) which tended to mask the personality characteristics of our
mothers.   This extraneous factor however would not account for
the extent of overlap.   In our opinion, the characteristics identified by Merrill and discussed by Spinetta and Rigler (1972) are
useful in diagnosis but misleading when viewed as discrete
entities.

Most mothers seemed highly defended against their feelings.   A
few resorted to projection and blaming of others which verged on
the paranoid.   Most used denial, dissociation and repression to a
powerful degree.   One of the fathers remarked, 'If she doesn't
want to know about something it's as though it never happened.'
It seems that in this way they not only shut out threats from the
environment but also thwarted their own disturbing impulses and
wants.   Many feared strong emotion and were unable to express
feelings.   This may account for their basic passivity and sense
of powerlessness and inadequacy in that such strong defences con-
sume a lot of energy.

It is not surprising that most mothers seemed depressed and
flat, overwhelmed by events rather than feeling in charge.   Over
half of the mothers displayed poor coping ability when faced with
problems of a practical as well as emotional nature.   It was as
though they hoped that by pretending bad things were not happening
they would go away.   A few took flight in fantasy 'when we win
the pools ...' or clung to magical, global solutions to their
problems, 'everything will be all right when we move.'   Planning
ability was poor or non-existent in over half of the mothers.
Those who could plan and organise their lives were very sensitive
to failure and usually found great difficulty in persisting with
the achievement of goals.   As one worker described:
'Mrs P showed some capacity to assess her own problems realisti-
cally and determine goals.   However, mixed in with her rational
ability was a fatalism and hopelessness which prevented her
from coping with her problems and she withdrew in apathy and
depression.'
A few were quick to feel frustrated when things went wrong
although sometimes believing that it was inevitable.   'Nothing
ever goes right for me.'   Many seemed to be out to prove this
statement, indulging in obviously self-defeating activities.   'I
think I am my own worst enemy' one mother ventured, and probably
this was true of the majority.

Feelings of futility were most acute in their roles as parents.
Many mothers felt 'overtaken' by parenthood and the fact that the
majority of battered children were either unwanted or unplanned as
discussed in chapter 4 meant that they probably did not have time
to grow emotionally into the maternal role.   However, to us the

problem seemed more fundamental than that.   It was as though, with
a few exceptions, our mothers were simply not equipped as people to
cope effectively with the task of child rearing.   A basic lack of
motherliness as a feature of abusive parents has been well documented in the literature (e.g. Steele and Pollock, 1968; Court,
1969a), and our impressions tend to confirm this as being central
to the problem of abuse.   One mother said, 'I don't feel I was
made to be a mother, I don't have the patience or understanding.'

Many of our mothers struggled hard with the idea of being 'good
parents', in some cases setting themselves very high standards of.
parenthood.   A lot of anxiety existed about fulfilling their responsibilities as mothers together with a strong sense of duty and
obligation.   Thus, anything seen as difficult behaviour on the part
of the child was, for the mothers, heavy confirmation of their own
inadequacies.   Lacking were feelings of empathy for the child and
the ability to enjoy the vitality of the relationship.   In fact,
the mothers often seemed threatened by the child's childishness
leading them to place considerable emphasis on discipline and control, even with young babies.   It is interesting that Carter
(1974) in a discussion of the relationship of child abuse and
powerlessness comments, 'the vulnerable parent stripped of his
ability to control a demanding and apparently powerful baby,
behaves like an insecure totalitarian ruler faced by an uprising.
The parent retrieves his shaky power by subduing the child in a
power game which goes too far.'

The mothers seemed predominantly to be out of touch with the
reality of their children.   It was as though they were playing a
game of being parents and treated their children as passive dolls,
fearful monsters or in a few cases, wise old men.   Correspondingly,
their own sense of being a mother felt at times unreal.   'I feel
funny sometimes when the boy says, "Mummy" and wonder if it's
really me.'   This indication of schizoid defences is perhaps a
clue to how the mothers managed to cope from day to day with a
task for which they seemed emotionally so ill equipped.   A few
of the mothers did seem to gain intermittent satisfactions from
child rearing.   Interestingly, they were mothers with three or
more children, who had found, with the exception of the battered
child, at least one of their offspring rewarding or enjoyed a
particular stage in his development.

On the surface, most of the mothers had a strong sense of gender
identity but also rigid conceptions of male and female roles.
There is some evidence to suggest that many of the mothers had
prematurely got themselves into the roles of housewife and mother
in order to avoid the turbulence of adolescence and the struggle
of establishing a firm sense of their own identity.   In this
respect they remained, with some measure of safety, submerged by
the demands of their roles.   Some complained of being 'tied down',
others professed contentment with what appeared to be restricted,
rather downtrodden existences, but there seemed to be resentments
uncomfortably buried within these claims.

Underlying the apparently firm identification with the female
role were indications of ambivalence and rejection of femininity.
This was more obvious regarding sexuality, discussion of which
seemed to provoke avoidance or confusion.   Some mothers presented

as dowdy or tomboyish, or asexual.   The few mothers who were more
aware of themselves sexually tended to be aggressively sexual or
narcissistic and manipulative.   However, this can be seen as just
one manifestation of fear of tenderness and closeness apparent in
their relationships with other people in general, including children.   Other adults were regarded with suspicion by most mothers
and not envisaged as providers of help and comfort;   rather they
were regarded as sources of criticism and blame to be avoided where
possible.   This reinforced their sense of isolation and loneliness
which most seemed to experience profoundly on a psychological as
well as the social level discussed earlier in this chapter.   It
also links with the low sense of self-esteem apparent in most of
our mothers.   The relevance of these concepts has been discussed
at length by Steele and Pollock (1968).

The fathers

The fathers on the whole seemed to be solitary figures.   Unlike
the mothers, they did not appear perturbed by their isolation but
instead were proud of 'going it alone'.   They tended to feel it
was 'feeble' to ask others for help and one father said with great
satisfaction: 'I have never needed to ask anyone for a thing.'
Over half were large and flabby in build, but most of them took
some trouble over their appearance and 'liked to look smart'.   A
few were scruffy and dishevelled, hunched up in corners away from
the world.   Several of the fathers, who on the surface appeared
neat and also competent, expressed a fear of dissolution.   'I
feel near to falling apart sometimes.'   In our opinion, this was
characteristic of the majority who used a variety of mannerisms to
conceal their vulnerability, ranging from brusque bravado to compliant charm.   Their self-righteous independence was probably a
desperate attempt to maintain face.
   The fathers' defences were predominantly denial and projection.
As we got to know them they gave the impression, with a few exceptions, of having big dependency needs, becoming demanding of
attention when it was immediately available, but were not prepared
actively to seek support.   Generally low tolerance of frustration,
inability to plan or even make an effort to meet commitments were
fairly common.   As with the mothers, this purposelessness was
sometimes combined with fruitless activity.   'I work hard all the
time but never seem to have anything to show for it.'   Underlying
their social facade, the majority of fathers seemed to have a
poor sense of their own value.   One or two made statements like,
'The wife and kids would be better off without me,' or, 'I'd be
better off dead.'   Many indicated that they felt themselves to be
basically 'bad'.
   Undoubtedly, many of the fathers seemed proud of their father-
hood which probably helped to give them a stronger sense of their
own identity.   However, our fathers, like most fathers in the
general population, in taking on the role of parent, had not
needed to change their lifestyle as much as their wives.   The few
fathers who did involve themselves intensively in caretaking activities took over the maternal role in such a way that their wives

were made to feel superfluous, inadequate and undermined.   In fact,
our impression was that most couples were unable to complement one
another in the parental role and that they derived little shared
pleasure from parenthood.

   As parents the fathers tended to behave like older siblings
towards their children.   Some fathers, like the mothers, seemed
to gain satisfaction from the power derived from parenthood.   They
tended to exercise this power in a playful way and enjoyed displaying their superior strength and knowledge in relation to their
children.   A few were teasing, provocative and somewhat spiteful.

   Several fathers seemed to have a need to continuously prove that
they were 'baby-makers'.   Although this need was probably compen-
satory, it struck us as reflecting more than anxiety about
potency.   For most of our fathers parenthood was perhaps a bulwark
against the purposelessness, low self-esteem and spectre of inner
dissolution which seemed to threaten them.

Medical problems

Over half of the fathers and most of the mothers mentioned some
form of medical complaint around the time of referral.   Many of the
complaints listed in Table 5.11 could be viewed as sub-clinical in
nature, but none the less resulted in considerable impairment of
functioning and well-being.

TABLE 5.11 Parents' medical problems (N = 43)

Complaints	Fathers (N = 19)	Mothers (N = 24)	Total
Migraine and other problems	0	5	5
Migraine only	0	3	3
Back complaint (non-specific)	5	3	8
Gastric problem	2	0	2
Obesity	0	3	3
Asthma	0	1	1
Depression	2	4	6
Anxiety state	0	3	3
Other	2	0	2
Sub-total	11	17	28
No problem noted	8	7	15

   From Table 5.11 it can be seen that the most common complaint
of the fathers was back problems and that of the mothers migraines.
Both conditions have been held to have a psychological component
in their aetiology and the other physical complaints listed are
also often described as psychosomatic (see Noyes and Kolb, 1963).

Ounsted et al. (1975) also report a high incidence of migraine
attacks amongst a sample of potentially abusive mothers.   It is
interesting that Noyes and Kolb draw attention to high parental
expectations, strictness and stifling of aggression in the early
background of many migraine sufferers.   'Migrainous patients
often disclose in psychotherapy hostile fantasies towards siblings
and other family members.   Frequently they have fantasised smash-
ing the head of the person toward whom they have felt hateful.'
    In addition, nine of the fathers were seen to have a drinking
problem.   In four cases this was considered serious in that the
use of alcohol considerably impaired their functionings, but none
of them had received any form of treatment for the problem.   None
of the mothers had a problem over the use of alcohol and none of
the mothers or fathers was known to have a drug problem, although
one mother was making heavy use of prescribed tranquillisers.
Details of the parent's psychiatric histories were patchy.   In
addition, when examining records, there was the problem of dis-
tinguishing between the occasional prescription of psycho-tropic
drugs for 'nerves' by general practitioners and the formal diagnosis of specific psychiatric symptoms.   As far as we could judge,
over half of the mothers and a few of the fathers were treated by
their general practitioners for psychiatric problems prior to
referral.   A few mothers and a few fathers had received treatment
from psychiatrists in the past, mainly at out-patient clinics for
anxiety states or depression, but none had a history of psychiatric in-patient care.   One father and four mothers were known to
have made some attempt on their own life prior to referral.

GENERAL COMMENTS

It is worth drawing together our scattered facts and impressions
of the parents and their backgrounds in an attempt to make some
cohesive comments about what had caused such serious parental dysfunctioning.
    As children, experiences of disrupted caretaking through the
loss of one or both parents or parental care of a distorted and
damaging quality were common; only one father and one mother remembered a happy childhood.   The majority of parents had therefore been denied the opportunity for forming adequate role models
for later life.   Many had virtually missed out on their adolescence through early pregnancy, over-heavy responsibility or
ongoing emotional disturbance.   Unplanned pregnancies frequently
precipitated marriage or cohabitation.   The majority of the
couples had frustrating and unhappy marital relationships, lacking
in mutual support, understanding or communication.   Sexual relationships were generally poor and unsatisfying; family planning
measures were often absent or inadequate.   Housing conditions
were poor and many lived in cramped space with little privacy.
Many fathers felt frustrated and dissatisfied at work; many
mothers felt isolated within their neighbourhood and community and
imprisoned in their homes.   Relationships with the extended family
were generally poor or non-existent; very few mothers or fathers
had either a relative or friend whom they could use as a lifeline.
Many suffered from recurring minor physical or emotional complaints.

Undoubtedly as a group of young parents the majority were and had
been deprived in many areas of their lives, emotional and practical,
in the past and the present.   An overwhelming conglomeration of
disadvantage and mischance had dogged their childhood and adolescence and still shadowed their adult lives: 'The complexity and
the interelationships of the factors that lead to child abuse'
described by Gelles (1973).   The clearest effects of this were on
their sense of their own value and their ability to relate warmly
and closely to others, demonstrated by embattled marital relationships and deeply stressful parenthood.   'I could never get close
and never get through', said one mother of her relations with
others.   Superficially, they appeared to function fairly adequately in other areas of their lives; for example, there was little
overt serious anti-social behaviour or severe psychiatric illness.
However, below the surface there was often evidence of quite
severe disorganisation and few parents were running their lives
in ways that were personally satisfying or rewarding.

Nevertheless, although the past helps one to understand why our
parents' lives had reached such an impasse and how they had come
to injure their children, some questions remain unanswered.   Why
was their deprivation manifested in child abuse rather than some
other form of deviant or disturbed behaviour?   Why did they, and
not other parents with equally impoverished lives, batter?

We do not feel that there is a simple uni-factorial answer to
these questions.   There is no single key that will unlock the
mystery of the 'battered baby syndrome', no one illuminating
factor alone that can distinguish and explain the 'battering
parent'.   Rather, we feel that the problem must be viewed in the
context of emotional and parental dysfunctioning and disadvantage
generally; that we must understand child abuse as an interplay
between emotional undernourishment and rejection in childhood,
unwilling parenthood, frustration and loneliness in adult relationships, particularly marriage, and the confinement and stress
of modern urban living.

Part two

Chapter 6

OVERALL MANAGEMENT OF CASES

EARLY MANAGEMENT

In January 1970 Denver House initiated its main therapeutic study,
with the provision of a community-based treatment service for
families in which a child under the age of four years was thought
to have sustained injuries inflicted by its parents.   Initial
responsibility for battered baby cases is essentially a clinical
one, the focus being on the child and identification and treatment
of its injuries (BPA, 1966).   We recognised, however, that a
multidisciplinary approach to the problem of abuse, with shared
responsibility and inter-agency co-operation and co-ordination is
imperative for adequate diagnosis, management and treatment of the
family as a whole (Court, 1971).
   Before opening intake we had made contacts with local hospitals,
general practitioners and Health and Children's Departments.   Our
purpose was to inform these agencies of the type of treatment service to be offered by the Denver House team, to explain our proposed treatment methods and the philosophy behind them.   We also
outlined our criteria and procedure for referral of cases, and in
addition, attempted to define the roles that we felt other agencies should play in their involvement with the families.   An
Inter-Agency Co-ordinating Committee had been formed, as has been
described in the Introduction.   Three major management decisions
were agreed by this committee.   First was that at this stage the
police should not be represented on the Committee and we would not
inform them of cases referred to us.   The second was that the
primary responsibility for casework with the families should be
ours.   Third, the institution and handling of Juvenile Court
action, if the necessity for this action arose, should be the responsibility of the local authority.   This arrangement ensured a
split in the function of the two social work agencies.   The theoretical bases for these decisions, and their operation in practice,
will be discussed in chapter 7.
   Decisions on early management of cases were based on two main
considerations, protection of the child and the provision of immediate help to the parents, in order to establish the basis for on-
going treatment.   Emphasis was placed on early diagnosis and

97

referral of cases to us, and a form of 'crisis intervention' was
advocated.   Referral agencies were advised that we operated a
twenty-four hour on-call service to ensure that a social worker
would be available to go out at any time of the day or night to
offer immediate support to the family.   They were also advised of
the need to treat the parents with circumspection, sympathy and
understanding.   Inquisitional and authoritarian techniques were
felt to be counter-productive and potentially harmful both to the
parents and the child (Steele and Pollock, 1968).   It was suggested that the referring agent should express concern to the parents
about their welfare and should refer to the puzzling nature of the
child's injuries.   It should be explained that it was for these
reasons that a referral was being made to a specialised social
worker from the community who might be able to help.   Finally, it
was felt that an introduction of the Denver House worker to the
parents by the referral agent would facilitate the acceptance of
social work intervention.

THE REFERRAL PROCESS

In most of the cases, referral to us was made during normal office
hours.   In less than half the cases, referral was made either
during the week-end or a week-night.   The majority of these were
hospital referrals of a child with serious injuries, the referrer
making use of the twenty-four hour on-call service to contact us.
   In seventeen cases, referral to us was within three days of the
diagnosis of abuse, and all but one of the fourteen cases of
serious injury were referred during this period, indicating that
there was a considerable amount of co-operation by other agencies
over our referral procedure.   However, a low index of suspicion
on the part of medical staff did account for longer delays in a few
cases.   The intervening processes prior to the first contact
between the family and the Denver House worker, sometimes led to
confusion and militated against easy access to the parents.   There
is some evidence to suggest that in nearly half the cases, the
handling of the parents by intermediaries or referral agents, and
the preparation for the initial contact with the Denver House
worker left a lot to be desired.   Although it should be remembered
that remarks made by parents might be exaggerated and should be
treated with caution, there is little doubt that some of these
highly sensitive parents experienced genuine distress because of
unsympathetic contacts, especially with hospital staff and in a few
cases, with health visitors.   One mother confessed that she was
completely alienated by the treatment of the consultant and found
her 'a frightening old bugger'.   Another mother complained bitterly
about the way she was handled by a casualty doctor at the hospital,
as he had indicated that she rather than the child needed treatment.
Others complained about medical social workers, 'she's always
following me around asking me questions', and 'she thinks I beat my
child so I told her a lot of lies.'   There were some examples of a
caring and concerned attitude towards the parents from hospital
staff and from health visitors, anxious to prepare the parents for
our intervention.   However, at times because of their anxiety,

they avoided discussion of the question of abuse and the child's injuries, and therefore the reason for referral to us.

Before our contact with them, parents were prepared for our involvement by referral agents in over half the cases and a professional person from the referral agency introduced us to the parents.   In the remainder, we had to introduce ourselves, often to clients with whom there had been no prior discussion concerning the child's injuries, and to a few who also had no indication that a social worker had been called in.   A case example illustrates the difficulty faced by a Denver House worker in making contact with highly sensitive and suspicious clients.   The health visitor who had referred the case, felt unable to tell the parents she had done so, had not discussed the child's injuries with them, and felt she could not introduce the worker to them.   There had been a delay of some twelve days in referral and as the child's injuries, minor bruising, had faded when we did make contact with the family, the worker did not feel able to discuss the real reason for his involvement with the parents, although telling them that he was from the NSPCC and was concerned for the welfare of the child.   These parents remained suspicious, defensive and aloof, and in addition, the battered child remained at risk in the home, the worker being unable to obtain the co-operation of other agencies at this late stage, in any plans to remove the child.

Successful introductions were usually those where the parents were carefully and sympathetically prepared for the involvement, often by a health visitor, who had a good relationship with the family, or a medical social worker or consultant, who had interviewed the parents at the hospital, perhaps on a couple of occasions before we became involved.

Time of initial contact with parents by Denver House worker

In most of the cases, we made contact with the parents on the same day as referral, and in three cases, the worker went out at night immediately after referral from hospitals, staying with the parents to offer comfort, support and practical help at a very critical time.   Short delays were caused in other cases while parents were prepared for our involvement.   In one carefully planned case for example, the parents were seen first by the paediatrician, who told the parents that the hospital would like the child to stay in a bit longer, that they were not happy about his injury and how it happened and would like them to see a social worker from the NSPCC.

POST REFERRAL PROCEDURE
Checking of information

On accepting a referral, we were responsible for checking records for information about the previous history of the family with the local health department, the maternity and child welfare clinic, the general practitioner, social services department and the local NSPCC.   The acquisition of all available background information on the family was felt to be an essential tool in the early

decision-making process.   However, the availability and adequacy
of information from records sometimes presented problems.   This
raises the important questions of confidentiality, methods of record
compilation and cross-indexing of information (Diggle and Jackson,
1973;   Oliver et al., 1974;   Parry and Seymour, 1971) and these
issues will be discussed in the final chapter.

The initial case conference

An early case conference with relevant agencies was arranged, so
that information could be exchanged and initial management and
treatment plans could be discussed and formulated.   This conference
was usually held within the first week after referral, following
our initial contacts with the parents.   We were then able to make
a preliminary psycho-social assessment, which provided a necessary
supplement to the medical diagnosis.   It was often found that if
there was a delay in calling the initial case conference, we were
left carrying full responsibility for the case and assuming roles
that we felt would be detrimental to the development of a therapeutic relationship with the parents.   In a number of cases the
seriousness of the situation warranted several case conferences in
the early period of treatment.   Minutes were taken of these meetings and were circulated among the agencies involved.

Initial management decisions and treatment plans

As previously indicated, the first priority for discussion and
decision should be the protection of the child.   Alternatives
regarding his placement should be carefully considered, with particular focus on whether there is a need for separation from the
parents, and if so, whether voluntary or legal separation by means
of Juvenile Court action is requried.   If the child is in hospital on referral, immediate consideration should be given to prolonged detention for protective purposes and also to enable the
social worker to make a clearer diagnosis.   This may sometimes
involve the institution of a Place of Safety Order in order to
prevent the parents from removing the child.   Other alternatives
include the provision of casework support to the family, with
emphasis on day nursery placement if the child is at home or discharged home, as the provision of casework help alone is not felt
to be sufficient protection for the child.   A final consideration
might be removal of the parents from the home by means of criminal
prosecution or through the provision of the Mental Health Act.
Discussion of the question of protection of the child and involvement of other agencies in plans for protection will be made in
detail in chapter 7, but it is appropriate to comment here that
this area created the greatest difficulties in early management,
because of the controversy and anxiety it produced, both in us and
other agencies.   This was graphically demonstrated in some cases
when we experienced problems in convincing the Children's Departments and medical staff about the urgency of protecting the child.
In one case, there were three case conferences in the first three

months and the worker comments, 'I found the hassle with the
Children's Department over whether they would or would not take the
case to Court almost as stressful as working with the family during
this period.'   Another worker comments, 'basically the two problems in getting my treatment plan (removal of the child) implemented were the professional "shyness" (including my own), regarding
abuse, and the formal procedure associated with other agencies,
especially the medical ones.'

Plans for initial treatment of the family were also made tenta-
tively at early case conferences.   It was generally found that
other agencies readily agreed that we should take primary responsibility for therapy, and were often relieved to give us this responsibility.   This sometimes resulted in other workers reducing or
sometimes unfortunately terminating contact with the families with
whom they had been previously involved.   It was emphasised that
other agencies should consult us before visiting the families in
order to avoid duplication, and also because it was felt that
over-visiting by a number of different agencies, especially at
times of crisis, might have an overwhelming effect on the family.
One worker described this 'gathering of forces' in a particular
case and added, 'at one point, having complained of social isolation prior to referral, the mother broke out sobbing to me,
"please leave me alone, please go away"....'   All other agencies
seemed anxious to make reparation to the mother, who had admitted
injuring the child, but presented as an appealing, helpless young
girl, herself needing protection.   The worker therefore, had to
undertake some of the functions of other agencies, and he felt that
this created confusion and apprehension in the mother and ambivalence towards him in his role as her therapist.

Our attempts to define the roles that other agencies should play
with the families did not necessarily resolve difficulties caused
by opposing theoretical standpoints and reluctance to become involved in cases.   This sometimes resulted in pre-judgment of cases,
refusal to participate in discussion, and hence inability to act in
the capacity defined.   In several cases it was apparent for
instance, that general practitioners did not want to become involved
in initial case discussions about the family, disagreed with the
diagnosis of abuse and, in some instances, refused to give further
treatment to the family having learned that abuse was suspected.
This is not of course true of all general practitioners, as some
were sympathetic and helpful, giving their full co-operation to the
worker.   In certain cases, hospital staff and paediatricians in
particular, were reluctant to take medical responsibility for cases.
In one case, where the consultant was asked to explain to the
parents the nature of the child's injuries and the need to detain
him, the worker comments, 'the main difficulty here was caused by
the consultant responsible for the case.   He found the whole
battered baby subject most anxiety provoking and apparently had
always tried to avoid being involved in such cases.'   After un-
willingly telling the parents of the nature of the child's injuries, the consultant was reluctant to have anything more to do with
the case, refused to participate in any case conferences and
refused to communicate directly with the worker.

LONG-TERM MANAGEMENT

Decisions regarding the long-term management of cases should have
as their main focus considerations concerning the continued safety
and future welfare of the battered child and his siblings.
Ideally, the aim is to make the home a safe and emotionally nour-
ishing place for the children (Davoren, 1968).   However, the long-
term placement of the children is a complex issue, and it is
apparent that careful and constant assessment and evaluation of
the family situation is necessary.   It is also important that
effective procedures for the on-going management and treatment of
cases should be evolved.

Intra-departmental management

In the recent report of the Committee of Inquiry into the case of
Maria Colwell (1974), the social work agencies involved were
criticised for deficiencies in intra-departmental management.
Particular reference was made to inadequate supervision of social
workers and an inefficient information flow within the departments.
   In the case of our project regular individual supervision
sessions and team discussions ensured that there was a constant
process of shared decision making and evaluation of cases within
the department.   Team participation enabled a greater clarity and
objectivity in evaluation, while also providing the individual
worker with much needed support in bearing the heavy responsibilities and coping with the anxieties aroused in working with these
cases.
   It was important that current information about cases should be
available to all members of the team, and it was therefore essential to keep detailed and up-to-date case records.   This was
necessary both for purposes of evaluation and also in order to
afford adequate coverage of cases at all times.   We continued to
operate a twenty-four hour on-call service and devised a duty rota
for dealing with cases out of office hours.   A worker on call was
usually aware of potential crisis situations in the families of
other workers and had been advised as to the course of action to
be taken in the event of a crisis.   However, it is not always
possible to predict crises, and crucial decisions may have to be
taken without reference to the worker involved in the case.
Access to relevant information assists in making appropriate
decisions at these times.
   During office hours our telephonist was a vital link between us
and the families and other agencies.   Telephone messages were recorded and immediately passed on to us for attention, thus facilitating a smooth flow of information within the department and
ensuring prompt action if necessary.
   We placed great emphasis on continuity of care for these families, and felt that questions of changes in personnel and termination of cases should be handled with sensitivity.   These issues
will be further discussed in chapter 8.

Inter-agency management

We continued the practice of holding case conferences, usually at
three- to six-monthly intervals in order to keep other agencies
informed about the progress of the families and to discuss their
further involvement in our cases.   Additional case conferences
were also called when crucial decisions had to be taken and plans
of action formulated.   Contact with other agencies was not restricted to case conferences, and often discussions with other individuals on a more informal level helped to produce greater clarity
and understanding and more co-ordinated action.

However, inter-agency discussion and consultation did not always
prevent difficulties in management.   Some of these difficulties
were practical in nature.   For example, we would have liked to
institute regular medical follow-ups on the children.   In practice
this was difficult to organise if the child was not in or had not
attended a hospital, or was not in care of the local authority.
We could not rely on parents' attendance at local clinics or visits
to general practitioners.   It was therefore important that we
should have good contacts with those in a position to observe the
children, and in our cases this responsibility often fell on
nursery matrons and other nursery staff.   In respect of our own
nursery, we did have access to a local doctor who was able to
observe, diagnose and treat or refer children for treatment at
times of illness or crisis.

In the long-term, differences in theoretical standpoints between
us and other agencies sometimes became more apparent, and led to
increased difficulties in management of our cases.   Narrow perspectives and polarized attitudes sometimes led to failures in
communication, serious errors in judgment and ill-advised independent action.   We would agree with the conclusions of the Working
Party recently set up to discuss the complex problem of management,
which warn against the dangers and possible fatal consequences of
unilateral decision-making (Franklin, 1975).   Where unilateral
action must be taken in the interests of the child the appropriate
committee should be informed.

It should be stated that in many of the cases, the growing dependency of the parents, and equally the burden of responsibility on
the worker, became so great that it was increasingly necessary to
share the load with other agencies.   The use of additional
resources in the treatment of the child and the parents will be
discussed in chapter 9.   However, in a few cases, it was difficult
to keep agencies involved once the initial crisis had passed.   One
worker described in the sixteenth month of treatment how she was
reduced to despair because other agencies, particularly the Health
Department, were reluctant to become involved and to take action
although conditions in the home were bad and the children were at
risk.   On the other hand, in a few cases, other agencies, though
not wishing to become directly involved, would from time to time
create a great deal of anxiety in the background.   This was felt
to be unhelpful to us and detrimental to the families.

Transfer of cases

In twelve cases, the responsibility for overall management of cases
was transferred to other agencies.   This occurred at varying
stages, as early as six months or as late as five years after referral.   Transfers only took place when distance after the family had
been moved, or a worker's departure, made continuation of treatment
by us impossible.   In six cases, the existence of a Care Order on
the child made it appropriate to hand responsibility over to the
Social Services Department.   The remaining cases were transferred
to a variety of local agencies for on-going treatment.
   We tried to prepare for transfers as carefully as possible by
discussing the situation with the parents and briefing other agencies fully about the history of the family and the current position.   We were sometimes able to organise introductory interviews,
and in some cases, the social workers from other agencies were
already known to the families.   In many cases we kept up contact
with the families by letter, telephone and occasional visits.   As
far as we know, the majority of transfers have worked successfully
and families have been able to accept workers from other agencies.

DISCUSSION AND CONCLUSIONS

It is difficult to make any clear assumptions about the success of
our referral procedure in relation to the accessibility of the
parents and acceptance by them of social work intervention.   Certainly, the indications are that immediate social work intervention,
as soon after the battering incident as possible, preceded by
efficient and sympathetic handling by the referral agency and other
intermediaries, is more likely to be acceptable, even to hostile,
heavily defended and inaccessible clients.   In addition, it would
seem that in some cases immediate referral to Denver House for
social assessment and co-ordination with other agencies might have
prevented serious mismanagement regarding both protection of the
child and successful intervention with the parents.
   We feel that it was to our advantage that we were a small team
and our caseload was restricted.   This facilitated greater cohesion
and mutual support between team members and allowed for careful
evaluation of each case.   However, even with small caseloads the
pressures on us were heavy because of the critical and long-term
nature of the work involved and because of additional responsibilities for education and research.   We feel that social workers
dealing with cases of abuse should carry only a limited number in
their caseloads, and other cases allocated to them should be
weighted accordingly (DHSS, 1974b).   Also, early closure of cases
should be avoided, as it seems certain that long-term support is
necessary in any attempt to prevent re-injury to the battered child
and his siblings (Skinner and Castle, 1969).
   It seems apparent that other agencies sometimes had considerable
difficulty in coping with the whole question of abuse and the responsibility this entailed.   Perhaps it is also true to say that we
had unrealistic expectations of the ability of other agencies to
perform their allocated roles, and also the level of co-operation

we demanded from them.   The greatest difficulties arose when plans
were made for their direct involvement with the parents in the area
of protection of the children and the provision of additional emotional and psychological support for the family.   It would seem
true to say that some agencies were rather in awe of the intensive
therapy offered by us and felt they could not compete or that they
could not waste their resources on a family already receiving
treatment.

To some extent we may have contributed to lapses in co-operation
of other agencies because of our possessiveness towards our cases
and perhaps our anxiety about confidentiality.   Also, in cases
where it appeared that events were running smoothly, we tended to
widen the time gap between case conferences.   This may have led to
false assumptions being made by other agencies regarding our cases,
because of inadequate or outdated information.   It is obviously
of considerable importance to develop an efficient system of recording and passage of information between agencies;   the Maria Colwell
inquiry (DHSS, 1974b) illustrated the potentially fatal consequences
of an inadequate system.

The management of battered baby cases has raised a number of
controversial issues, and these issues have aroused considerable
concern in the fields of law, health and social services.   In
addition, there has been press coverage of cases in which apparent
mishandling has sometimes resulted in the death of a child.   This
has provoked a public outcry against the professional bodies
attempting to cope with the cases, and a punitive retributive attitude towards the parents.   The Department of Health and Social
Security (1972, 1974a) has recommended the establishment of Area
Review Committees with the function of formulating general policy
on management;   also Case Conference Committees for discussion and
planning of individual cases.   We would agree with these recommendations.   In our experience, management of cases is greatly facilitated by inter-agency discussion and co-ordination.   However, we
feel that as a result of publicity, there may have been a dispro-
portionate emphasis on management and discussion of cases at the
cost of closer involvement with families and an analysis of effective methods of treatment (Jones and Jones, 1974).

Finally, we feel that plans cannot be put effectively into
practice unless goals are clear, procedures realistic, and there
is agreement between agencies regarding their roles and functions.
Failing this, committees and case conferences may serve little
purpose other than to raise anxiety and confirm that battering is
a problem.   'The management of child abuse generates a particular
and special form of anxiety in those who are charged with responsibility.   Agencies have developed techniques which are institu-
tionalised to facilitate the sharing of responsibility with others.
When such sharing is of information, the result can be useful to
the patient.   When the sharing is mainly of anxiety, then the
results are usually harmful to the patient' (Galdston, 1970).

Chapter 7

PROTECTION OF THE CHILDREN

LEGAL INTERVENTION
Use of the Adult Court and involvement of the police

When we started taking cases, we had not developed any clear plan
for working with the police.   Since our main emphasis was to be on
treatment and rehabilitation, we felt that we would prefer that
they were not involved with our families, as we did not believe
that they had a therapeutic role to play in battered baby cases.
Our intention was to avoid any direct interrogation about the circumstances of an injury, and we were therefore anxious that our
parents should avoid this experience from others.   We did not feel
that trial or punishment had any value in battering situations, and
believed that we would more easily be able to help the parents if
the police were not involved.

At the same time, we realised that the police had a legal right
to be informed of cases involving a possible offence and an obligation to make an investigation.   We considered the possibility of
building working relationships with our local police and a few preliminary discussions were held.   However, as the pressure of work
increased and our own therapeutic approach became clearer, the
possibilities of co-operation with the police did not develop and
their involvement in our cases was left to chance: by notification
from another agency or themselves picking up a case in the Juvenile
Court.

Amongst our families, there were fifteen cases which were not
taken before the Juvenile Court, in which the police were not involved in relation to the child's injury.

In a further six families, the child was taken before the Juvenile Court and the police were not informed prior to the Court
hearing, and did nothing further to investigate or follow up a case.

The police were involved in the remaining four cases.   In one,
they picked it up at the Place of Safety Order hearing and interviewed the parents twice, but took no proceedings.   The mother
told her worker with apparent nonchalance, 'Oh, did I tell you that
the coppers called round and told us we'd battered our baby? ...
must have been the welfare or the hospital put them on to us ...
told them he fell downstairs and if you don't believe me that is
your hard luck!'
106

In the second of these cases, the police were notified of the child's very serious injuries whilst he was still in hospital. They discussed the case with the Denver House social worker, who was anxious that the mother should not be interviewed if possible. A report from the Denver House psychiatrist, recommending that no action should be taken as the mother was suffering from a depression of the puerperium, was accepted by the police inspector.   He sent full details to the Director of Public Prosecutions adding that in his opinion no further police action was necessary.

The police were notified by the coroner in the third case after the child had died.   The police had three interviews with the parents, but were unable to find sufficient evidence to take any action.   In the fourth case, the police were informed by the paediatrician who feared the child might die, and the mother was charged with an offence under Section 20 Offences Against the Person Act, 1861 - Grievious Bodily Harm.   'They behaved like pigs at first.   They kept on at me and eventually I broke down and told them how it happened.   After that they were nice to me and gave me a cup of tea.'   At the Magistrate's Court hearing the mother was given an absolute discharge with an informal recommendation of social work and psychiatric help.

The nature of police involvement in battered baby cases is as yet unresolved in this country.   We would entirely endorse the words of an American judge, Delaney (1972), 'It can be seen that the criminal process as a solution to child abuse is usually totally ineffective.   Probably it has some deterrent effect on the parent capable of controlling his conduct but its chief value lies in satisfying the conscience of the community that the wrong to a child has been avenged.   That the true causes of the battering parent's conduct have not been sought out and treated is of little concern.' However, while the law relating to offences against children remains unchanged, it is clear that social workers and police must learn to communicate with and trust one another and that the present confused and inconsistent situation is unsatisfactory for all those involved in child abuse.

Use of the Juvenile Court

When we began work, we anticipated that the Juvenile Court would be used to protect seriously injured children.   It seemed clear from our study of previous NSPCC cases (Skinner and Castle, 1969) and from the experience of others in the field (for example Caffey (1957), Gwinn et al. (1961), Griffiths and Moynihan (1963)) that the risk of reinjury to young children was particularly high.   Also at the point of notification of an injury when a large number of interested professionals often descend on the family, the risks may be increased.

We were well aware of the disadvantages of removal of children: the risk of seriously alienating the parents by taking legal action, the emotional ill-effects on the child of separation from its parents, the lack of certainty about good residential alternatives, and the moral dilemma inherent in the removal of children from home against their parents' wishes.   Nevertheless, we felt

that the child's safety should be the main consideration and it was
our intention to consider removing all seriously injured children
by order of the Juvenile Court and work towards returning them home.
   In our preliminary discussions with the local authorities in our
area, we agreed that they would be responsible for taking legal
action in our cases.   We thereby hoped to test the ideas that had
been worked out by Kempe and his colleagues (1968) in Denver, Colorado.   Based on their assessments of the personality of battering
parents, they felt that the therapeutic and legal roles should be
separated, as the parents had a high level of hostility towards
authority combined with a poor development of basic trust and were
unable to tolerate feelings of ambivalence towards their worker.
We felt that other child protective workers in Britain might have
been handicapped in working with battering families by the need to
be both therapist and legal agent, and hence the local social services departments agreed to co-operate with us in an experimental
situation whereby they would instigate Place of Safety Orders and
Juvenile Court proceedings and we would take on the role of primary
therapeutic worker.

TABLE 7.1   Decisions about Juvenile Court action (N = 25)

A	Cases in which Juvenile Court action was not considered, since there was no injury at the time of referral	5
B	Cases in which Juvenile Court action was not seriously considered at the time of referral for one or a combina- tion of the following reasons: non-serious injury, child already receiving partial protection, insufficient medical evidence, no clear diagnosis of battering possible	7
C	Cases in which Juvenile Court action was considered at the time of referral as there was a serious injury. The Denver House worker recommended it in all these cases, but another agency disagreed. The Denver House worker then had to carry the responsibility for the child's safety	3
D	Cases in which Juvenile Court action at the time of referral was seriously considered and it was agreed that there was a need to remove the child from home, but the child was taken into care with the parents' consent (Section I, Children Act 1948)	3
E	Cases in which it was initially decided that the child should return home, but subsequent events soon caused Juvenile Court action to be taken	2
F	Cases in which Juvenile Court action was unanimously decided upon at the time of referral	4
G	Not applicable (child died)	1

   In three of the cases shown in Table 7.1 (two from Group B and
one from Group D), Juvenile Court action was taken after a period

of treatment (at-least two years) after a change in circumstances or
a deterioration in the situation led to re-injuries.   There were,
therefore, nine cases in all taken before the Juvenile Court during
treatment.

In general, we found local authorities somewhat reluctant to
consider taking Juvenile Court action.   In one case, for example,
where the child had very severe multiple injuries admitted by the
mother, and where, if she survived, permanent handicap was inevitable, the local authority queried whether there was sufficient
evidence for a Place of Safety Order.

At times their resistance was because of the difficulties of
proving cases in Court and the added problems caused by the change
in law (Section X, Children and Young Persons Act), requiring somewhat different legal test.   However, fundamentally there was a
general resistance to removing children against their parents'
wishes, and local authorities must have often felt frustrated that
Denver House was on the one hand offering intensive home-based
casework and on the other recommending removal.

Place of Safety Orders

Place of Safety Orders were obtained in all the nine cases taken
before the Juvenile Court, eight by the local authority and one by
an NSPCC worker, who had taken over the case when the family left
London.   All of these were for twenty-eight days, with one exception, which was unusually made for three days only.

In the cases taken to Court shortly after referral three of the
Place of Safety Orders were taken within a fortnight of the injuries occurring, one a month after referral and two after two months
had elapsed.   We found that in some cases we had to apply pressure
on local authorities even after the decision to seek an Order had
been reached.

Two of the orders were taken in order to remove a child from
home, six to ensure that he or she stayed in hospital and one was
to prevent the mother taking the child out of voluntary care, after
re-injuries had occurred during a week-end at home.   In four of
the six hospital cases, one or both parents were threatening to
take the children home, even though three of them were seriously
ill.

Outcome of Juvenile Court proceedings

In all cases there were several adjournments and interim orders,
either to give more time for the preparation of evidence or to
enable the parents to apply for legal aid.   These delays obviously
increased the strain for the parents.

In eight of the nine cases taken before Juvenile Court, a Fit
Person or Care Order was made.   In the one case which was found
not to have been proved, this was largely due to the successful
cross-examination and argument of the parents' solicitor.

Discussion of evidence

Our Juvenile Court cases illustrate different types of battering situation and types of evidence. Five involved very seriously injured young children, two of whose mothers had made partial or full admissions of responsibility for the injury, and four older children without current serious injuries.

Section I, Children and Young Persons Act, 1969, requires two conditions to be satisfied before the Court can make one of the five types of order open to it in care proceedings. In our Juvenile Court cases, the conditions which had to be satisfied were as follows:

(a) That the child's health was being or had been impaired or that the child was being ill-treated.

(b) That if the Court did not make an order, the child would be unlikely to receive the necessary protection.

Thus under this section (which came into force on 1 January 1971) it is not necessary to prove that the parents have injured or neglected the child; all that is necessary is to prove danger to health or life without pointing the finger at any particular culprit.   Inevitably, the Court would form its own conclusions about who might be responsible, but it would not have to pronounce on this point.   However, this point would be relevant to the second condition, because by making an order, the Court would in effect be saying that the child would be unprotected at home - i.e. that someone in the home would be likely to prolong or repeat the neglect or injury.

It is necessary for the medical evidence in the case of seriously injured children to be clearly and strongly presented. We found in several instances that paediatricians were unwilling to give this evidence, and some pressure had to be applied to persuade them to do so. They appeared to feel that they had played their role in identifying abuse and involving a social agency and did not wish to feel responsible for the outcome of their action: the removal of the child. They also understandably resented giving up valuable time to spending hours waiting in Court, with the possibility of several adjournments. This was especially true of consultants whose evidence was thought to be particularly valuable. They also felt at a disadvantage in Court due to their lack of legal expertise and disliked being cross-examined on medical evidence.

The case for the removal of the less seriously injured children had to be argued on the basis of one or several past injuries, a mother's admission of fear of injury, or a new crisis situation in the family, renewing the risk to the child.   Since medical data was not the foundation of the evidence in these cases, it was necessary for the social worker to submit a report and argue her case for the child's removal. We found that in several cases local authority social workers did not present evidence clearly and sometimes gave evidence at variance with what they had stated before the hearing.   This was sometimes due to a confusion and ambivalence about our role in Court (which will be discussed later in this section), and sometimes to lack of Court experience and inadequate preparation of the case by the local authority solicitor or court officer.   We felt that several local authority solicitors bringing cases to Court handled them badly, failing to present evidence clearly and causing unnecessary distress to the parents.

Reaction of parents to Court appearances

All the parents found their Court appearances a great strain.   In some cases anxiety was increased by a long wait and many adjournments.   (In one case, the interval between the Place of Safety Order and the Care Order being made was three months.)
   We collected parents from home and drove them to Court and they all clearly showed fear, tension and anxiety on the journey.   'I'm really dreading it.   All those people looking at me.'   'I feel ill - stop the car, I'm going to be sick.'   One father broke down just before going into Court, saying, 'You just don't know ... you shut your eyes for so long and don't see things you don't want to see ... but terrible things have happened.'
   The frequent period of long waiting on hard benches, in dirty, dreary vestibules and waiting-rooms, eyeing the other witnesses and watching policemen and unhappy looking people going in and out of the Court room increased the strain.   Many cigarettes were smoked and one thoughtful social worker took along a miniature of brandy in her handbag to support her clients and herself!   In several cases, the stress was worsened by the presence of the child, often crying inconsolably, in the care of residential or hospital staff, whilst the parents looked helplessly and angrily on.
   In Court, most of the parents were silent and withdrawn, although there were occasional angry outbursts.   Several mothers cried as the medical evidence was read out, hearing the parade of shocking clinical detail perhaps for the first time.   They all appeared apprehensive whilst giving evidence themselves.
   Afterwards, many parents felt angry at the way the case had been conducted.   'I felt very guilty in there - just like a criminal. We both felt on trial.   Why did they have to make it seem as though we were cruel parents?'   'I knew I couldn't win.   No one listened to me.'   'Is that all?   It wasn't worth it.'   '... that man up there deciding about children who he hasn't got the faintest idea about.'   All felt to some extent alienated and rejected by the experience.
   In seven of the nine cases, there was hostility or lack of support evident between the parents.   They were described, after hearing that their child had been taken into care, as 'crying separately', 'making no move to comfort one another', 'unable to cope with one another's grief'.
   It is often argued that a Juvenile Court hearing can be experienced by parents as a caring and understanding procedure, since magistrates try to appear human and the proceedings are supposed to be relatively informal and free from the usual pomp and ceremony of the operation of justice.   The police are encouraged to change into plain clothes, the press are not allowed to report names and addresses and the public are excluded from Court.   However, although one mother appeared to respond slightly to a magistrate's comment that 'you have been through hard times', all the parents

found the experience distressing and shaming and felt alienated from
the whole procedure.

Parents' legal representation

We found this another very difficult area in taking cases before the
Juvenile Court.   Workers already struggling with the attempt to
separate legal and therapeutic activities, and the inevitable blur-
ring of roles, then found themselves recommending and enabling
clients to secure legal representation which might result in children being returned home.   Particularly where parents denied injuring children and opposed Care Orders, this action was seen by them
as caring and in their interests, thus increasing their trust in
their worker, but it made the worker's position as the person most
strongly recommending removal of the child even more untenable.
It also led to difficulties with the parents' lawyers, who quickly
became aware of apparent conflict of role and attitude, and felt
confused about whose side the social worker was on.   'I wish I
knew what you were playing at', one solicitor said to a worker,
'who are you representing - or don't you know?'   In one case, it
seemed clear to the solicitors that a Denver House social worker
was hostile to his clients, even though they saw her as friendly,
and he advised them to refuse to see her, except in his presence.
    In two of the nine cases taken before the Juvenile Court, the
parents did not contest the case and were not legally represented.
    In a further three cases, the parents consulted a solicitor but
did not contest the case.   One father intended to contest, but
after listening to the evidence at the preliminary hearing, changed
his mind.
    In the remaining four cases, the parents opposed the Care Order
and employed a solicitor to attempt to demolish the local authority's case for removing their child.   All the solicitors were paid
from Legal Aid funds.   One of these cases was taken to Court after
several years of treatment, and since the social worker was able
to be open with the mother about his wish to remove the child, he
could be equally open in advising the mother to seek legal advice
and in communicating with the solicitor.
    The involvement of the solicitors in the other three cases proved
confusing and counter-productive.   It should be noted that none of
the lawyers involved was particularly interested or experienced in
Juvenile Court work.   Denver House workers were instrumental in
helping the parents to obtain a lawyer and all found themselves
distrusted by them and viewed as opposed to the parents.   In one
case, the solicitor at first assumed that the Denver House worker
was supporting the parents' case and that the local authority
worker was against them and he telephoned the Denver House worker
on several occasions to vent his feelings of identification with
the parents.   'I'm a parent myself and I can't sleep at nights
for thinking of how they must feel.'   His strong partisanship for
their cause increased the parents' hostility to the hospital and
local authority and made it even more difficult for them to express
their real feelings for the child.   However, when the Denver House
worker, under threat of sub poena, explained to the parents that he

would be giving evidence in the Juvenile Court, recommending the
child's removal, the solicitor felt confused and let down and warned
the parents not to trust the worker.   At the Court hearing itself,
the solicitor was shocked at hearing the medical evidence fully
detailed and commented upon, and muttered to the worker during an
adjournment, 'I don't know what to think now.   Do you think the
mother did it?'   In another case, a solicitor, whom the social
worker had previously described as 'crusading on behalf of the
parents', whilst questioning the mother, realised that she was
giving quite a different story to the one that she had prepared with
him.   After her evidence, evidently disillusioned, he advised the
parents to accept the Care Order 'for the best'.   Social workers
found themselves feeling acutely sorry for the solicitors as they
floundered in previously unknown emotional waters!

In the fourth case, the solicitor also strongly identified with
the parents against authority, successfully opposing the Care
Order, and the case was found not proved.

Whilst we would strongly endorse the human and legal right of
parents in such a situation to be legally represented, we found
that the difficulties of attempting to maintain our therapeutic
role were increased by the involvement of solicitors and that the
conflict between the interests of child, parent and social agency
were heightened.

We would strongly recommend that lawyers in child abuse cases
should have acquired familiarity with both substantive and proce-
dural law, should have learnt to read and evaluate medical, psychiatric, psychological and social work reports and should have
some knowledge of child abuse literature and treatment and placement
potentials.   As Isaacs (1972) observed, 'it is only by acquiring
some insight into the motivations which turn a parent into a child
beater that the attorney can achieve the level of understanding and
compassion that permits him to serve as an effective advocate and
counsellor.'

The separation of legal and therapeutic roles

As already discussed, we had hoped that it would be viable to separate these roles.   The current work on battering parents (for
example, Elmer (1967a) and Steele and Pollock (1968)) described
people whose lives had been a long chain of emotional deprivation
and rejection and who consequently were unable to invest trust in
other people and particularly those in authority.   It was felt
that if any kind of helping relationship was to be established,
this would be doomed to failure if the therapist had to become involved in questioning the parents about the injury, gathering
evidence and assuming responsibility for the removal of the child.
We had hoped that it would be possible to divide up social work
activities so that the local authority social workers would be
responsible for taking Place of Safety Orders, informing the
parents and discussing legal implications with them, taking cases
to Court, giving whatever social evidence might be necessary, and
we would be able to concentrate on forming a therapeutic relationship with the parents.

In practice, this split between the 'good' and the 'bad' did not
work out as we had hoped for a variety of reasons. We did not
find local authority social workers very enthusiastic about playing
the 'bad' role, whatever had been agreed theoretically in advance
with seniors in their departments. They were not necessarily convinced by the arguments; they resented, when already over-worked
having to give time to cases from which they would derive no reward
from clients, and they were sometimes unconvinced of the need to
take legal action at all. This is well illustrated by the example
of one local authority social worker, whose own impulse was to
return the child home, to put the parents 'on trust' and supervise
the situation. She was over-ruled by her senior and the Denver
House social worker and when the case went to the Juvenile Court
she consequently had to act in a way of which she disapproved.
She reacted by failing to communicate properly with the Denver
House worker and by acting, without consultation, in an attempt to
woo the parents. In another case, the local authority social
worker felt so resentful about her role that she tried to sabotage
the Denver House worker's relationship with the parents. In
several other cases, local authority social workers were unwilling
to communicate bad news to the parents, such as informing them
that a Place of Safety Order had been taken, or discussing legal
implications with them, and the Denver House social worker played
this role.

We had also not anticipated how often we would be the people
most strongly recommending removal of the child. Other workers
naturally then resented that we should be assigned the 'good' role.
As one Denver House worker wrote, 'my position as the person trying
to remain the good therapist and at the same time persuading all
the other workers of the need for them to take legal action of
which they disapproved became quite untenable at times.'

We found that the local authority solicitors bringing cases to
Court were even less likely to appreciate the therapeutic necessity
for a separation of roles than their social work colleagues. In
the early days of Denver House, we tried hard to argue our case
for non-involvement, but in every instance found ourselves commit-
ted to giving evidence in Court for the sake of getting the Order.
We were always able to tell the parents that this was under the
threat of sub poena and to discuss our evidence with them in
advance, but this did not undo the effect on the parents of hearing
their 'good' worker recommend removal of the child, and in two
cases give evidence of actual conversations. In one case, the
Denver House worker agreed to act as an expert witness and it was
thought (rightly) that the parents would find a general discussion
of battering more tolerable than a specific focus on them.

In the three cases brought to Court after a period of time in
treatment, the parents felt let down by their workers. We had
hoped that relationships established over at least two years might
be able to withstand the effects of the primary worker removing the
child, but this was not the case. 'You're meant to help people,
not make it worse.' 'You should never trust social workers - they
only bring trouble.' Although again the local authorities initiated and implemented Court action, we were seen as directly responsible and the clients felt betrayed, despite the fact that two of

the mothers were obviously relieved that their children were going into care.   However, workers in these cases felt that the situation was easier because of the established relationship and that parents could far more easily express negative feelings than to an unknown social worker.

In consequence, the parents were often mystified about the roles of different workers and responded in different ways, depending on their own emotional needs.   In one case only did the parents clearly uphold the separation of 'good' and 'bad' worker, despite the fact that the Denver House worker recommended the child's removal in Court and they opposed this.   They talked about 'us against them', clearly including the Denver House worker in 'us'. However, they had had previous bad experiences of the local authority before the case was referred.   In another case, the split was partially upheld by the mother, although she felt let down that the worker had to give evidence.   Her husband apparently felt both agencies were equally responsible for Court action.   In three cases, the parents   appeared to see all workers involved as reasonably 'good' and did not need to blame or dislike anyone.

We do not think it possible to draw conclusions from our experience of trying to separate the   legal and therapeutic roles.   We often found the mental and emotional gymnastics necessary a source of strain and guilt, and at times our position was quite untenable. Some of the difficulties we encountered could be removed;   it would help if there were a consensus   of opinion amongst co-workers on the need to remove a child and if there were greater expertise in preparing evidence and presenting cases in Court.   It would obviously be easier to operate a split if the two workers were in agreement and trusted one another, and this might be more easily achieved by two workers from within the same department.

Aftermath of Juvenile Court proceedings

The question of appeals against Care Orders, revocations and the return of children home will be discussed later in this chapter.

PROTECTIVE PLACEMENTS

In addition to the use of the Juvenile Court, we also tried to arrange protective placements for the children by hospital admission, voluntary residential care and various forms of day care. In all cases some kind of placement was considered necessary for the battered child, but this was not always possible to achieve.

Hospital care

Fourteen children spent some time in hospital during the first three months of treatment and a few were there throughout this period: two children were hospitalised twice.   Eleven of these children were in hospital with the injury(ies) that led to referral.   One child was detained in hospital for a prolonged period

after birth because of the mother's fears of harming him.   Two
children were admitted to hospital shortly after referral, one for
a paediatric assessment and one because of a minor re-injury and
for assessment.   We had a standing arrangement with several hospitals that children could be re-admitted for protective purposes
should a further crisis arise.   This happened in a few cases at a
later stage in treatment.

In the majority of cases, the workers felt that the hospital
atmosphere was reasonably friendly and relaxed and that the staff
made some efforts to encourage the parents to participate in caring
for the child.   However, it was often very difficult for the medical staff to contain their feelings in view of the injuries sustained by the children and the parents' apparent lack of concern.
In a few cases, workers noted that the hospital staff were suspicious and watchful or hostile and insensitive towards the parents,
who were highly aware of the reactions they evoked and made to
feel very uncomfortable.   In one case, in which the nurses were
obviously horrified and revolted by the extent of the child's injuries and the mother's rejecting behaviour, the worker observed
them forcing the mother to hold her very sick baby and commented,
'It was like a bomb being put in her lap.'   In another case, a
devoted mother was frozen out by nursing staff when her child was
admitted to hospital for the second time with a serious medical
condition because they had seen on the notes that she was a query
battered baby.

In a number of cases the nursing staff made useful diagnostic
observations, for example, relating to the parents' awkward handling or fear of handling the child, behaviour in the child that
seemed to irritate the parents and the way the child behaved in
the presence of his parents, including differences in his response
to each parent.

Parents' reactions to hospital care

Typically a child's admission to hospital, whatever the circumstances, is a time of crisis for the family.   Undoubtedly, for
parents who have injured their children, it is a very stressful
time, but the child's admission to hospital actually may be welcomed in that it provides them with a much needed break from caring
for the child.   However, it became clear to us that for most of
our parents, who were highly aware that the focus of professional
concern was the child's injury and future safety, any feelings of
relief were marred by their anxiety about what would happen next
both to them and the child.   This was particularly true of the
six families whose children were detained in hospital under a
Place of Safety Order.

Separation from the child was particularly hard for those
parents who closely identified with the child and wanted him home,
in contrast to their partners who showed little feeling for the
child.   We were aware that this led to a tremendous build up of
tension between such couples, who were quite unable to acknowledge
openly their feelings to one another.   Some parents understandably felt that the detention of their child in hospital under an

order implied condemnation of them as parents and became obsessed
with getting the child home.   It was evident that one young mother
wanted her child home in order to make reparation.   She was unrealistic when the worker tried to point out the enormous stresses
which she still faced.   She tended to idealise the child in his
absence, yet in practice found it difficult just to cope with his
feeds when visiting him in hospital and quickly became overwrought.
The father, who had a horror of residential care, was equally unrealistic and was preparing to fight the order as his wife had set
her heart on having the child home.   However, after the mother had
received constant reassurance and support from her psychiatrist and
social worker that she needed rest and respite from the demands of
the child, at least on a short-term basis, she was able to acknowledge that there were some advantages in transferring the child
from hospital to a residential nursery for a few months.

In over half the cases, workers remarked on the parents' apparent lack of affection for the child, lack of concern for the
child's suffering if there were injuries, and inability to sympa-
thise with what the child must be feeling on finding himself in
strange, new surroundings.   Ironically, some parents were noted
to be more interested in and empathetic towards other children in
the ward than their own.   In two cases, the mothers were described
as strikingly emotionally detached, negative and hostile towards
the children, almost as though they were blaming them for being
injured and causing so much fuss.   Some mothers expressed that
they were missing their babies and felt empty or without a purpose
in life, but they were preoccupied with their own needs rather than
the babies'.

A number of the parents were very critical of the care provided
by the hospital, including the food, clothes and routine.   Some
blamed the hospital for their children's unhappiness and boredom,
but were quick to sabotage any plans proposed by the hospital
staff to alleviate this.   Clearly, these were parents who felt
powerless and threatened by the situation so that resorting to
criticism was the only way of hitting back.   Some parents commented, with good reason, to their workers that they felt that the
hospital staff were witholding information from them, or felt
hounded by doctors who were anxious to seek information from them,
'nobody tells us anything, but everybody keeps asking us the same
questions and there doesn't seem any point in it.'

Voluntary reception into care

In six of our families, children were received into care with their
parents' consent (Section I, Children Act 1948).   These receptions
into care occurred at different points in treatment and for a
variety of reasons, ranging from a brief separation at a time of
personal crisis, to a wish for long-term separation from the child.
For example, one mother had arranged private fostering for her
child soon after birth.   Her health visitor later persuaded her
to cease this arrangement and place the child in day care.   An
injury noticed by the day nursery matron led to referral and it
was initially decided that day care should continue, while casework

support was provided.   However, a minor re-injury led to a reass-
essment of the situation and we accepted that the mother did not
wish to care for the child.   Voluntary reception into care was
arranged which continued for the next three years.

This was the only case in which voluntary reception into care
was necessary for a long period.   However, we occasionally had difficulty in persuading Social Services Departments of the need for
voluntary care because they feared that children would be abandoned.
In general, we found that voluntary reception into care only worked
successfully when the parents acknowledged the need for their
children to be away from home.   In all the other cases, this was
only acceptable because of an acute crisis situation in their
lives: either environmental, such as impossible housing, or emotional, such as a severe breakdown in their functioning.

It is often tempting for social workers who feel that children
should be removed from home for their own safety to try to gain
the parents' co-operation and acceptance in this action.   Although
we found this possible in some situations, in general, we felt with
the most seriously injured children and the most withdrawn and
suspicious parents that it would be a vain endeavour.   When
parents are unable to admit to others and sometimes to themselves
that they have been living under stress such that they have seriously injured their child, it is unlikely that they will co-operate in
an implicit admission of abuse.   Neither do we think that the type
of approach which combines an attempt at honesty with a veiled
threat is likely to succeed.   'I know what has happened, and I
feel that for both your sakes the child must go into care.   It
would be much easier all round if this could be done with your
agreement.'   This seems akin to the practice in mental health work
of encouraging patients to enter psychiatric hospital 'voluntarily'.
('If you don't, we'll put a Section on you'.)   We feel that it
lays too great a strain on parents whose feelings towards their
children are deeply ambivalent, and that to leave with them the
freedom to remove children from care places the child at too great
a risk.

Type of residential placement

Our general thinking at the outset of the project was that battered
children in care would be more appropriately placed in a residential nursery or children's home than with foster parents.   This
view depended on a successful prognosis for the child's rehabilitation with his family; we hoped that children would not need to
be in care for long periods and therefore considered the most
important factor in their residential placement to be the extent
to which the mother-child relationship could be encouraged and
enhanced during separation.   This seemed more likely in a group
setting than with an individual foster mother.   The strain on such
a foster mother of both offering warm mothering to the child and at
the same time giving understanding and sympathy to its battering
mother, whilst tolerating unpredictable visiting and forbidding
removal of the child, would be very great.   Natural parents could
easily feel threatened and undermined by the foster mother's com-

petence and the child's growing affection for the foster mother.
As one mother observed, 'the little bastard, he's all sweetness and
light with her.   She doesn't know what he's like with me.'   It
seemed much more likely that mothers would feel even more discouraged and rejected as they watched their child thriving in another's
care, and might cease visiting altogether as they sensed the foster
mother's natural hostility towards them and identification with
their child.   Residential staff are likely to be as child-orientated as are foster parents and as prone to hostility towards
battering parents.   However, where the child-caretaker relationship is more diffuse and individual attachment to the child less
intense, it is easier for there to be more understanding towards
the mother.

Therefore, with one exception, all our children in care were
placed in small residential nurseries or family group homes usually
run by the Social Services Departments.   Many of these placements
were successful in terms of the parents and most parents responded
well.   In particular, the parents needed to feel that they were
welcome to participate in caring for the child when they visited,
if they wished.   The least successful homes were those where staff
either put pressure on the parents to feed, dress and wash the
child when they visited or assumed all responsibility and did not
offer them the opportunity to look after their child.   'I feel so
spare when I go there,' said one mother, 'I'm not really needed at
all.'

For most parents, the smaller the institution the easier it was
for them to relate to staff and children.   A reasonably stable
child population seemed to help them feel that the staff cared for
the children as individuals.   In contrast, some parents who felt
particularly insecure as parents, preferred the relative impersona-
lity of a larger institution.   One mother said, 'Sometimes I just
feel like slipping in and nobody noticing me ... I don't always
want to be asked how I am and watched over.'

We felt at times that we had to act as a buffer between the
parents and residential staff;   a good deal of time was sometimes
spent in interpreting attitudes and expectations to one another.
This was particularly important when a parent was threatening to
remove a child from voluntary care because she felt slighted or
misunderstood by a member of staff.   Complaints about practical
arrangements and material details were frequent as the parents had
a strong need to retain some control over their children's lives.
In this context, it was important that staff should be as scrupu-
lous as possible in communicating necessary information to the
parents.   This was occasionally not done and parents felt
betrayed and powerless when they discovered that children had gone
on a day's outing or to the doctor without their knowledge.
Thus, it seems important that staff and social workers should do
their utmost to communicate consistently to parents about their
children, even in the face of criticism or coolness.

However, now that we can look back on the progress of our cases,
we feel that some retrospective comments should be made.   In
opting for group residential care in the interests of a reasonably
speedy rehabilitation, we were not using the child's immediate
emotional needs as the main criterion.   It could be argued that

these would be best served by placement with foster parents, particularly for babies. If a young child is likely to remain in
care for some time, such as one or more years, a consistent, warm
foster home would probably prove a more emotionally fruitful
placement than a children's home. Unfortunately, it is difficult
to predict the length of this stay when making initial plans, or
to guarantee the consistency of foster care. In the recent move
in child care thinking towards a greater emphasis on the rights of
the child as an individual (Goldstein et al., 1973), there has
been a tendency to assume that it is relatively easy to decide
that a child has no long-term future with his family. In our
experience, such a prognosis may be difficult to make until one has
known the family for some time; our emphases and decisions which
may appear over parent-focused at times were in fact made with the
child's long-term interests foremost. With hindsight, we now
feel that we were occasionally over-optimistic and that some situations could have been better resolved by the child's being permanently removed and offered a good alternative home. Such
issues, involving the need for improved initial prognosis and the
whole question of children's versus parents' rights and changes
in child care law, will be considered in our final chapter.

Drop-in foster mother

We also planned to provide occasional overnight or weekend care for
children normally living at home with their parents. We hoped to
find a woman living locally, with children of her own, who would
act as a drop-in foster mother, and to whom we would pay a weekly
retainer to ensure her availability in moments of crisis and at
short notice. She would need great qualities of tolerance and
understanding in order to care warmly and sympathetically for
possibly injured or unhappy children without making their mothers
feel inadequate or rejected. Advertisements produced a large
number of responses, but many of the applicants, in discussing the
issues involved, felt they would not be able to contend with their
own feelings against the parents.
   During a two-and-a-half-year period, we employed three drop-in
foster mothers at different times. All received regular supervision. They were used for a few of our families for the occasional weekend or night to give a mother some relief, and in one
case, for a longer period while a family awaited re-housing.
There were several difficult situations, particularly when they had
grown to know and love a child and had to observe harsh handling
from visiting parents. They sometimes found it painful to follow
our counsel and refrain from intervening between mother and child.
   Undoubtedly, the drop-in foster mother service proved useful in
some cases, but there were difficulties in administering this
scheme. Demands made on the foster mother were inevitably unpredictable so that she was either under-used or over-burdened at
times. However, we would recommend that child-protective agencies
should attempt to provide some kind of informal short-term residential care for at-risk children during family crises.

Parents' reactions to residential care

Of the thirteen children who were placed in some kind of residential
care, four were only in care voluntarily, two were in care both
voluntarily and under a Care Order, and seven were the subjects of
Care Orders alone.   Their parents varied considerably in their
reactions to separation from their children and to the establish-
ments in which the children were placed.   How they felt about the
situation seemed to depend on a number of variables: for example,
their willingness to have the child received into care and the
level of resistance to Juvenile Court action if this was instituted, their relationship with their social worker, how they were
treated by residential staff in Children's Homes, and, most importantly, the extent to which they felt they had already failed as
parents.   The most successful placements seemed to be those where
the parents were offered and could accept some 'mothering' and
caring for themselves and where visiting arrangements were
flexible.

Four parents visited their children in care frequently and
regularly, sometimes under difficult circumstances of distance and
expense.   However, their feelings about the experience and the
extent to which they participated in caretaking tasks varied
greatly.   In another four cases, three involving statutory orders
and one voluntary care, the parents' contact with the child was
spasmodic and often apparently out of a sense of duty rather than
a genuine desire to see the child.   One mother was unreliable
about keeping arrangements and the child was often disappointed
when she failed to appear.   She complained of headaches or minor
ailments as an excuse and was abrupt and ill at ease when with the
child.

The remaining five parents visited rarely, if at all.   In two
cases, they temporarily wrote off their children but were ready to
reclaim them when their lives were calmer.   Another child was very
seriously injured, requiring permanent institutionalisation.   In
the fourth case, the parents visited hardly at all, yet were the
only ones to run away with a child from a children's home, having
to be traced by the police.   In the last case, the mother was
encouraged to visit occasionally, but her visits were excruciating
for all concerned, as the child was shaken out of her routine by a
mother determined to 'show how it should be done' and the staff
stood by, trying hard not to intervene.

In a few cases, parents were able to acknowledge early on in
treatment that separation from the child was of value.   One mother
commented to her worker at a time of acute domestic crisis, 'I'm
glad she isn't here now, it wouldn't have been good for her and she
would have caught it by now, wouldn't she?'   In general, the
parents seemed more preoccupied with their own feelings than those
of their children.   'I'll just slip out ... it's better ... it
upsets me so when he cries.'   'They always seem to be putting him
to bed when I arrive - they know it's inconvenient for me.'
Criticism and complaints about such things as clothing, diet and
discipline were common, often demonstrating the parents' own feelings of having failed.   It was noticeable that there was far more
concern expressed about the children's appearance and material

needs than there was for their emotional wellbeing.   This was
obviously a delicate issue for residential staff.

Day care

When making initial treatment plans, day care for the battered
children and their siblings was seriously considered for all the
families whose children remained at home.   We thereby hoped to
afford the children at least partial protection and some stimulation
and warmth and to offer the parents relief from the full-time
demands of parenthood.   Day care was also used for children as
they returned home from care, sometimes as a condition of their
going home on trial.   In six cases, parents themselves had organised day care for their children prior to referral, but this had
not proved a sufficient safeguard.   Two of these children were
received into care, and for the other four, day care arrangements
were either extended or changed.   We arranged local authority day
nursery placements for ten battered children and seven siblings at
various points in treatment.   In addition, six referred children
and five siblings also attended our own nursery for varying lengths
of time once it had opened.
    In general, we found other agencies co-operative in arranging
day care.   Paediatricians were usually very willing to support
priority recommendations to the Health Departments.   Since day
nursery places are at such a premium it is encouraging that in all
cases where they were requested, they were provided.   In two cases,
health visitors were resistant on the grounds that the child was
too young to be separated from his mother, but this was eventually
overcome by persuasion.   The two main complaints about the
arrangement of day care were the length of time taken to get a
place and the question of payment.   In one case, a family had to
wait for a place for two months whilst tension mounted between
mother and child.   Problems were encountered over assessment and
payment, and several parents at first refused to entertain the idea
because of the charge.   An agreement was finally reached whereby
the Denver House worker wrote to the Health Department stating that
the child had been battered and was at risk at home, and the Health
Department would then waive payment.   They would not, however,
make a nil assessment and the parents were not to know of this
decision.   This led to a rather confused and unsatisfactory
situation.
    It was important to make sure that day nursery matrons were in-
cluded in on-going case conferences and management decisions, and
that they appreciated the importance of contacting us at once if
the child appeared with a fresh injury, or a parent or child's
mood and behaviour gave cause for concern.

Parents' reactions to day care

For the relatively few parents who could openly acknowledge that
they were finding the full-time care of their children a strain,
the provision of day care was very welcome and proved an acceptable

form of relief.   These parents were conscious of the fact that day
nursery places were at a premium and the obtaining of a place was
probably seen as the most meaningful aspect of the worker's intervention.   For example, one mother, who prior to the birth of her
baby had enjoyed a stimulating job, positively leapt at the offer
of a day nursery place, saying as if it were a death sentence, 'I
thought I would have to wait till she was at least two for that.'
The mother returned to work straight away and after several weeks
commented to her worker, 'You know, baby really appreciates us at
the weekends.   I think she really likes us then, but before I was
with her all day long.'   In such a case, even though the child's
injury was serious, day care proved an adequate protective measure
throughout treatment as it exactly met the mother's needs.

In several other cases, the offer of day nursery places proved
welcome to the parents in the later stages of treatment, for
example, when a new baby was born or when their child returned home
from residential care.   Certainly for those parents whose children
remained the subject of Care Orders, day care, even in the Department's own nursery, did not carry the stigma attached to residential care.

The majority of mothers, who initially expressed interest in
day care for their child, were in fact ambivalent about allowing
their children to attend once places had been obtained and were
often quite sabotaging in their behaviour.   It soon became clear
to the workers that they were torn between the internal directive
to be a good mother and to cope alone at all costs and the desire
to escape from full-time responsibility for their children.   Also,
these mothers were threatened by loss of control and/or love of
the child and by day nursery staff taking over their function,
when for example, they succeeded in toilet training the child, as
happened in several cases.

Eventually, after numerous delaying tactics, false starts, much
encouragement, reassurance and occasionally extreme pressure from
their workers, these mothers progressed from being able to leave
their children with the staff at Denver House, while they enjoyed
the exclusive attention of their worker, to accepting a trusted
worker's offer of baby sitting, to leaving their children at a day
nursery or playgroup.   Undoubtedly, in the later stages of the
project the facilities offered by our therapeutic day nursery were
particularly conducive to separating some very anxious mothers
from their children.   In several cases, the children's attendance
at day nurseries was erratic, reflecting the parents' continued
ambivalence and anxiety about separation and again highlighting the
need for flexible arrangements.

In three cases, the children remained in the home, without the
prtoection of day care throughout treatment or up to the time when
they started school.   For example, in one case, in spite of considerable efforts on the part of the worker, it proved impossible
to separate the mother and child for any length of time and it is
interesting to note that he even started school eight months late.

In a number of cases the fathers' views on day care were not
directly expressed to the workers and it is possible that they
were distorted by the mothers.   Some apparently remained singu-
larly uninvolved in plans made for the child, but in other cases,

the workers sensed that the fathers were doing their utmost behind
the scenes to obstruct their efforts at providing some relief for
the mothers.   Such fathers believed that a mother's place is full-
time at home with her child and lacked compassion and understanding
of the strains this imposed.   If their wives agreed to day care
they criticised them for being lazy and failing in their duty,
commenting on their heartlessness and increasing the mother's guilt
over parting with their children.   In addition, the mother's guilt
was exacerbated in some cases by the child's unhappiness at being
left or by staff reports of the child's extremely difficult
behaviour.

Denver House day nursery

In November 1971, two years after we had started taking cases, we
opened our own day nursery in premises close to the office.   We
had known for some time that we needed a day centre for children
and parents and had been waiting until a grant and building became
available.   There were four full-time members of staff, a matron
and three nursery nurses, all NNEB trained.   As the establishment
was for not more than ten children, this constituted a high staff-
child ratio.
    The premises consisted of a large children's playroom, a
kitchen, office, mothers' sitting-room, two rest-rooms for the
children, lavatories and bathroom.   The rooms were bright, cheer-
ful and modern and had previously been used for a residential
nursery.   One physical disadvantage that soon became apparent was
that the mothers' room led directly out of the children's room.
This meant that they were too much aware of each other: the children felt frustrated and rejected to know that their parents were
behind the often closed door, and the mothers felt that the children were encroaching upon them.   Ideally, such a mothers' room
should be as far as possible from the main hub of activity.
    The nursery was open from 9.00 a.m. to 4.30 p.m. five days a
week.   Over the next two years, six battered children and five
siblings attended at different times.   The number of our children
who attended was fairly low, since some were in residential care
and for others placements at local authority nurseries had already
been well established and it would have been unsettling to move
them.   No charge was made for attendance and a mini-bus collected
children in the morning and delivered them home in the evening.
We had learned from previous experience that payment and regular
prompt attendances had proved the main problems for parents and so
were anxious that children should receive the maximum possible
protection without having to rely on parental motivation.   We
could not insist on children coming to the nursery, but we encouraged and enabled parents as much as possible.   In the few cases
of irregular attendance, workers would visit the home when a child
had not appeared at the nursery to ask if help was needed or if
they could give the child a lift.   Occasionally the mini-bus
would return in the evening to an empty house and a staff member
would look after the child as long as was necessary.

The children

The aims of the nursery for the children were firstly, protective
and secondly, therapeutic.   The programme was designed to provide
an ordered and secure environment for the children, offering both
the opportunity for free play and for more structured activities:
organised painting or story telling, for example, and meal-times
and set periods of rest.   Initially, many of the children had no
idea of self-initiated play and would not attempt to explore or
try things for themselves.   Some of the older ones often violently
resisted the structured activities, causing scenes at meals and
refusing to stay on their beds at rest-times.

  The children attending the nursery ranged in age from a few
months to nearly five years; all displayed some form of disturbed
behaviour and appeared to be developmentally below average.   Some
were withdrawn and possessive, making no effort to explore or
initiate interaction with adults or children.   Others were highly
active, difficult to contain and often destructive towards people
and objects.   Many displayed beyond the appropriate age the
'grabbing reaction' referred to by Galdston (1973) which he des-
cribes as follows: 'grabbing of objects out of the hands of
another, biting the flesh of another, and shouting for the attention of another under certain circumstances ... it appears that
the crucial element was the relationship of the object to the
person holding it, that of belonging, of being the property of.'
This reaction, although it gradually became modified as children
got to know other staff and children, would return as new people
appeared who needed to be tested out.

  As the children became familiar with the environment and the
staff, changes were apparent in their behaviour.   They came to
relate more consistently to the staff, as they learned that they
could ask for attention and receive it.   The quieter, more withdrawn children seemed to respond better to the environment, gradually becoming more outgoing and self-assertive.   However, the
emphasis on group needs and an orderly routine meant that too
little attention was at times paid to individual children, and
the emotional difficulties of the more aggressive in particular
were not able to be tackled.

The parents

The parents were also encouraged to come to the nursery and use the
mothers' room for relaxation and conversation.   We were anxious
that parents might feel jealous and threatened by the attention and
care that their children were receiving.   To counteract this we
felt it was important to encourage their participation in the life
of the nursery and to meet some of their needs.   The staff were
asked to give time and attention to parents and to view the nursery
as their refuge as well as their children's.   It was not intended
that parents should receive direct tuition or guidance on child
care and development, as we considered that this would be fruitless.
Others in the field of child abuse (for example, Smith et al. (1973)
and Savino and Sanders (1973)) have written of the need for the

education of battering parents.   In our experience, although many
are ignorant of basic information on child care and development (as
are many other young mothers), this has not caused the flaw in their
capacity to be 'good enough' parents.   We would agree with Galdston
(1973) that 'cognitive enrichment will not replace a parent who cannot accept her child.'   Our intention was rather to attempt to
tackle some of the parents' emotional problems by means of the
primary therapeutic relationship and to offer the nursery as an
environment in which they could themselves relax and feel secure.
We hoped that they might also come to enjoy their children more in
a pressure-free situation, and that they might perhaps learn something about child care through identification with the staff.
Joint mother-child activity was encouraged but not forced; trips
and outings for all the children and parents were arranged.
Parties for Christmas and parents' and children's birthdays were a
regular feature of nursery life.

   Our general problem initially was the question of whether abuse
had been admitted and discussed.   Some mothers resented the fact
that the nursery was for 'battered children' and that this labelled
them as 'batterers'.   As one mother angrily observed, 'my child
only comes to this nursery because we haven't got a garden.'   A
television programme about battering, which included filming at
the nursery, aroused a lot of pain and anxiety.   Many of the
mothers had co-operated in making the film, although it had aroused
anxiety and conflict for them, and they felt let down when they
saw it because of its under-emphasis on treatment and prevention.

   The nursery atmosphere did not suit all the mothers; a few remained aloof and on the fringe of activities, preferring to use it
only for their children.   Only one father spent any time there
during periods of unemployment; the others all worked during
nursery hours.   For the majority of mothers whose children used
the nursery, however, it became in time almost a way of life.
They would arrive on the bus with their children and spend the day
there, chatting to the staff, drinking coffee, smoking, reading and
popping out to the shops.   Food was also available for the mothers
and for some the provision of lunch was an important service.   One
mother worked as a temporary staff member.   Since the staff were
encouraged to give attention to the parents, the mothers seemed at
times to want to take over from the children; the main area of
drama and interaction in the nursery would be the mothers' room,
as they regressed and demanded attention whilst the children
seemed dim figures, playing in the background.   This was very
difficult for the nursery staff, who were by training and experience
child-orientated in their approach and sometimes found it difficult
to meet the parents' demands.

Mothers' group

A year after the opening of the nursery, it was decided that a
regular mothers' group should be held.   We had always been hopeful
of running a group of some kind, but had felt that the parents when
we first met them were too untrusting and angry towards the world
to respond to such an experience.   We thought that many would be

threatened by the presence of others, that they would not be able to
tolerate any focus on child injury and that they would be so near to
traumatic events (the actual injury, hospital admission, Court proceedings) that their main need at the time of referral was for an
individual therapeutic relationship.

Thus, by the time the group started, all the mothers had established relationships with their own workers and some had been in
treatment for some time.   The setting-up of the group arose naturally out of a personal crisis for one of the mothers which disturbed the others who felt they would like a chance to discuss
things as a group.   Meetings were then held regularly at monthly
intervals; one of the Denver House social workers and the nursery
matron were present.   The length of the group meeting was flexible
and it continued as long as the mothers wanted, usually lasting
about two and a half hours.   For the first nine months or so, an
average of five or six mothers attended, involving a total of eight
who were present at different times.

Apart from occasional practical issues which needed to be discussed by the group, the leader did not initiate conversation, remaining passive and waiting to see what would arise.   There were
sometimes long silences.   In several of the early groups, there
was a lot of discussion about recent newspaper or television
reports of violence to children.   For example, one case of a woman
who had thrown her four-month-old twins into a brook, one drowning
and the other being saved, aroused a considerable amount of feeling
and anger.   In this and similar discussions mothers dwelt upon the
difference between 'impulsive' and 'cold-hearted' violence to
children.   The group leader tried to introduce the idea that other
parents experienced similar strains to their own and felt that
gradually as they began to accept their own potential for hostility
and violence they became more tolerant of others and their internal
stress was reduced.

The mothers were initially rather inhibited by the presence of
a social worker and the nursery matron from making negative comments about Denver House or the nursery, but as they became more
confident in the group setting and developed a sense of mutual
support, they began to voice criticism of their social workers and
the running of the nursery.   They complained particularly that
the staff were too brisk in their handling of the children and did
not supervise them adequately or pay them enough attention.
'They're too keen to put them to bed instead of playing with them,'
said one mother.   Some of the feeling behind these criticisms
certainly sprang from a sense of their own inadequacy and failure
as parents and the leader tried to help them to see this.   However, he and the matron also took seriously comments about the
running of the nursery and tried to be sensitive to the parents'
wishes.   A crisis when a child had to be taken before the Juvenile Court at a fairly late stage in treatment and the mother
angrily resisted it created an emotionally charged group.   The
other mothers, whilst offering the mother affection and support,
endorsed the need for children to be protected and sometimes
removed.

When the group had been going for ten months or so, Denver
House had to close, and a new social worker started work, based at

the nursery.   She has taken over the running of the groups which
are held fortnightly, or more frequently.   They are still continuing and now form an important part of the life of the nursery.
   Both the social workers who have been responsible for groups
consider that they have been valuable and that mothers, workers
and staff have gained from them.   Problems of sibling rivalry
between group members have arisen from time to time and one mother
has withdrawn, finding the focus on violence too threatening.   It
would perhaps be more valuable if such a group were to be run by
an outsider, neither the parents' social worker nor a member of
the nursery staff.

General comments

In retrospect, we now feel that we did not make sufficient provision at the nursery for the children's emotional needs.   They
gained security from a sense of routine and order; for some children whose home life had been disorganised and inconsistent, this
was particularly striking.   They improved developmentally (see
psychologists' chapter) through increased stimulation and contact
with other children, and in some cases the mother-child relationship became easier.   However, as many of the children grow older
they are showing signs of emotional disturbance and some are presenting behaviour problems at school (see chapter 9).   Other day
centres for battered children (for example Galdston (1973),
Ounsted et al. (1974), Ten Broeck (1974)) have included in their
programmes specific therapeutic attention for the individual children, realising that many need special understanding and treatment
in their own right.   We now think that such measures were lacking
from our own programme, and that we tended to over-emphasise the
therapeutic claims of the parents over the children, leading to
some degree of confusion and conflict for the staff.   Whilst some
formed special relationships with some children, they were not able
to provide the specialised treatment which many needed.   We now
feel that our dual and interlinked emphasis on treatment of the
parents and protection of the children neglected an important area,
the psycho-therapeutic treatment of the children, which could be
well provided in a day care setting.
   Ideally, such a day centre should be in the same building as the
social workers' offices.   Thus, the parents' needs could be met
primarily by their social workers and other office staff, with
their children near at hand rather than underfoot, and the nursery
staff would be able to concentrate mainly on the children.   The
social workers would have the opportunity to observe children, and
children and parents together, without having to make a special
journey.   Generally, we feel that such an arrangement would result
in a more natural, pressure-free situation, in which staff roles
and responsibilities would be more clearly defined and the needs
of parents and children would not be in conflict.

3   RETURN OF CHILDREN FROM RESIDENTIAL CARE

Inevitably in cases of battering the decision to return a child
from residential care is onerous and should only be taken after
inter-agency consultation and careful assessment of the case (see
chapter 4).   When assessing our cases we took note of criteria
already developed by other workers in the field, notably Johnson
and Morse (1968b) for determining whether it is safe to return a
child home.   These include: a reduction in social and environmental stress experienced by the family; changes in the parents'
functioning, including signs that they have found more ways of
getting satisfaction and pleasure in their lives and that they are
less socially isolated; changes in marital functioning possibly
involving the break up of a very stressful relationship or more
open expression of conflict between the partners, some acknow-
ledgement of what makes for dangerous situations with the child,
increased recognition of one another's problems and ability to
give mutual support at times of stress; the frequency and quality
of contact between parents and child while he has been away from
home, including signs of improvement in parent-child interaction
such as greater acceptance and increased enjoyment of the child;
an improvement in those aspects of the child's behaviour previously
seen as provocative by the parents; the development of a trusting
relationship between the parents and the worker to the point where
the parents can turn to the worker at times of stress; the availability of a lifeline for the parents to use in crises; the
availability of acceptable forms of relief from the child such as
day care or week-end care, once he is returned home.
     It will be recalled that thirteen children were placed in resi-
dential care voluntarily or under Care Orders at some point in
treatment.   When children were placed in voluntary care, their
parents were free to remove them at any time.   In situations
when we felt this action was premature we tried to dissuade but
ultimately could not prevent them form having the child home.   In
contrast, in cases where separation was legally enforced we could
exercise control over the timing and way in which a child was re-
united with his family.   We had no fixed ideas on the optimum
length of separation for children in care under orders.
     Wherever possible rehabilitation was carefully planned with the
parents and the child was reintroduced to the home over a period
of months.   We arranged for the parents first to take their children out for odd days, gradually progressing to overnight stays,
long week-ends, holidays and finally to having the child home
permanently.   It is particularly important at this stage for
workers to try and discern whether both parents genuinely seem to
want the child home or are requesting this because they feel
exposed to public or family disapproval; or whether one partner
is pressing for the child back, while the other realises that the
return of the child would result in impossible stress.   In some
cases where we became aware that although the parents had pressed
to have the child home they were actually very apprehensive when
this became a realistic possibility, we intensified support during
this period.   In other cases, however, we sensed that the level
of anxiety in the parents would be raised by workers increasing

their visits.   The feelings of some parents for their children
continued to fluctuate considerably.   For example, on one occasion a mother confided with joy to her worker, 'I had my first
really positive feelings for Sally today.   She really feels
part of the family.'   Whereas the following month the relationship deteriorated rapidly at a time of a family crisis and she
reported, 'Sally is like a stranger here now, I just don't know
how I'm going to cope.'   This highlights the need for flexible
arrangements, for slowing down the child's reintroduction to the
home and for a willingness to consider returning the child to care.
     It is vital too that the child's feelings about and reactions
to visits home should be taken into account.   In the case of
Maria Colwell disregard of the child's extreme reluctance to
return to her natural mother had disastrous consequences and is
rightly criticised in the Report of the Committee of Inquiry
(DHSS, 1974) as inexcusable.   In our cases as most of the children were in the younger age range, we needed to rely more on
behavioural indications of feeling than on verbal expression.
Hence we often involved ourselves in taking the child backwards
and forwards between home and residential care.   This provided
valuable opportunities for observing firsthand how the parents and
child reacted to one another and how the child appeared to have
been affected by the visit.   Also we asked residential staff for
their observations on the child's behaviour after visits home.
     Once a child is returned home on a permanent basis his progress
continues to require careful monitoring.   Workers need to be
alert to the fact that although there may be a honeymoon period
during which everything seems to be going well between the parents
and the child and they seem to have little need of the worker,
this is often followed by a gradual deterioration in the parent-
child relationship and interaction.   The parents may again begin
to see the child as unsatisfying and unrewarding and for example,
a particularly dangerous situation may arise if the child re-
gresses in his behaviour.   This underlines the need for continued
support to be offered to these families after the child's return
not only to consolidate improvements already made in their functioning but also to avoid a reversal to previous destructive
patterns of interaction.

Children in voluntary care

In three cases voluntary care was used intermittently at times of
family crisis.   Typically the children returned home after two
to three months in care when their parents indicated that they
felt ready to cope with them again.   All were subsequently provided with places at Denver House Nursery.   In another two cases,
where inadequate accommodation was a major source of stress, the
children spent approximately twelve months in voluntary care and
went home when their families had been rehoused.   They were also
offered day care.   Only one child remained in voluntary care
over a prolonged period of time.   After three years, during which
she experienced three changes in placement, workers became increasingly concerned about her future care.   The parents were

asked to consider whether they would like the child home or
whether they would prefer a long-term foster home placement to
be found for her.   They decided to resume care of the child,
who was by this time attending school.   At the time of writing
this arrangement seems to be proving satisfactory, although when
the child went through a phase of regression, the parents found
this difficult to tolerate.

Children in residential care under orders

In two cases children were returned home earlier than the workers
had intended because of decisions reached on legal rather than
casework grounds.   In one case where following an Interim Order
the Juvenile Court decided not to make a Care Order, the child
was returned home seven months after referral.   The other was
the only case where the parents lodged an appeal against the Care
Order.   This was due to be heard at Quarter Sessions (now the
Crown Court) but was withdrawn at the last minute after an agreement had been reached out of Court between the lawyers that the
child should start going home for weekends immediately and should
be allowed home on trial in a few months' time.   He was returned
to his parents' care ten months after referral and they accepted
the offer of a day nursery place for him.   It is interesting
that once the parents had achieved their objective of getting the
child home they were no longer concerned about the existence of
the Care Order.   Approximately two years later, after the worker
had initiated discussion about revocation, which temporarily re-
awakened considerable anxiety in the parents, the order was
revoked.
   In both cases described above, the parents had consistently
asked for their children home from the moment they were taken into
care and were bitterly opposed to the enforced separation.   They
denied that they had caused the injuries, denied any problems with
the child and were reluctant to accept social work help.   The
workers in these cases were extremely anxious about the children's
safety once they returned home, but against all the odds these
parents made a concerted effort to care for their children and no
re-injuries occurred.
   Of the other four cases in which Fit Person Orders or Care
Orders were made at the time of referral, one child was too
seriously damaged to be cared for at home and until his death
received special care in an institution.   Another child, who also
suffered residual damage from her injuries, spent two years in
residential care then was placed with her maternal grandmother but
remained subject to the Care Order.
   The other children were both returned home on trial with a day
nursery or nursery school place; one after twenty months and one
after twenty-four months.   The orders were still standing at the
time of writing.   However, the parents of one of these children
were angrily questioning the necessity for the order to continue
as the child had been home on trial for three years.   They were
desperately seeking reassurance that if they applied for the order
to be revoked they should not meet with opposition.   In this case,

while the risk of physical injury was considered to be low, continued concern about the child's emotional development meant that
the agencies involved were unwilling to recommend revocation.
Understandably one of the consequences of the Maria Colwell Inquiry
has been an increasing reluctance to recommend revocation of Care
Orders in such situations.

Of the three cases in which Care Orders were made at a later
stage of treatment, one child was placed in a local authority
children's home, one child was returned home on trial from residential care when she started school, approximately twelve months
after the order was made, and the other was placed in a residential school for maladjusted children.   The latter was the only
case in which the worker concluded at the time the order was made
that permanent separation was desirable.

Without a long-term follow-up of the cases included in our study
it is impossible to say how successful we have been in our attempts
to rehabilitate children with their families.   An important conclusion from our experience is that the severity of the injury to
the child has little relevance to a favourable prognosis.   We
have found the criteria outlined at the beginning of this section
useful for determining whether it is safe for the child to be returned home.   However, we wish to emphasise that even if there is
evidence to suggest that the risk of physical injury has diminished,
there still remains the question of whether the home is conducive
to the child's emotional development.   With hindsight, we now
feel that in several cases, the child's interests might have been
better served if the focus of our intervention had been on helping
the parents to accept permanent separation rather than on working
towards rehabilitation.   In future, if the proposals of the new
Children Bill (1975) are implemented, it is foreseeable that other
more drastic measures, such as the termination of parental rights
by the Courts, may be adopted to safeguard long-term placements.

Chapter 8

THE PRIMARY THERAPEUTIC RELATIONSHIP

AN OVERVIEW

> The therapeutic person is one who uses himself as a human being in the healing process.   (Kempe, 1970)

In our search for a long-term treatment strategy we were fortunate in having the work of a number of experts on which to draw: (Steele and Pollock, 1968); (Davoren, 1968); (Kaufmann, 1966); (Wasserman, 1967); (Kempe, 1969, 1970); (Steele, 1970); (Galdston, 1970). Their observations and reflections on child abuse in general led them to attach great importance to the personality characteristics of the parents in the causation of abuse and the need for direct therapy with the parents to assume a prominent position in any proposals for treatment. The development of our own views on treatment, based on this work and other research in the field has been discussed in detail elsewhere (Court, 1969, a,b, c); (Okell, 1969); (Court and Okell, 1970); (Okell, 1972); (Kerr and Court, 1972); (Jones, 1973), but can be summarised below.

It was assumed that abusive behaviour hinged on the fact that battering parents did not experience 'good enough' mothering when they were young, particularly in the early phase of their development. This would impair their ability to care for their own offspring. Having little to offer the child, the parents also made inordinate demands on him by expecting him to provide the love and affection which they had never known (Morris and Gould, 1963). Disappointment, frustration and eventual battering would be the likely outcome of such an impossible situation.

The therapeutic relationship was intended to provide for some of the parents' unmet dependency needs. In fostering the parents' emotional development, it was hoped that their capacity to care for the child would improve. In addition, it was felt that the provision of an alternative source of satisfaction for the parents' needs would have a direct impact on the skewed dynamics of the parent-child relationship by decreasing the parents' unrealistic demands of the child and the concomitant risk of abuse for failing to meet them.

It was believed that unless this was done the parents were likely

133

to remain unchanged in their potential for abuse.   Other plans for
management and treatment were not in themselves able to offer lasting safety to the battered child and his siblings.   Removal of
the child or the abusive parents from the home, even with legal
sanctions, is rarely a permanent arrangement.   Convictions for
child abuse result in time-limited sentences, and parents can apply
to have a child returned home and are frequently successful.   In
addition, we were aware of the dangers to other children in the
family (Skinner and Castle, 1969) and the proclivity of abusive
parents to carry on producing more children in an impossible attempt
to satisfy their own needs.   Thus, the provision of a therapeutic
relationship for the parents was seen as essential if the abusive
pattern were to be broken.   The extent to which these views
changed in the light of experience will be documented as treatment
processes are discussed and evaluated, in this and subsequent
chapters.

Casework strategy

The task of engaging the parents in therapy was not expected to be
easy.   Their lack of basic trust and fear of any close relationship was well documented in the literature.   As Steele (1970)
observed, 'The very idea of help is foreign to them because they
feel that the ones to whom they look for help are the ones who
will attack them.'   We did not expect the parents to be motivated
(McHenry et al., 1963) and we anticipated hostility, avoidance or
passive compliance on their part.
   We proposed not to accept such attitudes at face value, but to
reach out to the parents in an uncritical, undemanding way on
whatever terms they could tolerate.   We considered that abuse of
a child (or fear of abuse) and the process of referral would constitute a crisis in the lives of our families (Caplan, 1961).
The first few contacts with the parents could thus be very important and we could take advantage of the view that during a crisis
habitual defences are disrupted and clients are more amenable to
help.   Persistence was necessary, but over-visiting was to be
avoided for fear of 'hounding' the parents.   A twenty-four hour on-
call service was to be manned to provide them with a lifeline in
times of stress.   Casework was seen as an essentially long-term
restitutive process in which we would imaginatively nurture the
deprived areas of the personality.   Since the deprivation of
abusive parents was hypothesised to be of early origin, we
believed that, at the outset, discussion of problems and interpreta-
tion were likely to have limited value.   Initially, demonstration
of concern in action and attitude was what appeared to matter most
and listening was envisaged as the important ingredient.   We
envisaged that as treatment progressed and the parents began to
develop trust such techniques might appropriately be used with
caution.   We had in mind the parents' low sense of self-esteem
and their penchant for self-defeating behaviour.   Competent
practical help was seen as necessary but advice-giving was regarded
as a trap likely to confirm their fear of domination.   We planned
to be on hand to help the parents work through their own
difficulties.

As can be imagined, the social workers preparing themselves for this task were subject to a high degree of anxiety.   We expected our capacity to be loving and giving to be taxed and needed to create a very supportive atmosphere in the team.   Probably our greatest fears were of being excluded by the family, or failing to establish any contact that was meaningful for them, thus leaving the children exposed to further danger.   Skinner and Castle (1969) had already documented the pitfalls of providing an adequate service, the high rate of re-injury to the children and the likelihood of the families moving without trace.   Against this background we set out to test what we hoped was a positive alternative.

Evolution of treatment

We provided a treatment service of at least eighteen months' duration for most of the subjects in our study, extending to over three years for some.   Many different factors were operating within this period, including major changes in family composition owing to the absence or change of a father figure, the birth of another child, or the removal or return of the abused child.   Rehousing sometimes to new areas, changes in employment, including those which affected the balance of the marital relationships when wives began working, are some other examples of fundamental changes in lifestyle.   Such factors undoubtedly influenced the nature of the primary therapeutic relationship whilst at the same time they may be seen as indicators of the effects of treatment and are used as such in evaluating progress in family functioning (chapter 10).   Other concrete changes such as the involvement of other agencies, changes of personnel within our Department and placements for the battered child and his siblings also impinge on the therapeutic relationship, governing the type of interaction required or accepted.

In addition, our treatment approach undoubtedly changed as the project evolved and we gained more practical experience.   Although we still held to a psychoanalytic model of changing abusive behaviour by modifying the underlying pathological need, we were concerned that our non-critical stance might be seen by the parents as condonation.   We began openly to place greater emphasis on the physical safety of the child and his other needs.   Our earlier hesitance about separation when we felt a child to be at risk diminished and more pressure was brought to bear on the parents and other agencies to ensure temporary or long-term, day or residential care in such situations.   We also became less anxious about exclusion or rejection by the families and began to clarify the parameters of our nurturing role and explore the use of a more challenging attitude towards the parents.   We realised that we could briefly postpone a visit or refuse a request without destroying the therapeutic relationship, provided that we remained sensitive to the parents' feelings.

Changes of personnel

We felt that continuity of care was of primary importance for the
establishment of a meaningful worker/client relationship.   Disruption of care could repeat for many of these parents their
experiences during childhood, leaving them feeling mistrustful,
insecure, isolated, criticised and rejected (Zalba, 1967;
Wasserman, 1967).   We felt that the worker who was initially
allocated to a case should continue to work with the family for as
long as possible, thus providing an experience of a prolonged,
stable and caring relationship.   In over half the cases, the
original worker with the family was still involved eighteen months
to two years after referral.   Five of these families had experienced continuous care from the original worker for a period of
three years and over.

   In only five cases was care of the family transferred to
another social worker within the Denver House team during the
course of treatment, and in only one of these cases was this change
effected during the first year.   Reasons for transferring cases
were because the original worker with the family ceased employment,
because of administrative changes within the Department or because
of the family's increased demand for attention.   In only one case
was there more than one change in Denver House social workers
involved during the course of treatment.

   It was usual for transfer of cases to be arranged over a period
of time so that clients were gradually prepared for the change.
We were fortunate in that there was always an overlap of workers,
so that the original worker could sometimes choose and could
always know to whom the case was to be transferred.   The family
could then be told about and introduced to the new worker by the
original worker before he or she left, thus facilitating a smooth
transition of care.   In one case, the new worker was eagerly and
easily accepted by the family as he had previously substituted for
the original worker when the latter was on holiday, and had helped
during a time of crisis.   In a few cases, the families had
casually met the new workers during visits to Denver House or
Denver House Day Nursery, and if they had not communicated, at
least knew their faces.   In two cases in which a change of worker
was partly effected as a result of pressure exerted by the
clients, their familiarity with Denver House and the friendliness
with the staff seemed to compensate for insufficient preparation
for the change.   All but one of the families appeared to experience no great difficulty in accepting or relating to the new
workers, though a few had become greatly attached to and dependent
upon their original workers.   The one family who rejected the new
worker had also resisted contact with the original worker.

   It would seem that we were able to convey to most of the
families that they could seek help and support from all the members
of the Denver House team.   The 'on-call' service meant that a few
families made contact with members of the team other than their
main workers, sometimes during times of crisis.

   In most cases, we also continued to substitute for one another
during holidays; also a locum was employed for a period of four
months when one worker was away, in order to ensure that his cases

were adequately covered.   In a few cases where families remained
resistant to our intervention or the parents said they would prefer to manage on their own, we felt it inadvisable to introduce
another worker during holidays.   However, some were able to per-
ceive the Denver House setting as a secure and friendly base and a
second home, visiting the project co-ordinator and the other staff
while their own worker was away.

Phases of treatment

Changes in the nature of any close relationship are not easily
discerned by the people involved.   If the changes are gradual and
contact fairly frequent as in our study, the task becomes more
difficult.   However, before we began to study our material more
objectively in retrospect, we had the impression that there were
different phases in the therapeutic relationship with the passage
of time.   We felt that the initial three months of treatment were
used to establish the best possible contact with the families.
The rest of the first year of treatment was a time when we were
busy with the task of using the contact to nurture the parents and
help with practical problems, some of which had been raised in the
initial period.   It seemed that the second year was used to consolidate our nurturing role and to work in more depth and detail on
the specific problems which each family raised.   The third year
was a weaning period in which ties between worker and client
loosened but we were still available to help when needed.
     The term 'phase' is intended to have a flexible connotation in
this context.   The time periods were selected around prominent
features which emerged in each phase for most families.   As with
child development, each phase did not totally eclipse the others
and features of all phases were to some extent present throughout
the whole period of treatment.   Also, some families appeared to
make more rapid progress through the phases whilst a few, chiefly
with mothers identified as resistant, remained predominantly in
the first or second phase.   The first and probably most precarious
phase has been dealt with in detail as it was regarded as the
proving ground.   The subsequent phases are considered in summary.

THE FIRST THREE MONTHS OF TREATMENT
Crisis intervention and how we introduced ourselves

It would be true to say that the first interview was a time of
crisis for the child, the parents and equally for the worker.   We
had to try to convey to the parents that we were there to help and
not to punish them.   We were therefore very cautious in our
initial approach, as we did not wish to jeopardise our chances of
continued success with them.   With the first few cases, this
brought about initial hesitancy in introducing ourselves as social
workers from a child protective agency, involved because of the
child's injuries.   Other cases presenting particular difficulties
to us were those in which recent injuries were not visible on referral, or where parents had not been informed about our involve-

ment.   To these parents we tended to introduce ourselves as social
workers from a small research team, who wanted 'to try and help
families who had similar problems to them with their young children.'   However, these 'problems' were not made explicit.   One
worker remarks, 'I was desperate to give a plausible and fairly
honest account of why I was there, but expected from what others
had said that the mother would be hostile; I was afraid of
threatening her and being denied access.'   The first interview
with this mother was conducted on the doorstep, the worker being
greeted by the abrupt words, 'What do you want?'   Another worker
who decided that the first interview with a very resistant mother
was 'the wrong time to come clean', subsequently wrote her a
letter explaining 'the hospital asked me to see you because your
baby had a couple of injuries and it can be difficult to be a
young mother on your own a lot, with a young baby and maybe not know
whom to turn to if you need help.'   As we grew more confident, and
as later cases tended to be those with serious referral injuries,
we were less hesitant about identifying ourselves and our agency
during the first contact with the parents.   We also made early
reference to our specialised interest in helping families where
young children had been injured.

     Probably at no time were we more concerned to convey ourselves
to the parents as a caring, undemanding presence than during the
first interview when stress was at or near its peak.   A dramatic
illustration is provided by a family referred before midnight.
The baby had just been admitted to hospital in a critical condition and the mother was waiting in the ward.   The social worker
visited within the hour and sensed that the mother could not face
what was happening or what had led to the child's admission.   The
mother wanted to talk about mundane topics such as the price of
vegetables and simply have someone wholly with her.   The worker
stayed chatting with her for most of the night until the mother
felt comforted enough to allow exhaustion to take over and was
driven home to bed.   The development of a good therapeutic relationship was dependent to some extent on the circumstances surrounding our intervention as discussed in the chapter on early
management.   Undoubtedly prompt referral and prompt visiting as
in the above case made for much better initial contact.   In contrast delays in referral of only a few days seemed to foster
avoidance and resistance in the parents.

     The help we offered in the crisis period was obviously dependent
on the particular problems presented by individual cases and the
emotional state of the parents at the time of intervention.   However, the primary focus in all cases was on providing a 'life line'
for the parents ... 'I gave her my card, described how the on-call
system worked and suggested that as she got to know me better, she
might feel able to call and get someone to visit if she was feeling at the end of her tether with the kids or wanted company.'
Another important focus was the provision of relief in caring for
the children in the home, usually through the offer of alternative
care for them ... 'my first offer of help was a day nursery placement for a purported hyperactive child.'   During this early
crisis period our offers to approach other agencies on their
behalf were an important means of gaining the parents' trust,

while often the offer of practical help was the first acceptable
way of demonstrating our concern for them.   In all cases, we felt
that one of our most valuable functions was attentive listening
and providing the opportunity to share anxiety and release pent up
emotions.

There is no doubt that in some cases, our anxiety about the
initial contact was exacerbated by difficulty in communicating
with the parents.   A few interviews were described as 'the hardest
half hour of my life ...'; 'an uphill task ...'; 'fraught and
difficult'.   This applied equally to interviews with one parent
alone or with both parents.   However, a few joint interviews were
particularly difficult, either because of the parents' constant
competition for our attention, or the complete withdrawal of one
partner.   However, in most cases, our caring approach and the
nature and immediacy of help offered seemed to facilitate communication, relieve pressure and pave the way for further contact.

Frequency of contact with the parents during the first phase of
treatment

How often we saw the parents depended mainly on how much contact
they could tolerate.   Often we had to push the pace beyond their
initial resistance but with caution.   A compliant attitude on the
part of one mother led the worker to visit practically every day
during the first two weeks until she finally moaned, 'I just can't
stand it any more.   Please go away.   Please leave me alone.'
Conversely, a few became excessively demanding and in practice
workers found they had to set some limits.   In one atypical case,
there was a need to regulate the relationship closely in order to
to bring some kind of order and structure into this family's
chaotic life.   The optimum rate of contact was about twice per
week.

Total numbers of contacts per family ranged from four to forty-
five times during the first three months of treatment (average
twenty).   Most of the interviews were with mothers on their own
(average twelve), but quite a number of joint interviews with both
parents were carried out in this early phase of treatment (average
seven).   Fathers were only seen about once on their own and
eleven fathers were never seen individually.

Most families failed at least one prearranged appointment and
two families failed over ten.   The average number of appointments
failed per family was three and it was extremely rare for the
parents to bother to get in touch to set another date.   In fact,
very few appointments were initiated by the parents.   Over half
never attempted to arrange an interview and on average this
occurred only once per family with the remainder.   Over half did
use the on-call service however, telephoning out of office hours,
on average on one occasion per family.   Many seemed glad of its
existence and though infrequently used, it provided extra
security.   'It's knowing where to ring and that someone will
answer.   I mean it's the chatting that helps ... to feel there's
someone there who understands.'

Whereabouts of the interviews during the first three months

We felt we could not expect parents to seek us out and keep office
appointments, and on average over half of the interviews were conducted in the home.   We hoped gradually to encourage families to
visit Denver House and find there a caring atmosphere which might
be viewed as a refuge.   However, the fact that many parents did
not visit emphasises the importance of reaching out to them.   In
most families, some interviews were conducted elsewhere, for
example, at hospitals, the average number being five.   This was
a demonstration of our feeling that it was important to accompany
parents when facing stressful situations.

The treatment process

Whatever their reaction to the worker, it was assumed that all the
parents had a need for individualised care and concern but that
their need for love would be painful to acknowledge and was ob-
scured by the fear of loss should they become dependent.   Practical help was offered as fully as possible in all cases and ranged
from running errands to arranging re-housing.   The workers' cars
were important tools in this process, enabling lifts to be given
to the parents and a justification for increasing contact.   Sometimes the ice was broken on such journeys.   Appointments with
other agencies were organised by the workers when parents needed
them and usually the worker accompanied the parents.   Generally,
the workers acted as a buffer between the families and other
agencies.
     In spite of the dangers of advice-giving, some workers found it
necessary to use a certain amount of direction and authority over
specific issues, particularly those relating directly to the protection of the children.   This included urging parents to make
use of day nurseries.
     Gifts were used sparingly, but to good effect, in some cases
where a plant or push-chair was just what the family wanted and
could accept at that particular point in time.   A few were confused by our approach and did not know whether to regard us as
friends or professionals.   Most families seemed comfortable with
our informal approach.   Some families preferred regular prearranged appointments, others did not.
     Efforts were directed primarily towards the mothers in all but
one case and most fathers eluded our less concentrated offers of
help.   The mothers seemed to fall into three groups: being fairly
accessible, ambivalent or resistant to treatment.   Good initial
contact undoubtedly made for a better on-going relationship, but
this was not necessarily progressive as some mothers became more
defensive through time in this initial period.   In this sense
breakthroughs could appear misleading and in all cases the
workers had to strive to some extent to maintain open contact with
the families.

Accessible mothers

A few of the mothers were motivated and accessible.   These were
the only mothers who viewed their problems with the child as a two-
way process, showing concern about their ability to mother.   They
were all poignantly aware of social isolation and acknowledged a
desperate need for someone to talk to.   One mother said to her
social worker: 'I am not really worried who you are or where you
come from, so long as you are willing to help me.'
   Their own appraisal of their problems was inclined to be comprehensive and included a more open acknowledgment of marital problems
and past or current difficulties with grandparents.   They were
aware of relationship problems as well as the more obvious, concrete ones.
   In addition, this group of mothers, in contrast to the others,
displayed overt signs of distress and disturbance, particularly
anxiety and depression which they were able to express, 'I got up
with a terrible tightness in my chest and couldn't breathe.'
   The accessible group of mothers did not require the workers to
direct all their efforts towards maintaining some kind of contact.
These mothers made some use of support from the start.   Reaching-
out was still necessary to sustain the relationship but the predominant techniques were encouraging ventilation and attentive
listening, with tangible demonstrations of concern.   'I was fairly
passive and mainly acted as a sponge for the mother's outpourings.
On days when the mother was very depressed, I sat out long
silences with her in an accepting kind of way.'   Although one
mother was articulate and had some insight into her problems, the
worker was careful to respond 'primarily in an empathetic, supportive manner, rather than with a desire to clarify or interpret ...
I aimed to help the mother to pay more attention to her own needs
and wants and encouraged her to care for and value herself more.'
Similarly, another worker with a very communicative but anxious
mother, 'had often to reassure mother that she was a person of
value within her own right' and 'tried to demonstrate that my
giving was not conditional on her giving to me'.
   The following extract is taken from the eleventh interview with
a family six weeks after the case was referred.   The referred
child, a girl aged three, did not have an injury on referral, but
the mother's rejecting behaviour, the history of abuse and the
child's retarded development led to the child being admitted to
hospital for protection.   The interview took place in the home.
   'I visited Mrs B. in the late afternoon and immediately sensed
an "atmosphere".   She was extremely depressed, and in what I
would describe as her sabotaging mood.   She announced that she
was going to the hospital to take her daughter home the following afternoon and then produced a letter from the Health Department.   This said that there was no place available at present
for her daughter at the day nursery, that she would be placed
on a waiting list and if she did go, she would have to pay
£1.25 per week.   Mrs B. said she could not understand this as
she had been told there was a place for her child.   I said that
as far as I knew that was true and there must have been a mis-
understanding.

She then said, "What's the point of her going there anyway?
It's my relationship with her that needs mending and when she
comes home, I'll be at my most tired and irritable and will have
to get the other children to bed."   I suggested that if she was
relieved of some of the pressure of caring for all the children
throughout the day she would probably find she could enjoy her
daughter more in the evening.   Next she said, "If she learned
to talk at a day nursery, I'd feel jealous, wouldn't I?   So
there's no point and anyway, we can't afford it."   I didn't
attempt to contradict her at this stage.

Shortly Mr B. came in with some shopping but left almost
straight away.   He asked Mrs B. to give him a kiss and she refused.   Then he pecked the children on their cheeks and said,
"Mind how you are with them, see you tomorrow."   When he had
shut the door behind him, Mrs B. burst out crying, picked up
the baby and buried herself in him.   Her other little boy
immediately stopped demanding attention and pressed against
her leg.   I moved closer to comfort her so that we were all in
a huddle around her.   She seemed to find this physical contact
reassuring and gradually stopped crying, saying between sobs,
"everything's been terrible!"

She told me about some of her other worries and then stopped,
saying, "Anyway, you'll be away tomorrow and the next day,
won't you?   You said so before."   I stayed quite a while
until Mrs B. had cheered up enough to listen to my suggestions.
I said that when I got home, I would make some 'phone calls
for her and then I would get a colleague whom she knew to call
round in the morning and I would let him know that she had got
a lot of troubles on her mind.   She seemed reassured by this
and I left her to think about the arrangements for her
daughter.'

Resistant mothers

A few of the mothers were described as resistant and very hard to
reach.   An extreme example is the family whom the worker visited
nineteen times, leaving notes in between, and was allowed in on
only four occasions.   Another mother did not like 'people prying
into my private life'.   Two of this group were initially more
accessible, owing, it seems, to a prompt referral.   However, this
was not sustained once the crisis had passed.   At the point of
crisis one gave the worker a glimpse of the broader extent of her
problems.   These included social isolation, a need to work, and
problems with the battered child.   The remainder were terse in
describing their problems and confined them to one or two areas,
housing being the most common.   Only one mentioned marital difficulties saying with a challenge, 'it's my husband I need help
with!' (not the children).   Toward the end of the three month
period, some of the resistance in these families had sufficiently
thawed to make them more accessible to the workers, but any discussion of difficulties was still inclined to be cursory.   The
workers, however, felt that problems in these families were just
as extensive as in the other sub-groups and the defensiveness only
heightened the difficulties of providing effective help.

In one extreme case this was not possible, 'I attempted to offer
a warm, trusting relationship to the mother and looked around for
practical areas where help might be valued, but every approach was
rejected.'   The need not to force the pace of the relationship and
to avoid a sense of intrusion was uppermost in our minds.   'I
quickly sensed that the mother was heavily defended against dependency and did not find it easy to accept help of any kind.   I concentrated on offering friendship and support, adopting a caring
attitude, but was careful to "mother" her only in subtle ways.
Through lack of response, I quickly gave up trying to get the
parents to voice their difficulties.   Instead I concentrated on
just being available to them and keeping "a foot in their door".'

In these more difficult cases some kind of practical help
usually provided the workers with a focus around which they desperately tried to build a link with the family.   Although workers
were avoided, kept on doorsteps, or virtually ignored if they
managed to get into the home, through persistence they usually
managed to sustain some kind of tentative contact during the first
three months of treatment.

The following interview was the thirteenth, two months after
referral.   The parents had been avoiding the worker for several
weeks and having got no response from the offer of an appointment,
the worker called on chance at the home.

'Eventually Mrs K. came to the door and jumped about three
inches when she saw it was me.   She looked colourless and
tired and was temporarily thrown off balance as to what to do.
She asked me in and got me to perch in the kitchen while she
fiddled with things, straightening them, picking a leaf off a
plant, etc.   I said I had tried to 'phone her as she asked
but couldn't get through so perhaps they had popped out.   Mrs
K. said, "Oh, no, we were in, but silly of us, we did not have
the 'phone switched through properly.

The telephone then rang and when she came back, she mentioned
it was her aunt who was depressed at the moment.   A brief discussion about somebody else's feelings seemed to help Mrs K. to
settle and she invited me into the sitting room.

Ambivalent mothers

The remaining mothers in the sample, that is over half, acknowledged
difficulties with their children.   They were inclined to see them
as 'problem children' but did not recognise their own part in
creating a difficult response.   Marital problems were hinted at
rather than openly discussed and tended to take the form of complaints about particular behaviour of their husbands rather than
constructive evaluation.   With the ambivalent mothers, considerable efforts were needed to get a therapeutic relationship established.   Some kind of acknowledged crisis or situational stress
frequently enabled the workers to prove they could be useful.
For example, two mothers were desperate to separate from their
cohabitees and were helped to reach and act upon this decision.
By the end of the three-month period, most of these mothers had
begun to make active use of the help offered.

Mrs O. seemed very ambivalent about our offer of help.   The
family was referred because their three-month old daughter had
multiple injuries.   We thought that the direct provision of food
might give us a chance of reaching the parents at their level of
need and this mother was invited to lunch at Denver House.   It was
the tenth interview, two weeks after referral.

'Mrs O. brought her mother along who was staying with her.
She did not seem very relaxed over her food, but her mother sat
back and ate with relish.   Mrs O. said, "You've got some un-
usual things.   You must like the same food as my mother."   I
smiled and asked what sort of food Mrs O. liked.   She said,
"Just plain and simple things."   I said I would remember that
for the future.

Mrs O. told me how the baby was getting on in hospital, how
much she enjoyed feeding her and how well she was doing.   She
then talked about her little boy and how he would like the toys
she noticed in my office.   I said I had brought them up
because I thought he might be coming with her.   She then said,
"He would probably smash them all to bits."

After a while I raised the question of her seeing a solicitor as I had been finding out about one for her.   She was
reluctant to agree a time when she could see him and because
there was some urgency, I suggested that I ring him now.   He
had some free time this afternoon and Mrs O. halfheartedly
agreed to go to see him and her mother left.   As we walked
over to this office I mentioned that I had a long journey to
work and would probably be moving soon.   She suddenly looked
alarmed but did not say anything.   I said that it would be
much easier if I moved nearer to work and she said with relief,
"Oh, you're not going to change your job then?"

We waited for about ten minutes at the solicitor's office
during which time she became more and more tense and seemed on
the verge of tears.   She looked pale and I asked her whether
she felt frightened.   She said that she was a bit, "I don't
like the thought of going over it all again."   We sat it out
in a grim sort of silence.   I was not sure whether to go in to
see the solicitor with Mrs O. but decided in favour of it.
He was a bit brusque at first and Mrs O. became tearful so I
put my arm around her, but she did not seem to notice.   He
laboured the question of legal aid and as we came out Mrs O.
seemed flat and depressed.   She said she wanted to go off and
do some shopping, and walked away on her own.'

Social worker's contacts with the children

Several social workers specialising in the field of child protection have advised that it is extremely unwise to have the child as
the focal point of the interview, even though his safety is the
reason for the contact.   Davoren (1968) states that if the worker
gives any attention to the children, it can be very threatening
for the battering parent.   'He also begins to feel frozen out by
both you and the child, and returns to the horrible nightmare feeling of being unwanted.'   The Denver House social workers, bearing
such advice in mind, proceeded carefully in this delicate area.

Within the sample, there were a few cases where caution was unnecessary as the parents seemed sufficiently secure to tolerate
and positively encourage the workers to show direct interest in
their children.   In one case, the worker noted that the parents
would have been very offended if he had failed to pay attention
to the children.   In another case, the worker commented that his
interaction with the children provided light relief for all concerned as contact with the parents was often strained and punctua-
ted by long silences.   In a further few cases, the parents'
reactions to any contact between the worker and the child were
tinged with ambivalence.   One mother vacillated between trying to
shut the child out of the interview altogether and forcing the
worker's attention on the child while she encouraged him to
perform.

With over half of the sample, workers instinctively avoided
much interaction with the children, merely acknowledging them and
responding to them in subtle ways.   This was because they could
sense straight away that this would prove too threatening for the
parents.   Generally workers limited their involvement to positive
comments about the children's appearance or developmental progress, empathising with the parents when the children's behaviour
was proving troublesome.   This often proved exceedingly difficult
for the workers as many of the children welcomed their arrival as
a diversion and made overtures to them for kisses and cuddles.
Because of the parents' intense need to be the focus of attention,
often the only time the workers felt it was permissible to interact with the children was when they were left alone with them,
for example, during a mother's hospital appointment or when they
were transporting the children somewhere.

A few parents were extremely competitive with their children
and became furious if they received momentary attention from the
worker.   It is interesting to note that one mother, when angry
with the worker for focusing briefly on the child, would occasionally retaliate by reading the child a story and shutting the
worker out completely.

Rough handling of the children

While it seemed unlikely that the parents would batter a child in
our presence, we anticipated some degree of rough handling of the
child by the parents in the course of our interviews.   Davoren
(1968) recalls how in her early experience with abusive families
she tried to restrain the parents from being rough with their
children.   She soon realised that although this afforded the
child protection whilst she was there, the parents were likely to
see such intervention as a criticism of them and might well take
revenge on the child once she had left.   One mother in our
sample resorted to handling her child roughly both as a means of
distracting the worker's attention from her husband and to retaliate against what she considered as criticism from the worker.

The Denver House workers were exposed to a high degree of
anxiety when witnessing rough handling.   Generally, we refrained
from any direct intervention, but attempted to distract the parent.

Also, we were perturbed when the parents seemed insensitive to the
child's needs.   For example, many parents did not respond to their
child's desire to be comforted and instead made fun of them,
showered them with sweets, or completely ignored them.   Sometimes
the situation felt unbearable and workers suggested 'maybe he's a
bit tired and wants to lie down' or with a mother getting distraught
over food refusal, 'perhaps she's just not hungry and you're getting
yourself upset.'

Many parents whilst engaged in rough behaviour seemed oblivious
of the worker's presence.   This extract from an interview with a
mother during the thirteenth contact two months after referral con-
veys something of the dilemma.   The child in question was only
ten months old.

'As we passed the baby's bedroom, Mrs T. said, "Can you hear
the monster?   What a bad girl!"   She then got the baby and
brought her into the sitting room.   She always places the
baby between herself and me and I often feel I have to try to
relate to her through the baby.   She was pleased I noticed
that the baby had grown.

Before we had a chance to resume our conversation, the baby
started to irritate Mrs T.   Apparently she had pulled the
standard lamp over the evening before and as she made a move
in that direction, she was pulled back.   She then grabbed an
ashtray on a stand and Mrs T. put it behind the door.   Next
it was the wastepaper basket and Mrs T. triumphantly put it on
the mantelpiece.   When the baby got a tile from the fireplace,
she was smacked and pushed into the middle of the floor.   The
baby babbled as her mother told her off and Mrs T. said, "Just
listen to her.   You're not going to answer me back like that,
my lady."

Mrs T. began to seem glad of my quiet companionship and we
chatted socially about holidays and Europe.   She then talked
about the baby, picked her up, and began tickling her.   At
first the baby laughed and enjoyed it, but Mrs T. went on
until the baby got short of breath and was crying with frustration.   She then said to the baby, pulling her up, "Come on,
stand up without using your hands."   The child's legs soon
caved in and Mrs T. got angry saying, "Come on, don't be lazy,
stand up properly!"   I diverted her by asking her about her
work and as usual, she was glad to have a chance to talk about
this.'

In the most extreme case the mother virtually persecuted the
battered child and her sibling and treated them both in a harsh,
cruel manner for no apparent reason.   She enforced an extremely
strict regime and for example made the children stand up while
they ate.

On one occasion when the battered child had been looked after
at Denver House, she started to cry when it was time to leave for
home.   The mother remarked furiously, 'she's always doing this
when we go anywhere' and yanked hard at the child's arm to drag
her away.   When the child resisted, she roughly bundled her out
of the room, and tightly gripping her hand, bounced her down the
stairs with her feet lightly touching about every fourth step.
The worker commented, 'during such incidents I did very little

except to distract the mother by making sympathetic remarks to her or simply keeping quiet and hiding my disgust.   I am convinced that my intervention would have made matters worse for the child as the mother seemed to need only the slightest bother over her to start persecuting her again.'   In two cases, rough handling was precipitated by the worker's casual enquiries about earlier unexplained injuries and this does emphasise the need for caution in this area.

Discussion of abuse in the course of treatment

We did not intend to concentrate on finding out from the parents how the child was actually injured.   We felt that an interrogatory approach was bound to be charged with accusation for the parents which would impede therapeutic progress.   Generally, apart from an initial enquiry in which we would not press for detail, we intended to avoid direct questions about the battering incident but to leave the parents free to raise the subject themselves.   This approach is in keeping with the views of Steele and Pollock (1968) but runs counter to the treatment philosophy of some other workers in this field.   For example, Ounsted et al. (1974), treating selected families in a residential setting, state, 'It is useful to go over each violent act and elicit in detail what really happened.'   Probably one factor which influenced our attitude in this matter was our lack of control over the treatment situation.   In over half the cases our interaction was dependent on the parents' co-operation and we were afraid that they would suddenly break contact if we attempted to penetrate their defence prematurely.   Not only might this expose the child to further danger, but also the parent to possible personality disintegration.

    In practice, however, the workers' approaches varied from avoiding any discussion of injuries to fairly detailed questioning about how they occurred.   Parents also varied in their degrees of reluctance to talk about the reason for referral, the extent of the damage to the child being an important factor.   Where the child did not have a current injury (five cases), the parents could obviously be expected to discuss their fear of causing harm or past incidents of abuse as this was the reason they were accepted for treatment by the Department.   Often they referred to the general taboo on expressing violent feelings towards young children which they felt extended to professional people.   One mother who graphically described ramming a feeding bottle into her baby's mouth commented, 'You can't tell many people about these things because they'll think you are peculiar.'   Even with our specialised focus we felt some awkwardness about the subject, experiencing a tendency to accept that there was a problem without focusing on it unless the parents wanted to be specific.

    As mentioned in chapter 2, there were a further five cases with current injuries where parents admitted that the child had been abused.   One case entailed a moderate injury, where the mother was both openly guilty, 'Will I ever get it off my mind?' and expressed a desire to make reparation.   Another at first made

a tacit acknowledgment and when the worker later asked how it
happened, described the incident in a very cursory fashion. It
was very important to this mother for others to recognise that she
had not deliberately injured her child. The worker coped with
this by telling her that other people had done this kind of thing.
Although this mother was matter-of-fact about the whole business,
she developed considerable depression and a variety of psychosomatic
symptoms. Another mother only admitted abuse in the course of
police investigations, and then confessed to the worker. She
was terrified of rejection, asking, 'Will you and the health visitor still come to see me?' The fathers in these three cases
tended to be unsympathetic or even fairly punitive towards their
wives.

In Not all the remaining parents, who did not openly admit to
abusive behaviour, were cool and impassive or anxious and compliant. Some, who at the outset adopted these attitudes, later
became defensively angry. 'If the child had pneumonia instead
we would be left alone. There has been no bashing about, you
know!' or openly hostile, 'Can't have much bleeding confidence in
anybody, can you?' A couple of families were challenging from
the start - 'Still, you haven't come here for a chat, let's get
down to business!' All of the foregoing quotations in this
paragraph were from fathers. Mothers on the defensive tended to
be less critical and displayed hurt feelings - 'Well, it's not
very nice you know to think someone thinks you bash your baby';
or, 'They all accuse me. I don't want to beat him to kill.'

In a few cases, owing to avoidance by the workers and reluctance of the parents, injuries were never discussed at all. When
workers were explicit about the injuries they were careful to
stress their primary aim of being helpful and not condemning, and
in all but a few cases, the parents accepted this. As one worker
put it, 'I told the mother it was not my intention to accuse,
criticise or get angry, but to get some help to you.'

During the course of treatment several parents expressed
oblique anxiety about their children's safety or revealed that
they had violent fantasies about them, morbidly referring to
domestic dangers, etc. One father from a family in which abuse
had obviously been occurring for a long time, referred to the
care his children had received from a daily-minder in the past -
'they kept coming home with bruises and you really couldn't say
anything. She had so many children to look after that she
couldn't keep an eye on them all.' Another father played out a
sick kind of game in the worker's presence asking, 'Shall I beat
baby up? I go up to her doing a karate chop, she laughs, she
thinks it's a game, but one chop and ...' Another parent, on
learning that a minor reinjury to his son had been noted, went up
to him and said, 'You look as if you've been in a scrap, don't
you?' He then started to make boxing gestures at the child
with clenched fists, jokingly saying, 'I'll bash you, I'll get
you one - I'll bash your face in.'

A few parents who probably feared rejection and condemnation
appeared to raise the topic of abuse to test out the workers'
reactions, subjecting them to close scrutiny. One mother asked
the worker if she saw many bad cases of abuse, 'people who kill

their babies and babies with their heads bashed in all oozing with
blood ... I can't think how you can do your job.'   The workers
were often able to make good use of these opportunities to state
that they felt sympathetic towards such parents and wanted to help
them.

Two mothers referred to TV programmes or newspaper articles on
battered babies which they had seen.   One mother, who had watched
a battering mother being interviewed on TV, said that she had
really felt sorry for her.   In contrast, several of the parents
who denied any knowledge of the cause of their children's injuries,
dissociated completely from parents who damage their children and
were unable to accept the worker's suggestion that extreme pressures might lead people to do this unintentionally.   They intended
to adopt a self-righteous, punitive attitude, saying, 'Well, I
wouldn't speak to anyone who had been cruel to their child -
people who cause injuries to their children should have the same
done to them.'

The parents' development of trust

We felt that the parents' development of trust in the workers
would indicate the establishment of the therapeutic relationship.
Lack of basic trust is said to stem from fears of abandonment and
rejection (Steele and Pollock, 1968; Court, 1969b).   The sur-
facing of such fears was taken to be further indication of a
developing attachment.   With all the families, we were careful to
leave notes about failed visits and prepare the parents for
absences by telling them in advance when we would be away.   Substitute workers from the team were provided for holidays and
longer absences and postcards sent whenever they occurred.   At
the end of the three months our efforts seemed to have been rewar-
ded by the mothers but not the fathers.

The fathers

Apart from the few trusting or ambivalent fathers, most remained
mistrustful throughout this period.   They seemed wary of forming
any relationships and avoided contact.   Some remained openly
hostile, others were innocuous and 'pleasant', or silent when
seen.   A typical comment from one worker was 'avoided dependency
and though he became a bit more candid, he was still tense, mistrustful and defensively aloof'.   A few seemed glad of the
advantages of practical help (although a few were also somewhat
threatened by this) but made it clear that they wanted to keep
things at that level.   One father showed willingness to accept
help only because of a crisis and needed to maintain control by
feeling he was manipulating the worker into doing what he wanted.
A few were actively sabotaging, jealous of the attention given
their wives, yet resisting contact and battling to keep their
independence.   This rather grim picture may in some part be a
product of our mother-focused approach but virtually all fathers
were reached-out to and no attempt was made to exclude them.

This could indicate that on the whole the fathers were more damaged
emotionally than the mothers.   It also seems to stress the need
for individual attention for these parents from one person they can
call their own.   From the start some social workers were conscious
of mothers wanting them all to themselves and subtle forces of
jealousy and possessiveness were probably operating within the
families against the inclusion of the fathers in therapy.   We were
prepared for this and discuss our attempts to get round this
problem in chapter 9.

The mothers

The accessible mothers seemed to be ready for a dependent relationship and quickly invested trust in their social workers.   They
seemed to want to share their lives with the worker, one mother
bringing out photographs of her childhood.   They were interested
in the workers' personal lives and began to form strong attachments
and identifications.   They demonstrated strong fears of abandonment, several asking questions early on about how long the social
worker was likely to be around.

The mothers in the ambivalent group were more cautious.   They
would not dare to believe at first that anyone could care about
them because they felt worthless and inadequate.   Gradually most
in this group began to invest trust over the three-month period
and also to show fears of being 'let down'.   One mother showed
her attachment by literally holding on to a present given by the
worker and imitating her clothes.   Another mother said she wanted
to take her social worker on holiday with her!

A few of the mothers who were ambivalent at the outset were
still ambivalent by the end of the three-month period.   One was
depressed at the time of referral and grateful for the empathy and
uncritical caring that was shown to her but did not seem to become
attached.   Another began to trust but then withdrew after the
worker had been on holiday and seemed to resent her earlier
dependence.

The resistant mothers remained mistrustful throughout this
period.   They seemed fearful of rejection and criticism in spite
of evidence to the contrary and maintained emotional distance,
though a few appeared compliant.   One viewed the worker as someone
with power whom she could use to manipulate other agencies, but
would not let the worker nearer when he did this.   Fears of
abandonment did not arise with this group and most made it clear
that they would be only too happy to be left alone.

There was no marked variation in the fundamental problems perceived by the workers across the full range of families.   A
relationship problem between mother and the battered child, marital difficulties, particularly lack of support from husbands, and
social isolation were noted in nearly all of the cases.   In quite
a number, unresolved conflicts with grandparents appeared near the
surface, and material stress was often a feature.   Most of the
above were recognised by those mothers who were accessible and
only one or two, particularly material stress, of these factors
were admitted by the resistant mothers.   This endorses the need

for a careful psycho-social evaluation in all cases, particularly
those families in which the parents are insistent that 'everything
is fine', a phrase used by several of our most resistant mothers.

By the end of the first three months of treatment, over half of
the mothers were engaged in a meaningful relationship with their
social workers and only a few remained suspicious and inclined to
avoid contact.   We were greatly helped by other researchers in
the field, who had attempted to document their experiences and
opinions.   This gave us a theoretical foundation, which provided
guidance and heightened our sensitivity about how to approach
families involved in this distressing problem.   It also acted as
a bulwark against the intense anxiety we all felt in coming to
terms with and trying to ameliorate parental violence towards
infants.   All theoretical models however can only act as a guide.
They cannot tell a therapist how to be, and do not remove the
struggle of evolving a personal way of relating to clients in a
helping capacity.   The variations both obvious and subtle in
family situations and parental needs were striking.   Our most important task in the first three months was to make connections with
the parents which were meaningful in their terms.   This entailed
a need for imagination as much as knowledge and, above all, an
ability, in the midst of rejection from the clients, to be patient
enough to see their needs.

Workers often felt denigrated, impotent or, occasionally, overwhelmed by the families.   One worker felt resentful of a mother's
pressure to give false assurances during the course of many crises
and 'the fact that they seemed to want me to remove altogether
the source of their worries rather than help them to cope with or
find solutions to their problems.'   In spite of feeling debilita-
ted, with most families, workers were able to retain a sense of
optimism even when the task was most daunting.   'Caring for this
mother was practically a full time job in itself.   She presented
as rootless, lost, childlike, insecure and unhappy, with immense
dependency needs.   Her message came over loud and clear, "feed
me, feed me" on all levels and this I attempted to do.'

SUBSEQUENT PHASES OF TREATMENT
Subsequent pattern of visiting

There were wide variations in the frequency and whereabouts of
interviews with each family, but some trends did emerge.   The
most obvious and expected change with time was the decline in the
number of contacts per family as treatment progressed.   Whereas
the average number of contacts per family per month was seven in
the initial three months of treatment, visits fell to an average
of four per family per month during the remainder of the first
year.   In the second year, contacts on average were two per family
per month.   For families in treatment for a third year, the
average number of contacts was one per family per month.

Other changes occurred in the pattern of interviewing.   There
was a more active use of our service by the clients shown by a
decrease in the number of appointments failed and an increase in
the proportion of interviews initiated by clients throughout the

three-year period.   The use of the emergency telephone service
progressively increased during the first year of treatment, but
in the second and subsequent years it was rarely used at all,
implying that such a service is of maximum value in the earlier
stages of treatment.   The proportion of visits by clients to
Denver House gradually increased with time as home visits decreased
but the proportion of interviews conducted elsewhere, at hospitals,
nurseries, etc., remained roughly the same.   There was a very
slight decrease in our limited contact with fathers on their own
and also in the proportion of joint interviews after the initial
three months of treatment.   For the rest of the period, these
figures were fairly stable and overall, joint interviews constituted about 20 per cent of our contacts with the families.

THE SECOND PHASE: 4-12 MONTHS

It is clear from our analysis of case summaries that this period
was marked by the development in the clients of dependency on the
social workers.   Whether this was the tentative beginnings of
attachment displayed by the resistant mothers or a deeply felt
bond expressed by the accessible mothers, the workers emerged as
important caring figures in their lives.   'I don't know what
would have happened if I hadn't met you.   I would probably be in
jail by now.'   'I can't see anyone else keep coming like you do.'
.Such comments seem to reflect the feelings of most of the mothers,
even if they remained unvoiced.
   It was often difficult to see the signs of attachment, partly
because we were so close to the situation, but also the client's
continuing defensiveness and lack of trust created a negative
impression.   For example, the worker who felt frustrated and of
little value to a family because interviews continued to be limited
to awkward silences or superficial chat about the same seemingly
insignificant topics, was surprised when the mother asked with
great concern, 'You will still come to see me when we move, won't
you?'
   Workers were on the whole very active in providing practical
help during this period which undoubtedly fostered a good relationship.   We arranged to ferry children to and from day nurseries
and to hospital appointments, helped a substantial number of
families with rehousing and gave financial assistance when needed.
We made liaison with other agencies to ensure that the families
were getting the maximum benefit from available services and sometimes acted as a buffer between the family and the demands of hire
purchase companies, housing authorities and the fuel boards.
Without such opportunities to demonstrate our concern, relationships tended to progress more slowly.   In writing about one
family, the worker remarked, 'They did not seem to need much practical help and I did not seem to get any further with this family
as regards helping them with problems on a deeper level.   They
continued to keep me at a distance.'
   Sometimes practical problems provided the only meaningful
points of contact.   Another worker writes, 'There were continued
periods of withdrawal and I only really felt able to get through

in moments of crisis when practical help was needed, otherwise I
seemed to be having little impact on the client.'   The provision
of practical help did not automatically ensure the growth of a
relationship.   'In spite of abundant practical help, there remained
much passive resistance from both parents with some more positive
feelings emerging towards the end of the first year.'   It was a
case of practical help being one aspect of our care and attention
which provided tangible benefits;   unlike a compassionate smile, a
hug, or whole-hearted attention, the results of practical help
were less likely to vanish once the social worker had left.   One
mother remarked, 'A lot has happened since I was last in the car
with you.   I'm on the pill, I've got new teeth, and the baby is
all right.   You're a good friend and always a help when I need
it.   Nobody listens to me except you.'

Another feature of the relationships during this period was the
extensive use of ego-building techniques.   We were keen to discover the accomplishments and achievements of the parents, however
minor, in order to give praise and encouragement which would
mitigate low self-esteem.   We also tried to lower the high standards they set for themselves and ease the resulting self-condem-
nation when they were not met.   We suggested more realistic
alternatives and fiercely defended their right to attach importance to their own needs and wants.   These attempts to relax the
pressure of a punitive superego were very significant in combating
the feelings of powerlessness and hopelessness which pervaded the
first year of treatment for many parents.   Work in this area when
coupled with support, often led to parents' making major re-eval-
uations of their lives.   They moved towards the resolution of
chronic conflict situations, for example, in their relationships
with grandparents, with spouses, or over the use of contraception.
By the end of the first year, many of the mothers, with the confidence gained from dependency and support during the four to twelve
month period, were moving into a more self-assertive phase.

THE THIRD PHASE: 13-24 MONTHS

This period was marked by a much greater sense of ease in the
worker/client relationship.   Dependency was openly acknowledged
and began to be taken for granted even by the resistant mothers,
sometimes grudgingly.   'Well, I've got no one else to turn to.'
Fears of abandonment diminished and parents were able to tolerate
changes of appointments and absences for holidays well.   Often
parents reflected on the development of their relationship with
their worker, recalling earlier events, particularly crises, with
perspicacity or talking about how they felt when we first introduced ourselves.   For many mothers, and a few fathers, workers
were seen as part of their extended family or perhaps came to
represent the 'good' parents they had never had.   One worker was
entrusted with the keys to the home in order to call and feed the
cats whilst the family were on holiday.   In another case, the
worker acted as a witness at a wedding and often we played a part
in important family occasions.   At the crisis of the birth of a
new child, a worker and her husband spent the night with the other
children in order to avoid disrupting their lives.

Many contacts became simple, friendly social events over cups
of tea, during which we casually shared experiences, for example,
over TV programmes or our food preferences.   Such interviews were
interspersed with focused discussions about specific problems
where feelings were explored in much greater depth than in the
earlier stages of treatment.   Though adhering to an informal
approach, workers felt able to develop a more active role, direct-
ing the mothers' attention to areas which they seemed to be
avoiding, challenging some of their statements and occasionally
making interpretations.   Workers also began to raise more uncomfortable topics for discussion.

Crises still occurred but tended to be emotional rather than
practical in nature, such as anxiety over handling feelings towards
the children, the spouse or the extended family.   Practical help
continued to be offered but clients began to gain more satisfaction
from managing their own affairs.   Similarly, they began to make
active demands on other agencies without our help and became
challenging when their needs were not met.   This self-assertion
and growth of competence was very heartening to witness, but they
still needed to feel that we were behind them.

As we fostered the development of autonomy in the client, feelings began to emerge directly.   Most striking were the occasional
negative outbursts towards the primary worker, 'I'm going to tear
you off a strip', other agencies, or the spouse.   Several mothers
also began to acknowledge negative feelings towards their own
parents or parents-in-law which seemed to represent a very healthy
step.   Mothers spoke much more about how they felt, and seemed to
be becoming aware for the first time in treatment of the importance of emotions in their lives.   'I felt embarrassed' ... 'I
really did not like it when ...' 'I was furious ...' 'I felt very
sorry for ...'   Comments were often prefaced with remarks such
as these which seemed to indicate a newly found openness and
self-awareness in the lives of the mothers.

THE FOURTH PHASE: 25-36 MONTHS

The third year was a time when those parents still in treatment
(sixteen) seemed to achieve a fuller independence and acted without reference to their workers.   They tended to cope with their
own problems and tell us about them after the event.   There
appeared to be a definite growth in the resourcefulness of the
parents and their need for support and nurturing had diminished.
For example, even with a family where both parents operated on an
infantile level, the worker noted that they were 'now more adult
and responsible' and had even managed to arrange and pay for
their own holiday.

During this year, and earlier with some cases, we began to
question the therapeutic value of the roles we had assumed with
the family.   As the need for nurturing and support diminished,
new needs did emerge and more complex but specific problems came
to the fore.   For example, with several mothers, previously described as resistant, deep-seated marital problems began to emerge.
It was felt that the effective handling of new needs of the

parents required a different approach based on more firmness and
detachment on the part of the workers.   We found it extremely
difficult to develop such qualities in the wake of a close,
nurturing involvement with the family.   Techniques certainly
changed and workers continued to challenge and confront the
parents more, but such tactics did not seem to produce the kind
of reflective reaction and emotional development in the client
which would normally occur had the relationship been in its
infancy.   It was almost as though our caring attitude had been
absorbed by the family, or at least the mothers, to such an extent
that our challenging comments had little therapeutic impact, and
lacked for them the clarity and provocation with which remarks
from an unfamiliar worker would have been endowed.

TERMINATION OF TREATMENT

We expected our treatment commitment to the families would be of
long duration.   Assuming that serious emotional damage was a
feature of the parents' early background, restitutive nurturing
is essentially a long-term process.   Families who moved out of
the area during the life of the project were usually transferred
to other agencies.   Premature loss of premises in November 1973,
interrupted the service provided.   We continued to maintain as
regular a service as possible.   Where appropriate, families were
transferred to the social worker attached to the Denver House Day
Nursery, which continued to function in the area.   Few cases
were closed, and even when they were, or with families transferred,
occasional contact by letter, telephone or a visit was maintained.
Table 8.1 gives the disposition of cases in December 1974.

TABLE 8.1   Disposition of cases (N = 25)

	Number
Still open and requiring treatment in December 1974, to be referred to another worker	5
Still open in December 1974, and in treatment with social worker attached to Denver House Day Nursery	5
Referred to another agency when family moved or social worker left	9
Closed (in 3 cases after two years and in 1 case after one year)	4
Contact lost (in 1 case after a few months, in the other after two years)	2

It can be seen that there were only four cases we considered
ready to be closed.   All the other twenty-one families continued
to require help, although two severed links themselves with our
service.

DISCUSSION

There was much to suggest that most of our therapeutic energies went
into the first year of treatment when we embraced a primarily
nurturing role.   Although we found it possible to enable parents
subsequently to loosen gradually the ties and establish some
measure of independence, we found it very difficult to bring forth
other therapeutic skills needed to cope with the new problems which
emerged.   It may be that the social workers were so engrossed in
the nurturing process that we failed to respond to the new needs
which arose.   This was probably part of the problem but there is
also evidence that the parents strongly resisted any changes in our
approach.   It seems that our relationship was used to develop some
measure of basic trust in the parents and allow them to fulfil some
of their current dependency needs.   From this they developed self-
assertion and moved towards independence.   Such a process, even if
only partially achieved by most mothers, represents considerable
emotional development and in itself a cycle of growth.   In our
experience this process exhausted the therapeutic potential of the
primary relationship.   If the client wanted to continue working
on other problems which had been unearthed, then another worker
was needed to provide the therapeutic stimuli.   Probably another
agency with a different ethos was needed.   For our part we felt
that to a greater or lesser extent, we had fulfilled our basic
therapeutic intention but were frustrated when recognising the
many remaining problems in the family, particularly the emotional
problems in the parent-child relationships, that we could do very
little directly to help.
    It is of interest to compare our findings with the work of
Reiner and Kaufmann (1959) in the field of delinquency.   Using a
psycho-analytic model, they elaborated the therapeutic problems
posed by parents with character disorders and Zalba (1966) has
written of the relevance of their work to child abuse.   Although
our theoretical formulation of our parents' personality problems
based largely on the work of Steele and Pollock (1968) and Steele
(1970) differed, our approach to treatment bears many fundamental
similarities and the theoretical differences may lie more in terminology than with practice.   Reiner and Kaufmann emphasise the
provision of more than simple support, practical help, or clari-
fication of the client's problems.   They recognise the key
importance of the therapeutic relationship itself and feel that
the initial task of establishing that relationship is probably the
most difficult stage in a treatment process that is essentially
long-term.   Problems were also encountered in treating fathers
and although some involvement of the fathers took place, treatment
was focused on the mothers, as in our project.   They have identified four stages in treatment: establishing a relationship, ego-
building through identification, helping the client establish a
separate identity, and, helping the client gain self-understanding.
    In the second stage, we have stressed the importance of depen-
dence on the therapist rather than identification with him.
Although some valuable identification and modelling undoubtedly
took place, a much more prominent feature of this period was the
fact that the parents allowed some of their dependency needs to

be met.   Perhaps, because of this, we also noted two stages in the
development of independence.   Apart from these differences, our
description of the treatment process in terms of emotional growth
has much in common with Reiner and Kaufmann.   Where we seem to
have foundered is in the fourth stage they identified as helping
the client to 'gain some understanding of his behaviour and its
roots in the past'.   Certainly, such understanding did develop in
some of our clients but the gains were implicit rather than an
overt function of our work.   Using the analogy of the adoles-
cent's relationship to his parents, Reiner and Kaufmann state that
the establishment of independence 'does not require renunciation
of the relationship', and argue that the therapist takes on a new
role which distinguishes him from the early nurturing and weaning
functions.   It may be that our informal approach and very close
involvement with the family meant that we were unable to make this
transition.   Like many parents of adolescents perhaps we remained
too closely associated for the clients with infantile needs.   It
seemed that our clients needed to turn to peers and fresh authority
figures to tackle the problems posed in this stage of their
development.   The question remains open whether our main emphasis
on a nurturing role in the early stages served the long-term
interests of the clients.   A further question is their capacity
to have coped with any other kind of approach.

Chapter 9

THE USE OF OTHER WORKERS -
PROFESSIONAL AND UNTRAINED

From the beginning we considered it most important to introduce
other people into the therapeutic process, in addition to the
primary worker. We thought that many parents might not be able
to share their worker, and that we would need workers to play other
roles: as marital co-therapists, as child care workers when
children were away from home, as legal agents in Juvenile Court
work, and as non-professional friends and supports. Our success
in involving others was mixed, depending partly on personalities,
our own, our co-workers' and our clients', and partly on the
situations, of the individual case and of Denver House as it
developed.

Co-therapy with the other partner

We very much hoped at the outset to work with both parents, as we
were aware of the ease with which fathers slip into the background
of a treatment situation. We expected that some fathers would be
the batterers, and planned to offer two Denver House workers to as
many families as possible, as we could also work in the evenings
and at weekends and had time and workers available. In some
cases, we thought it might be more appropriate to use a co-
therapist from a Social Services Department, and as our commitments
increased this became the rule when a co-therapist was needed.
  However, as is often the case, we were not able to reach the
majority of our fathers; in only one case was the main therapeutic relationship with the father. By the end of the first three
months of treatment, the fathers had been seen on average once
individually, eleven never having been seen alone and the mothers
had received an average of twelve individual contacts. Some
fathers had been seen in joint interviews with their wives and a
few we had not met. In eleven cases, we did not try to introduce
another worker for father (or in one case mother). Three of
these families permitted us too tenuous a footing to dare bring in
yet another social worker. In another case, the father left home
soon after referral. In two further cases, the mothers were considered so accessible and the marriages so relatively stable that

another worker was not necessary.   The remaining three fathers and
one mother seemed remote and unwilling to become involved.   As
treatment progressed, we did get to know some of these fathers
better, but it is now clear that once a pattern had been established
that the mother was the client, this was very difficult to change.

In nine cases, we tried to introduce a local authority social
worker as a co-therapist for the other partner.   Only two of these
succeeded at all and neither developed into consistent marital co-
therapy.   Difficulties arose because of Social Services Departments' pressure of work, unwillingness by fathers to be involved
and sometimes a lack of understanding between workers.   In some
cases there was a tendency for clients to try to play workers off
against one another;   this could be difficult and confusing to
handle and communication between co-workers was of great importance.   Where there was a child in care, the local authority
worker had an important child care role and it was difficult for
the parents to see her or him otherwise.

In five cases, there was an attempt to introduce two Denver
House workers into the family as co-therapists, one to work with
each of the parents.   Three of these failed totally, two fathers
failing to co-operate and drifting firmly back into the background,
and one shouting, swearing and threatening violence against anyone
who wore a suit!   All these couples had troubled marriages, and
the fathers were unhappy and confused as individuals;   nevertheless, repeated attempts to offer a worker for fathers were unsuccessful.   In the remaining two cases, two Denver House workers
were successfully introduced into the family, in both a male
worker for the father and a female for the mother.

In retrospect, this failure to involve the fathers seems an
important shortcoming, particularly as we were aware how many of
the marriages were unhappy.   One can now see that the focus on
the mother was often established at the beginning as she was the
more easily accessible and available, and that we as much as the
clients became set in this pattern.   It must, however, be added
that some of our mothers were jealous or suspicious of a desire
for contact with their husband and that other workers (for example
Davoren (1968) and Paulson and Chaleff (1973)) have encountered
the same problem.   In addition, it is our impression that some of
the fathers, although as confused and emotionally deprived as
their wives, found it much more difficult to accept dependency and
appeared to be more defended against their emotional needs.

Use of other workers with child care functions

In eleven cases, a local authority social worker was involved with
a family because the child was in care, either voluntarily or
through the Juvenile Court.   These collaborations worked more
successfully than the attempts at marital co-therapy, although
they meant that the mother now had two workers and the father
still remained out of the picture.   In most cases, the local
authority worker's task was to arrange, co-ordinate and communicate
about the child's care, although when the Juvenile Court was involved, role difficulties arose, as already discussed in chapter 7.

Other professional workers' involvement in cases

Seven of our cases were referred by health visitors, and in the
majority of others a health visitor was already known to the family.
We were anxious that they should be involved in case conferences,
and encouraged them to continue to visit families as they had an
important therapeutic function, and also had access to resources
such as day nursery places, medical attention from clinic doctors
and family planning facilities. We also hoped that they would not
drop already established relationships with mothers on referral to
us.   In six cases, health visitors became most important co-
workers for the mother, offering much support and working well with
us.   In one, the health visitor was far more successful in keeping
a relationship going than we were.   In the remaining cases, health
visitors did not become meaningfully involved; the families were
sometimes difficult and suspicious, and occasionally the health
visitor's child-orientation made it difficult for her to accept or
understand mothers.   Sometimes they withdrew with relief once they
knew the case had been referred to us.   In none of our cases was
a GP involved in the on-going treatment situation, although some
were helpful and co-operative as crises arose.

Psychiatric treatment

In a number of cases, in addition to our casework support, parents
and children received psychiatric treatment.   Symptomatic relief
and the additional focused support undoubtedly helped these
parents.   However, the function of psychiatric treatment seemed
complementary to our service and did not replace the parent's
need for a long-term mothering relationship with a community-based
social worker.

In-patient psychiatric treatment

Three parents were admitted to mental hospitals in the first twelve
months of treatment.   All were voluntary patients and remained in
hospital for periods of less than six months.   One parent was
suffering from reactive depression after making a suicide attempt.
There was considerable confusion about the diagnoses of the other
parents, one of whom was assessed for temporal lobe epilepsy.   The
initiative for liaison with hospital staff was left entirely to
Denver House workers.   However, our continued involvement with
these parents was welcomed and we visited them regularly.   We
found that the parents, who were often bored, lonely and ill at
ease in the hospital surroundings, were responsive to us and we
quickly were able to consolidate our relationship with them during
their time in hospital.

Out-patient psychiatric treatment

Two mothers received occasional psychiatric support on an out-
patient basis at times of crisis.   Another mother received supportive psychotherapy for approximately eighteen months.   Close
communication about the mother's progress was maintained between
the psychiatrist and the Denver House worker.   Initially there
was duplication of roles but this dependent mother seemed glad of
intensive support from more than one source.   At a later stage
in treatment the worker acted as a buffer between the psychiatrist
and the mother, who was upset by and resistant to the psychiatrist's
increasing use of interpretative techniques.   From this examination of methods came the realisation that the mother could make
little use of further psychiatric help and the treatment was
gradually discontinued.

    Joint supportive psychotherapy from a psychiatrist and a psy-
chiatric social worker was offered to and accepted by a couple
with serious marital problems, when they moved some distance from
the project area a few months after referral.   The two Denver
House social workers involved in the case continued to visit for
a year, then gradually withdrew.

Families with children attending child guidance clinics or
special schools

In four cases it was possible to arrange for the battered child or
other children in the family to attend Child Guidance Clinics for
therapy soon after referral.   In one case, the child psychiatrist
worked together with the mother and child, who was in care under
an order, to try and improve their relationship and interaction.
The other mothers were seen by the psychiatric social worker while
the children had sessions with the psychiatrist alone.   In one of
these cases, after the family moved away from London, the children
were made the subjects of Care Orders and whilst in care, received
individual therapy, arranged by the local Social Services
Department.

    In several cases, as treatment progressed, we became increas-
ingly disturbed by the continued distortion in parent-child
interaction and concerned about the children's emotional development.   In one such case the day nursery matron reported that she
and her staff were having great difficulty in containing the
child, who required constant supervision because of her disturbed
aggressive behaviour, culminating in an incident when she tried
to strangle another child.

    As our own involvement with these children continued to be
relatively limited, for reasons already discussed (see chapter 8),
we were anxious for them to receive treatment in their own right.
Thus, therapy at a Child Guidance Clinic was arranged for the
child described above and another extremely provocative child.
Also their mothers were seen by the psychiatric social workers,
who focused directly on their parenting problems, especially
matters relating to discipline and control.   In another case, the
battered child and his siblings were psychiatrically assessed and

both were placed in a boarding school for maladjusted children; the
battered child under a Care Order and his sibling with the mother's
agreement.   In a further two cases, however, our attempts to
arrange specialised help, including speech therapy, for the children
proved unsuccessful because of parental resistance.

THE ROLE OF THE PSYCHIATRIC CONSULTANT TO THE DEPARTMENT

We also employed a psychiatrist on a sessional basis and were
fortunate to have the services of a consultant forensic psychiatrist, with long experience in the field of child abuse and murder.
We hoped that he would be able to fulfil a variety of functions
for our unit; some of our demands upon him changed as work progressed and the needs of the Department became apparent.

i Psychiatric assessment of parents

Seventeen of the fifty mothers and fathers in our sample were seen
by the psychiatrist, twelve mothers and five fathers.   Thus at
least one partner in thirteen of our twenty-five families was
seen.   Other parents referred to our unit and not included in the
present sample were also seen by the psychiatrist.

In the cases referred later in the project, parents were seen
shortly after referral as part of the initial diagnostic procedure.   We were rather cautious in our handling of our earlier
referrals and became more confident with later referrals that an
interview with our psychiatrist could be accepted fairly readily.
In fact, few people seemed to object to the idea, some supplying
their own reasons when they met him.   'Oh, yes, I'm seeing you
about my headaches, aren't I?' as one mother said.   Many parents
responded well to a fairly structured interview, talking quite
freely and sometimes supplying information they had not given to
their social worker.   Thus, some parents were seen near to the
time of referral and we feel that this should have been our procedure in all cases.   The remainder were seen at the request of
their social worker because of a specific concern, in two cases a
request for termination of pregnancy and in one to support a child
guidance referral.   In others, the social worker was worried about
a parent's state of mind, for example, about the effects of a past
head injury or about a possible psychotic delusion.

In no case seen by our psychiatrist was a diagnosis of psychosis
or acute depression made.   Generally, his comments on the parents
he saw were such as, 'immature personality', 'has large personality problems', 'feels very inadequate', 'has a strong need to
lean on others', 'is not depressed in a psychiatric sense, chron-
ically discouraged would be more accurate'.   Additionally, he
felt that many of those he saw were treatable by our kind of
method; both because of obvious social problems which could be
remedied and because he considered that the kind of inadequacy and
immaturity he saw would respond to long-term support, warmth and
availability.   'He needs someone who will spend a great deal of
time with him, listening, showing him how to deal with day-to-day

problems, making him be realistic, helping him to face up to things
and not run away.   Once a week chats would be of very little use.'
In several cases he stressed the need for a 'forgiving and reassuring father (something she has never had)'.   In general, he did
not think that our parents would respond to traditional psychiatric
treatment in the sense of regular out-patient appointments.   'All
your tender loving care is the real medication together with a continued nursery accommodation for the child and resumption of work
for her as soon as possible.'

Thus, his diagnosis of the parents and advice on their treatment
generally endorsed our handling of the situation.

ii   Treatment of our parents

Generally, it was not envisaged that the psychiatrist would be
involved in treatment;   it was agreed at the outset that his time
was too limited and his place of work geographically too distant.
If psychiatric treatment was considered necessary, a local psychiatrist was sought.   However, with one family which was rehoused after referral to our psychiatrist's area, he and his
psychiatric social worker took on the case for ongoing treatment
and continued to be involved over a period of some years.

iii   Psychiatric consultation for the department

The psychiatrist regularly attended inter-department case conferences.   His diagnostic experience was particularly valuable in
the initial stages of the project.   However, as treatment progressed and we gained confidence, we felt more of a need for a
psychiatrist who could be available for crisis consultations than
for routine case discussions.

iv   Medical and psychiatric support for termination or
sterilisation referrals

As already mentioned, the psychiatrist saw some parents specifically
to consider a request for termination of pregnancy or sterilisation.   This was very valuable, as it is often difficult to obtain
medical and psychiatric support for such requests from young
mothers with few children.   The parents' GP valued advice from a
psychiatrist with experience in the field of child abuse.

v   Support over legal questions

In one case, our psychiatrist agreed to act as an expert witness
for the Social Services Department in recommending a Care Order.
He was able to draw on his experience of child abuse in general
and the likelihood of re-injury, presenting his evidence in a
manner sympathetic to the parents.   Undoubtedly his support of the
case helped the magistrates to decide that a Care Order should be
made.

In another case of a mother seen shortly after referral, he wrote a report for the police who were considering prosecuting her, recommending that no action should be taken on medical grounds.   This advice was followed.

This also provided a most useful back-up service, as Courts and police tended to pay more attention to our views if psychiatrically supported, and our psychiatrist had much experience of court and police work.

vi   Requests for medical information

When writing for medical details about parents for research purposes, for example to obstetric departments, the psychiatrist would sign such requests.   This helped in gathering valuable material as doctors proved more willing to release information to another doctor than to a social worker.

General comments

In general, we found it valuable to have a psychiatrist attached to the Department who could make psychiatric referrals and recommendations, and request confidential medical information.   His experience in the field was helpful, particularly in the early stages, as was his legal support.

However, we would recommend that child protective workers should try to obtain the services of a local psychiatrist with relevant experience who could be readily available for crisis consultations and support for workers and diagnostic assessment and treatment for parents.   Obviously such a psychiatrist would be best fitted to offer support if he had an appreciation of social work practice.

THE USE OF LAY STAFF
Mothering-aides

An important aspect of our treatment programme was the idea of employing untrained local women as mothering-aides.   We hoped to find women, preferably mothers themselves, with natural resources of sympathy, motherliness and good humour, whom we could introduce to our families once the main worker had established a relationship.   The aims were: to extend the mother's range of relationships and provide her with extra 'mothering', to take some of the weight of visiting off the social workers' shoulders, to have another person available to help with practical tasks, taking children to nursery or mothers to hospital appointments, and to experiment with the use of untrained workers with battering families.   When applicants were seen, we were careful to explore their feelings about and attitudes towards parenthood and child abuse, as we needed people who were sympathetic, non-judgmental and relaxed and happy about their own children.

Over a three-and-a-half-year period we used three women as mothering-aides.   They received regular individual supervision from a social worker and were paid by the hour for flexible amounts

of time.   They all had cars available, which they were able to use
in their work with us.   They were involved with eight of our
families, to a greater or lesser extent, depending on the needs of
the individual and the situation.   In three cases, they visited
regularly, forming a good relationship and offering additional
support, friendship and practical help.   They became adept at
sitting and listening with affection and attention, and tolerating
attitudes and sometimes behaviour which could be harsh and unattrac-
tive.   In two cases, they regularly ferried children - one to
weekly child guidance appointments and the other daily to nursery.
In three more families, they were used occasionally as a crisis or
specific need arose.

There were of course problems from time to time: sometimes a
mothering-aide could not tolerate a particular client and such a
relationship could not be forced.   They sometimes suffered from
difficulties in identification: where should their loyalties lie?
This was particularly true in situations where a mothering-aide
was told about an injury or observed very rough handling;   their
brief from us and their inclination had been to befriend the
mothers and they felt they were betraying trust if they 'told on
them'.   Similarly, there were sometimes problems for them in
knowing how much of their own lives and experiences as mothers
they should share with clients.   We felt that these dilemmas
could be resolved if regular supervision was available and the
mothering-aide was able to share and expose her feelings.

In general, they all felt somewhat under-occupied, and probably
we were too wary about using them and need not have been so protective of our clients and our staff.   Good support and supervision from trained staff are essential if understanding and
potential are to be developed and this could be well provided by
a small group setting, if several mothering-aides were working at
the same time.   Ideas on the use of lay staff are fully discussed
by Kempe and Helfer (1972).

Drop-in-foster mother

Another lay worker we used was the drop-in-foster mother, whose
function has already been described (chapter 7).

Denver House staff

Finally, something must be said of the therapeutic contribution
made by our office staff, project co-ordinator, secretaries and
telephonist.   Our aim was to create a warm and friendly office
atmosphere for clients, with the minimum of formality.   The office
staff were encouraged to put clients' needs before typing and
office tasks.   Parents were encouraged to drop in when they felt
like it, or to park their children whilst they shopped or had a
break.   We decided not to have a separate waiting-room, and
clients were received in the project co-ordinator's room, where
they could chat with somebody and have coffee.   Amongst her many
other administrative functions, the project co-ordinator was also,

most importantly, the first person clients met and provided their
first impression of the office.   The five different project co-
ordinators all brought their own style to the job and developed
their own relationships with different parents, as did the secretaries and telephonist.   One co-ordinator excelled in providing
food for clients at the right moment, another secretary formed
excellent rapport with the younger mothers who would come to see
her for a chat, another mother became very friendly with our telephonist and would often come to see her and her dog.   One project
co-ordinator in particular gave much time and attention to clients,
and did individual work with several families, such as visiting
whilst a social worker was on holiday or helping an over-protected
three-year-old to separate from his mother when she brought him to
the office.

    Some clients did not come to the office at all, either because
the journey was too difficult or because they could not venture
far from their homes.   Some had to be wooed cautiously before
they would enter the building.   Some, however, either immediately
or after some persuasion, came to like and trust the people and
the atmosphere and came often for conversation, coffee and comfort.
We see it as important that an informal, comfortable atmosphere
should be created and that everyone in the building should be prepared to give of themselves to clients.

Chapter 10

EVALUATION OF PROGRESS IN FAMILIES

METHOD

There are many difficulties inherent in any attempt to assess
changes in family functioning over a period of time when the
families are being studied in depth.   With very detailed material,
indicators of change can be seen to comapre many complex variables
which do not readily lend themselves to simple quantification.   A
few simple facts could have been chosen for comparison before and
after treatment.   We have included such hard data in our evaluation but felt that on their own, they would not do justice to the
complexity of the material under study.   The reliability of this
method is also dependent on the sample, which in our case is
limited.

   The repeated interaction between social worker and client tends
to blur the worker's ability to assess change over a lengthy
period of time, as well as making the question of validity highly
problematic.   There are several ways of avoiding these problems.
External interviewers could have been used to apply a standardised
questionnaire to each family at several points in time.   It would
in our view have been useful to have such additional information,
but only as a supplement to our more subjective data, because we
feel that problems of internal validity would have been great.
In addition to the problem of taking simple facts as indicators
there would have been difficulty in devising or selecting a suitable questionnaire which captured the causative factors in child
abuse at a time when these factors are still unknown.   Further,
we feel that independent interviewers, given limited contact with
our parents, would have experienced difficulties in gathering
accurate information from them.

   We did consider the use of external judges to assess our case
records.   Even detailed records such as ours suffer from grave
omissions of fact which tend to be retained in the worker's head
rather than placed on paper.   We also felt that external asses-
sors would do little to counter worker bias, as case records
probably reflect changes in the attitudes and development of the
social worker as much as changes in the family.   The schedules
which we decided to use, though biased, did call upon the training

167

which all social workers receive in objective assessment whilst at
the same time drawing on their intimate knowledge of the family.
We felt that these were the best tools at our disposal for evaluating our treatment service.

We were aware that Hunt and Kogan (1952) have discussed the use
of a 'movement scale' in casework evaluation.   This entails the
social worker responsible for the case making quantified judgments
about changes in client functioning.   Usually two points in time
are selected similar to those chosen in our study, one in the early
stages of treatment and the other after considerable treatment has
been given, in order to provide a before/after comparison.   We
felt, however, that with such a case by case method, where workers
rate the second point with reference to the first, there would be
strong tendencies to record some degree of change whether it had
occurred or not.   As we had already devised instruments for classifying diagnostic information, this provided us with a basis for
a second assessment of the families at a later stage in treatment.
It had the advantage of application without reference to the
earlier ratings for the families thus reducing the possibility of
bias.   Quantifiable items were selected from the diagnostic
schedules applied to the families at referral, for repetition at
a later stage in treatment.   The period of eighteen to twenty-one
months after referral was chosen in order to yield, over the maximum period of time, the maximum number of cases still in regular
contact with the project.   Twenty-one families were available for
re-assessment in this way.   Two of the other families had not been
in treatment for long enough to be included.   In another case, the
worker had insufficient contact at this time to make an evaluation,
and the remaining family had not been engaged in active treatment
at all, having moved from the area without trace.

Use was made of the detailed system of recording which had been
in operation since the inception of the project.   Each social
worker re-read his own reports for the 18-21 month period and used
this information to complete the schedules on the state of the
families at that point in time.   Problems of bias did not arise
from this retrospective approach as we were unaware when recording
interviews during this period that they were to be chosen for
evaluation.

The selection of items from the original schedules for repetition was governed by two factors.   The first was the relevance
of the topic for child abuse according to our own impressions and
those of other researchers in the field.   Thus ratings of parent-
child interaction were particularly important and as many items
as possible were included on this topic.   The other selection
criterion was the original diagnostic validity of the item.
Without this, there seemed little point in repeating the item some
eighteen months after referral.   For example, because of the
small numbers of families with siblings, little quantitative information could be gathered on differences between the quality of
their care and the care of the battered children.   Thus, no
attempt was made to re-evaluate this area at a later stage.
Similarly, variables with a low response rate or a wide spread of
answers at the diagnostic stage were excluded.

The variables fell into three main categories: social circumstances, marital interaction and parent-child interaction, and the findings are accordingly grouped under these headings.   Where it was shown on inspection that statistical tests were worth doing, they have been carried out.   In each of the three areas of family functioning specified above, variables were assessed in terms of the degree of change shown.

CHANGES AT 18-21 MONTHS
Social circumstances

No changes after treatment were apparent in respect of the number of fathers with drinking problems, rate of unemployment amongst fathers, or the long hours worked by many fathers.   The parents remained isolated from the extended family and still received very little support from their siblings.   Financial disorganisation remained a marked feature in the lives of nearly half of the families.
   There were slight changes in the mothers' working patterns. Fewer mothers were working after eighteen months of treatment and fewer had ambitions to work.   Fathers were somewhat less isolated at work and also in the local community.   More substantial changes occurred in other areas of social functioning.

TABLE 10.1 Fathers' satisfaction at work

	0-3 months (N = 25)	18-21 months (N = 21)
Strong dissatisfaction	15	5
No marked dissatisfaction	7	12
No information or not applicable	3	4

$x^2 = 4.5$ $p < 0.05$

   A significant difference was shown in the level of satisfaction which fathers gained from their work.   Thus there was less dissatisfaction amongst the fathers at the later point in time.

TABLE 10.2 Mothers' relationships in the local community

	0-3 months (N = 25)	18-21 months (N = 21)
Contact and support	4	7
Contact, but little support	9	10
Virtually no contact, no support	11	1
No information or not applicable	1	3

$X = 9.3$ $p < 0.01$

   The mothers were significantly less isolated from their local communities after treatment.

TABLE 10.3   Standard of housing

	0-3 months (N = 25)	18-21 months (N = 21)
Family inadequately housed	18	3
Family adequately housed	7	18

x^2 = 13.08   p < 0.001

Most families were adequately housed at the later point in time, and as the table shows there was a significant improvement in the standard of housing after treatment.   In addition, we noted general improvement in the atmosphere of the home and more personal possessions in evidence.

Marital interaction

Most indications of change occurred in respect of the marital relationship, but they took the form of trends rather than statistically significant results.   Four couples had separated by the twenty-one month point in treatment.   We continued to work primarily with the mothers, some of whom found new partners.   Our impression was that for three families the dissolution of these relationships had been a positive event, at least for the mothers, and indirectly, the children.

In the relationships which survived, fathers spent more time in the home and the mothers' resentment which formerly arose over the amount of time they spent drinking with friends naturally decreased.   Mothers also seemed less frustrated in respect of their own interests.

TABLE 10.4   Amount of contact between parents

	0-3 months (N = 25)	18-21 months (N = 17) *
Oarents rarely together	16	6
Having average amount of contact	4	10
Having excessive contact	5	1

x^2 = 8.6   p < 0.02
* Four cases were single parent families in this period.

The parents were spending significantly more time together after treatment than they were at referral.

TABLE 10.5 Extent of mutual support between parents

	0-3 months (N = 25)	18-21 months (N = 16)*†
Mutually supportive	3	9
Not supportive	22	7

x^2 = 11.5 p < 0.001
* Four cases were single parent families in this period.
† For this variable one case could not be rated.

   Significantly more parents were providing mutual support in the
18-21 month period.   In addition to the increase in mutual support, there were some indications that fathers were less undermining in their attitudes towards mothers.   There was also a non-
significant trend towards improved communication on everyday
matters between parents but little improvement in their ability to
communicate their feelings to one another.
   Fewer fathers were physically violent to their wives during the
latter period.   There were fewer parents who did not sleep
together and more parents had their own bedroom.   This variable
is of course related to improvements in accommodation.   There
were slight indications of more parents gaining sexual satisfaction from the marital relationships but this information was very
limited.

Parent-child interaction

The results from these items relating primarily to the interaction
between the mothers and the battered children were disappointing.
Only slight positive changes were noted in most aspects of these
relationships, leaving many doubts about the effectiveness of our
treatment service in improving the quality of mothering.   As a
point of interest five mothers gave birth to additional children
during the twenty-one-month period after referral.
   A few more fathers showed greater acceptance of the battered
child and there were slight changes in the rejecting attitudes of
mothers.   However, the majority of mothers could not be termed
even fairly accepting of the battered children after twenty-one
months of treatment.   Similarly, mothers were only slightly
warmer in their physical handling of the battered child.   They
were a little more encouraging, empathetic, less critical and
their expectations of physical and emotional performance were
somewhat reduced.   However, five mothers were still seen as predominantly insensitive and another twelve only displayed empathy
sporadically, depending on their mood.   The mothers' attitude to
discipline remained fairly harsh or inconsistent, but fewer children appeared over-controlled or confused about maternal discipline.
There was slightly less conflict between parents over discipline.
There was no change in the use of physical punishment as a form of
discipline.   Only three mothers never used physical coercion in

this way. Mothers were taking a little more care in monitoring the child's environment but a third were still rated as fairly neglect-ful and there was no noticeable improvement in their standard of mothercraft. The feelings of jealousy between parents over the battered child remained a feature in over half of the intact families. None of these items showed statistically significant results.

It is our impression that some positive changes did occur in the quality of the relationships between mothers and the battered children. The degree of change however was generally minimal, and diffused over several items. Our instruments were not sensi-tive to such slight changes on a broad front, as they were designed with the aim of capturing significant changes or trends. These did not occur and the following comments from workers give some idea of the shifts we observed.

'The parents still have high expectations on all fronts but they appear less extreme now that the child is no longer a baby.'

'A bit of improvement on all sides. The child is less provoca-tive, more independent and contained. Mother is somewhat more relaxed and finds him less of a strain.'

'Both parents had shifted a bit from sheer ambivalence to being fairly accepting towards the child. They were also beginning to show signs of gaining pleasure from their relationship with her.'

'Both parents still relate to the child in an odd kind of way - giving all kinds of confusing clues. They also try quite un-realistically to get her to make decisions, offering multiple choices which she is incapable of understanding.'

Our assessment of positive movement is disappointing at this stage of treatment. In only a few items could the changes be termed 'marked movement': in fathers' job satisfaction, mothers' relationship with people in the local community, adequacy of accommodation and several variables associated with a somewhat closer and more harmonious marital relationship. The major cause for concern was the minimal improvement in the quality of inter-action between mother and children in the majority of cases.

Further progress

In addition to the structured evaluation at 18-21 months, team discussion of cases at the end of the project provided a useful overall assessment of movement. Although unquantified, we felt that team evaluation of cases by workers would reduce the bias that might arise from automatically recorded changes. We wanted a flexible evaluation of movement in the sample as a whole, as well as case by case, and used a simple means of enquiring into which families had or had not changed in specific areas of functioning. At the same time it was also possible to speculate about why move-ment had occurred in certain cases or in certain areas and not others. The task of attempting this on a more rigorous, quanti-fied scale was felt to be beyond the scope of the project, except in the area of subsequent injury to the battered child and siblings.

THE CHILDREN
Subsequent injury to the battered child

In recording subsequent injuries, we included all those for which
there was no definite proof of accidental cause.   On reflection,
this criterion may have been too rigorous in that any external
marks, be they scratches, bumps or bruises, were listed if no
adequate explanation was given.   Many children in the age range
of the study group frequently and unknowingly incur this type of
injury during the rough and tumble of their lives.   It is under-
standable that with our high index of suspicion, we did not give
our parents the benefit of the doubt, but this being the case, the
estimated rate of subsequent injury may be misleading.   Full
details regarding the nature and degree of subsequent injuries and
the age of the children at the time will be found in Appendix A.
   During the three-year period after referral, twenty-two children were available for possible injury in the home.   Of these,
twelve received injuries for which there was no adequate explanation.   Comparison of our figures with those reported in other
studies would be misleading because of differences in time periods
and criteria used for recording and defining injuries.   Although
our figures appear to be high, in fact only two children suffered
a serious injury and three moderate injuries during this period.
Most of the children suffered minor injuries which did not warrant
medical treatment, and none sustained permanent physical or mental
disability as a result of post-referral injuries.   The highest
rate of injury occurred during the first year of treatment.

Subsequent injuries to siblings of the battered child

Out of a possible total of thirty-two, seven siblings were thought
to have been injured by their parents during the three year period
following referral.   One child received moderate injuries and the
remainder minor injuries, with two children suffering recurrent
minor injuries.   The fact that siblings were also injured lends
support to the view that there is little difference in parental
treatment of the siblings and the battered child.

Rehabilitation of the battered child

At the time of writing, twenty battered children were living at
home with their parents.   Some of these children had been separated from their parents during the course of treatment.   Full
details regarding periods in care and the process of rehabilitation will be found in chapter 6.

Physical and emotional development of the battered child

This section is based on our impressions of the children at the
time of last contact with the family or information available to
us at the time of writing.

Four children were described as 'pale and deprived looking',
generally underweight, undernourished and somewhat lethargic.
They displayed varying degrees of withdrawal and anxiety in their
behaviour, especially when with their parents.   Most of the remaining children seemed to fall into two groups, the introverts
and the extroverts.

The Introverts: These were children who at the time of referral had seemed withdrawn, controlled, wary and generally lacking
in energy and interest.   Now they appeared healthy, but delicate,
fairly spritely and spontaneous, aware of themselves and sensitive
to their surroundings and other people.   A few of these children
showed traits of obsessive neatness in their behaviour, wariness
of their parents and perhaps an over-eager compliance and willingness to please others.   They seemed to be 'holding in' their
feelings, but the appearance of recurrent problems such as enure-
sis, food refusal and sleeplessness, suggested that these were
highly sensitive and anxious children.

The Extroverts: This group consisted of robust, hyperactive
and clumsy children, careless of personal danger in the environment and often prone to accidents.   Some were aggressive or destructive, uncontrollable and prone to temper tantrums.   They were
easily frustrated and distractable and unable to involve themselves with others.   Interaction with groups of children or their
parents tended to trigger this reckless, violent behaviour which
seemed imitative of their parents or siblings.   Though many of
these children had shown similar characteristics at the time of
referral a few developed them at a later stage.

In our estimation only eight out of a possible twenty-three
children seemed to be making reasonably satisfactory and sustained
developmental progress.   Of the remainder, a few had serious
emotional problems which caused grave anxiety about their future
development.   A few were like weather vanes who reflected the
moods of their parents by regressing or displaying disturbances
when the home situation was particularly stressful.   Morse et al.
(1970), in a three-year follow-up study of children hospitalised
for abuse or gross neglect, reported that 6 out of 21 were ad-
judged to be 'normal'.   Of the remainder, nine were mentally
retarded and six emotionally disturbed.   They comment that a
common characteristic among those children who appeared to be
developing normally was a good mother/child relationship as perceived and reported by the mothers.

THE PARENTS
The marital relationship

At the time of writing, ten of the original twenty-five couples
had separated.   Seven of these were married, most of whom are
now legally separated or divorced.   Similarly, Johnson and Morse
(1968b) in their study have reported that 30 per cent of
marriages ended in separation or divorce.   The separations in
our sample occurred at varying times during treatment, four within
the first year and the remainder during the second or third year
after referral.   Typically, the woman left the man or forced him

out of the home.   In some cases this action seemed indicative of
personal growth, as evidenced by an improvement in self-image and
self-confidence, the ability to cope with serious relationship
problems and to envisage living independently.   This improvement
in functioning was sustained after the break-up of the relationship.   However, in a few cases it would seem that stress in the
relationship had become so unbearable that it resulted in serious
dysfunctioning and the ultimate collapse of the partnership.   It
is of interest that in three cases a situation of acute crisis and
eventual breakdown of the relationship seemed to coincide with re-
injury to the battered child.   A few of the separated mothers
have established long-term relationships with another man;   one
married her new boy friend and others have had relationships with
a number of men.   A few mothers have remained on their own.
    Amongst most of the fifteen couples who remained together and
those who formed new liaisons, the improvements described at the
18-21 month period were sustained and there were a few couples who
showed considerable improvement in their relationships.   However,
with some couples the situation remained highly stressful and unsatisfactory, often reaching breaking point.   Although a few of
the mothers and fathers in these latter cases seemed better able
to cope with the stresses and were not overwhelmed by them, they
did not have sufficient resources to make the ultimate break.

Parental roles

There was one area in which the parents did appear to have made
considerable progress and this was in the area of family planning.
Most of the mothers had started using regular methods of birth
control, mainly the pill, by the end of the first year of treatment.   In addition, five mothers were sterilised at some point
during treatment.   Only eleven mothers had another child or
children during the whole period of treatment.   Six families increased in size after the initial 21-month period following
referral.
    As to the ability to assume or accept parental roles, in a few
cases this seemed to be related to the state of the marital relationship.   Greater support and understanding between partners or
a positive ending of the relationship seemed to lead to greater
complementarity in parental roles, improved interaction with the
children and greater enjoyment of them.   However, it seems fair
to say that many continued to be reluctant parents and to show
considerable ambivalence towards children whom they felt duty-
bound to accept.   Only one mother was finally more able to
acknowledge that she did not want her children and was able to
separate from them.   Others continued to have unrealistically
high standards for themselves as parents and were naturally unable
to meet these standards.   In most cases, practical care of the
children remained good or adequate, but most of our parents
demonstrated a low level of adequacy in providing for the emotional needs of their children.

Interaction between the parents and the battered child

As previously indicated, at the time of writing twenty battered
children were living at home with their parents. It is not
possible to add a great deal to the conclusions reached at the
18-21 month period regarding the nature of parent/child interaction, when slight positive changes in some areas of the interaction were noted. A few parents seemed to be genuinely more
understanding, attentive and responsive to the child's needs.
Some parents were more able to admit that they had problems with
their children and showed a growing awareness of their own contribution to these problems. However, most of the parents were
still ambivalent towards the child and inconsistent in their
handling especially in the area of discipline.
    Finally, workers remarked that in many cases where expectations
of the child's physical and emotional development seemed less
exaggerated, this often reflected an increase in the child's age
rather than a basic change in attitude and action towards the
child.   Pollock and Steele (1972) suggest that rapid improvement
in the attitude and behaviour of parents towards the battered
child must be regarded with caution. It may reflect the parents'
desire to please rather than a basic change. It is our impression that only a few families showed a genuine and sustained
improvement in this area.

Social situation

There was less financial disorganisation and an improvement in
general household management after the 18-21 month period. Also,
a few more mothers had started working and were gaining considerable satisfaction and confidence from this. For many couples a
more settled home environment encouraged the development of
interests and the creation of a more supportive social network.
A few parents became integrated in the community to the point of
joining local action groups or becoming actively involved with
their unions at work.   The formation of a supportive network was
also facilitated by the mothers' group meetings at the nursery.
These mothers began to make social contacts outside the nursery
and to call upon one another at times of crisis.
    In some cases there was a definite improvement in the relation-
ship with grandparents. A few mothers in particular felt less
oppressed and overwhelmed by their parents and were able to act
independently of them.

Psycho/physical functioning

The mothers: Many mothers became more consistent in their appearance as they developed a greater sense of identity. They also
seemed more aware of their sexual identity and their attractive-
ness to men, and were better at acknowledging their own sexual
desires. As their self-image and sense of value improved, many
mothers' level of energy and motivation increased and they were

better able to assert themselves, to set and achieve their own
goals and to deal with crises and stress.   This did not necessarily involve a disappearance of self-defeatism or denial, but a
relaxation and opening up to the possibility of change.   These
improvements seemed to us to reflect a higher level of emotional
maturity in many cases.   These mothers were also gradually able
to wean themselves away from us.   In a few other cases, we feel
that the mothers had been so seriously emotionally damaged in the
past that they would never be able to sustain significant personality growth.

Most of the mothers were physically healthy although a few who
had initially been hypochrondriacal still complained at times of
stress of recurrent ailments, particularly migraines.   Although
anxiety and depression were still experienced by a few mothers,
the majority were less prone to mood swings and were more emotionally stable.   Generally, the mothers were more able to discuss
their feelings and emotional problems on a deeper level.   Interestingly, though able to discuss abuse more openly as the climate
of opinion became more favourable, the number of mothers able to
acknowledge their involvement in abuse remained unchanged.   Most
were obviously still highly sensitive to the stigma attached to
them as battering parents.

The fathers: Of the fathers who had initially seemed highly
defended, a few remained rigid, denying and unreachable.   Others
began to crumble emotionally when confronted with crises, especially in their marital relationships.   Among those who had
appeared highly immature, ineffectual and lacking in resources,
there had been little change by the end of treatment.   In the
remaining cases there seemed to have been a gradual improvement in
psycho/physical functioning in the areas already discussed when
describing the mothers.   In summary, they seemed more emotionally
mature, able to open up more about problems and feelings, and
better able to cope with crises on their own.

None of the fathers suffered serious physical ill-health, but
in a couple of cases there was an emergence of serious psychological disturbance during treatment.   However, at the time of
writing, these fathers seemed to have accepted that they were vulnerable and were better able to avoid stressful situations.

DISCUSSION AND CONCLUSIONS

The main areas of functioning in which we expected change have
already been outlined in this chapter and include parent-child
interaction, family functioning, social, emotional and physical
functioning of the parents and development of the battered child.

With regard to parent-child interaction, we agreed basically
with Steele and Pollock (1968) that there should be a 'change in
the style of parent/child interaction to a degree which eliminated
the danger of physical harm to the child and lessened the chances
of serious emotional damage.'   As we have seen these expectations
did not materialise to any great extent.   Although there was a
diminished possibility of serious injury to most of the children,
and milder forms of physical punishment were used as a means of

discipline, in only a few cases did we feel sufficiently confident to state that the risk of injury to the battered child or siblings was eliminated.   Also, improvements in emotional interaction were only slight and it would seem that our parents continued to experience difficulty in acknowledging their parenthood, and accepting and enjoying children as individuals 'with age appropriate needs and behaviour' (Galdston, 1973, Steele and Pollock, 1968). In terms of the treatment service we offered to our families (see chapters 6 and 7) our expectations for improvement in this area might have been unrealistic.   Other workers have attempted to focus more directly on problems in parent/child relationships (Galdston (1973), Paulson and Chaleff (1973), Savino and Saunders (1973), Ounsted et al. (1974)) using methods of group therapy and providing education in child care.   They have claimed some success with these methods but evaluation over the long term is still in progress.

With regard to family functioning, we expected 'an improvement in the marital relationship, in other interpersonal relationships and in dealing with problems of everyday living' (Steele and Pollock (1968)).   We were somewhat surprised by the extent of change or improvement in the marital situation, as we rarely attempted direct marital therapy.   Similarly, positive changes were noted in some cases in relationships with the extended family, although unlike other researchers (Davoren, 1968) we did not expect a great deal of change to be reflected in this area because in many cases, grandparents were abroad.   An improvement in economic stability with increased job satisfaction and general improvement in home management and living conditions certainly suggested an ability to deal with everyday problems more effectively.

It would seem that these improvements in family functioning were related to change in the social situation and emotional growth.   'The parents should show an increased ability to make social contacts outside the home and relate to wider social milieu for pleasurable satisfaction and a source of help in times of need' (Steele and Pollock, 1968).   The gradual progress in this area with the establishment of a more meaningful and supportive social network was certainly evident in our families.   Davoren (1968) speculated that the development of a relationship of trust and friendship with the social worker might facilitate the development of outside interests and other social contacts.   This occurred in many of our cases, and the therapeutic relationship also helped parents to approach others in authority more readily in times of need.

As regards the parents' emotional and physical functioning, we anticipated that there would be improvements in emotional growth and stability;   improvement in the self-image and 'an ability to deal fairly adequately with crisis on their own' (Steele and Pollock, 1968, 1972).   Changes in this area were already taking place at the 18-21 month period, and in most cases, there was a sustained improvement in emotional and physical functioning.

We hoped that the battered children would be generally less controlled by their parents and interact less warily and more warmly with them and others;   also that emotional and physical

development would be age appropriate, and that there would be a
lessening of marked psychological disturbances such as depression,
acute anxiety symptoms and acting-out behaviour.   It seems
apparent that in many cases improved environmental stimulation
outside the home facilitated both physical and emotional development in certain areas.   However, this was not sufficient to
counteract the effects of an unfavourable home environment and we
felt that in many cases there was a serious risk of permanent
emotional damage.   It is necessary to reiterate that the majority
of the children did not receive individual therapy, and we are
aware that insufficient provision was made for their needs (see
chapter 6).

There has been little attempt to assess the effectiveness of
treatment services for abusive families.   Pollock and Steele
(1972), expect reasonably satisfactory results in 80 per cent of
families using their techniques of supportive psychiatric and
social work help, but have not clarified what is meant by satisfactory results.   Johnson and Morse (1968b) in their study of
eighty-five abusive families treated by the Child Welfare Service
reported that with supportive social work help akin to our treatment service 'though significant improvement in ability to function
and in ability to care for children occurred in many families, most
were still at a low level of adequacy, at the time the service was
discontinued or at the end of the study.'   Other studies have
dealt with the whole spectrum of neglect which may have included
abuse.   For example, Young (1966) reports on protective services
offered to 125 families in which there was neglect of the children,
combining casework with group work, group education and 'services
adapted to the changing needs of the individual and the family
unit'.   In 90 per cent of the cases, deterioration stopped by the
end of the first year.   During the second year, 60 per cent of
the families showed progress in at least one area of family functioning, usually income management and household practices.
During the third year there was more family cohesion, increase in
own achievements and more interest in community activities.

One problem which remains is the extent to which changes in
family functioning were directly connected with the service which
we provided.   This we cannot know.   As Hunt and Kogan (1952)
state:

It can probably be justifiably assumed in many cases that
marked improvement would not occur except through the intervention of casework, especially when other therapeutic influences
are not present.   However, for the lesser degree of movement
in both a positive and a negative direction it is entirely
possible for non-casework factors to have been the primary
forces responsible for the changes that occur.

In considering our service as a whole and not simply the casework process in the narrower sense, there were few other therapeutic agents in contact with the family.   Psychiatric treatment
was provided for brief periods for several of our parents but in
only two cases can the provision be viewed as anything more than
symptomatic relief.   Regular day care or periods of residential
care were provided for children in most of our families.   This
can be viewed as part of our recommended service whether provided

directly by the project or obtained from another agency.   Help
with rehousing and other forms of practical assistance were certainly viewed by us as an integral part of the casework process
although they do not constitute in themselves the 'relationship
therapy' which we endeavoured to provide.   Whether improvements
in individual and family functioning were effected more by
concrete provisions than by the emotional support and nurturing
which we gave is open to debate.   Certainly, rehousing had many
repercussions;   in relieving frustration between parents and child
and marital tension by providing more space, and in conferring on
the family an enhanced sense of achievement and self-image.

   It could be suggested that with abusive families, treatment
goals are inevitably conservative and achievement should be seen
in terms of prevention of further deterioration rather than marked
improvement in family functioning.   This is a view which should
be given more weight in the light of our findings.

Part three

Chapter 11

PSYCHOLOGICAL ASPECTS OF BATTERING PARENTS

The purpose of the project reported in this chapter was to provide some objective quantifiable indices of psychological and social factors associated with battering derived from a controlled comparison with non-battering parents.

The numbers involved have been necessarily small as patients of long standing could not be included and the author was not appointed until half-way through the main investigation.

Up to that time little quantitative work of a psychological kind had been undertaken.   Those studies using intelligence tests by Cameron et al. (1966), Bennie and Sclare (1969) and Gibbens and Walker (1956) suggested that a more detailed measurement using an individual intelligence test would be valuable.   Work by Elmer (1967a), Melnick and Hurley (1969) and Schneider in Kempe and Helfer (1972) suggested that objective personality tests on a British population would fill an as yet unfilled gap.

The project fell into two distinct parts.

METHOD

In the first part of this investigation three psychological tests were given to twenty battering parents and twenty matched control adults to be described in the following section.

The tests used were a short form of the Wechsler Adult Intelligence Scale (Wechsler 1958), Cattell's Sixteen Personality Factor Questionnaire (Cattell et al. 1970) and Schaefer and Bell's Parent Attitude Research Instrument (Schaefer and Bell, 1958).

The choice of these tests was dictated in part by time factors, hence the selection of a short form of the WAIS, which included five only of the ten available sub-tests.   These were Comprehension, Similarities and Vocabulary sub-tests, from the Verbal Scale, and Block Design, and Object Assembly sub-tests from the Performance Scale.   Reliability and validity of this short form of the full test are reportedly acceptable (Wechsler, 1958; Doppelt, 1956;   Maxwell, 1957).

A further consideration was that techniques should be both objective in their administration and evaluation, and quantifiable.

Accordingly Cattell's Sixteen Personality Factor Test (1970) was
chosen to provide a basic set of personality trait measures
together with second-order scores.   By comparing the profile of
scores obtained by battering parents and non-abusive parents it
was hoped to highlight both their similarities and differences.
Form C, for average adults, was thought to be the most appropriate.
     The Parent Attitude Research Instrument (Schaefer and Bell,
1958) was the final choice.   It was hoped this test would tap
another level of personality functioning, namely surface attitudes
toward child rearing in particular, and family life in general.
Originally devised to assess normal maternal attitudes it has been
used in a number of other settings, notably by Elmer, in a study
of abusive and neglectful parents in the USA (Elmer, 1967a).
     These three tests were administered in the order in which they
have been described but not always in one sitting.   This depended
very much upon the co-operation of the subjects and especially
with the experimental group, several visits were sometimes required to avoid fatigue and discouragement.   Such clients were
often anxious to discuss the events which led to their referral to
the unit, and whatever the dictates of method, it would have been
impossible as well as counter-productive to discourage such discussion.   In the second part of this investigation a specially
devised questionnaire was used by Health Visitors as the basis for
an interview in the client's home.   It was hoped to provide information to aid differential diagnosis of battering from accidental
injury by means of this questionnaire.
     The choice of questions was dictated by a number of likely leads
derived both from the literature on the battering parent and also
by a close reading of case studies.   Although several of the
questions were not easy for health visitors to introduce, in fact
their inclusion appears to have been justified by the results.
Elaborate coding had to be avoided in this part of the study since
it was essential for questions to be easily introduced into a
normal interview, and their replies remembered until they could
be noted down after the interview.   While methodologically such
an approach has many pitfalls, it has the great merit of using
interviewers who are acceptable to their respondents and therefore
likely to get truthful and co-operative results.   Examples of
questions included in the questionnaire are given in Table 9.

THE SAMPLES

Two separate samples make up the subjects of this report.   The
first sample of tested subjects was drawn for the most part from
a London population.   The experimental subjects consisted of
twenty clients referred during 1971 and 1972 to the NSPCC's
Battered Child Research Department.   At the time of the study
this department drew its referrals from the three London boroughs
of Camden, Kensington and Chelsea, and Westminster.   Most referrals were from hospitals in the area; some were through local
Health Visitors or Social Service departments.
     It was ascertained before testing began, that in ten out of the
twelve children whose parents formed the basis of this part of the

study, severe injuries had preceded their referral.   In the other
two cases one child had been the recipient of repeated minor burns
and other deliberate hurts, while the other child's parent had
sought help out of her own fear of doing her child serious injury.
The degree of confidence with which the diagnosis of batterings
was made was also ascertained and was in every case high in the
ten battered cases.   The control subjects with whom the battering
parents were compared, were adults living in the same areas, pair
matched on the following criteria:
1   Age of child.
2   Age of each parent.
3   Ordinal position of the battered child.
4   Nationality.
5   Type of living accommodation.
Details of age matching are shown in Table 11.1, from which it may
be seen that no significant age differences occurred.

Ordinal position of child

Most of the children in both groups were only children and only
two mismatches occurred overall;   a second out of three battered
children matched with a singleton control, and a fifth control
matched with a second of two battered children.

Nationality

Nationality was overwhelmingly British in both groups.   One
Hungarian family in the battering group was balanced by a Yugoslav
control.

Accommodation

The final criterion was chosen to provide some control over social
class in addition to equalising the effects of housing conditions.
Later, inquiry at time of testing revealed no significant difference in occupational social class.
    The numbers of mothers and fathers in the tested sample are
unequal owing to the fact that two of the mothers were without
partners (and were accordingly matched) and two fathers refused
to be co-operative.   These two were matched with two control
families in which the husband refused to take the tests.
    The testing of these subjects was not as standardised as might
have been preferred, as more of the control subjects were seen at
the department than was true of the battering parents.   In order
to obtain their co-operation it was usually necessary to visit
their homes, a fact that had not been appreciated at the outset,
and which led to many of the control parents having already been
seen at the department.

TABLE 11.1 Ages of subjects receiving psychological tests

	Mothers		Fathers	
	Battering (N = 12)	Control (N = 12)	Battering (N = 8)	Control (N = 8)
Mean age	22.3 yrs	24.8 yrs	23.7 yrs	25 yrs
SD	3.72	4.02	3.15	2.66
t	-2.0757		-0.786	
P	0.1 > P > 0.05		0.5 > P > 0.1	

	Children	
	Battered (N = 12)	Control (N = 12)
Mean age	15.3 mths	15.3 mths
SD	12.7	11.4
t	-0.042	
P	P > 0.5	

   The second sample, subjects of the Health Visitor Questionnaire, formed an independent sample and were drawn from the County of Surrey's Register of Accidents in the home to Children under the age of two years.   Of some 500 reported during 1972, fifteen were thought by a medical officer, to whom the child was referred, and a subsequent case conference of concerned professionals, to have been non-accidentally injured.   These cases were compared with an equal number, drawn at random from this register, and were parents whose child was confidently supposed to have been accidentally injured.   No attempt was made to match these cases for age as one of the intentions of this part of the inquiry was to discover whether accidentally injured children differed in age from battered children, and whether their parents differed on this same variable.   The range of ages in both cases was likely to be fairly limited, given the fact that, by definition, all the children were under two years of age.   Details of ages may be seen in Tables 11.10 and 11.11.

   All the subjects were visited in their home by their usual Health Visitor who carried out an interview in the course of which the questions already described in the previous section were put. The Health Visitors involved in this study had themselves had the opportunity to criticise the suggested questionnaire, and were indeed a fruitful source of suggestion for ways of improving the technique finally employed.   Unfortunately, it was not possible to have the interviews conducted 'blindly' and Health Visitors usually knew whether the parent was suspected of child battering.

THE RESULTS

The results of this project will be discussed for each of the techniques used and their inter-relationships reviewed in the section which follows this one.   Results reaching a significance level at or beyond the 0.05 level are marked thus *.   Fuller details may be found in Hyman (1973b).

THE WECHSLER ADULT INTELLIGENCE SCALE

The results of the short form of the WAIS are shown in Tables 11.2 and 11.3   They show few major differences in intellectual ability between battering and non-battering parents.   All the parents scored within the normal range although battering parents were relatively less able in their command of verbal concepts than in their practical abilities, whereas the reverse was true of the control parents.   This suggests a rather 'concrete' style of thinking in the battering parents consistent with relative diffi-culty in seeing the consequences of actions and in controlling impulses to act.

TABLE 11.2

	Battering mothers	Control mothers	Battering fathers	Control fathers
Mean verbal IQ	97	108	93	111
SD	18.4	26.6	13.0	17.3
T	1.5126		2.4707	
P	0.5 > P > 0.1		< 0.05 *	
Mean performance IQ	100	96	101	108
SD	10.5	18.6	15.7	12.7
T	-0.8915		0.8074	
P	0.5 > P > 0.1		0.5 > P > 0.1	

TABLE 11.3

Verbal/ Performance	IQ Differences for battering and control parents			
	Battering mothers	Control mothers	Battering fathers	Control fathers
Difference	-3	+12	-8	+3
P	0.5>P>0.1	< 0.05 *	< 0.01 *	0.5>P>0.1

THE SIXTEEN PERSONALITY FACTOR TEST

Fifteen factors only were scored for this test, factor B, general
intelligence, having been omitted as offering a less valid measure
than the WAIS already described.

Of the fifteen factors covered by the test only five showed
reliable differences between battering and non-battering parents.
These were factors A, C, E and M, and F for the fathers only.

The raw score results are tabulated in Tables 11.4 and 11.5 and
STEN values are shown graphically in Tables 11.6 and 11.7   These
STEN or standard scores are based on tentative American norms, no
British norms having been available on this form of the test.

TABLE 11.4 Matched fathers' mean raw scores on 16 PF test

Factor	Battering Mean	SD	Control Mean	SD	t	P
A	7.1	1.6	9.7	1.8	5.62	0.001 *
C	7.1	1.9	8.0	1.1	2.16	0.05 *
E	6.4	1.8	5.5	2.0	2.15	0.05 *
F	5.4	1.9	8.1	2.7	4.28	0.001 *
M	5.6	1.9	4.0	2.0	3.03	0.01 *

TABLE 11.5 Matched mothers' mean raw scores on 16 PF test

Factor	Battering Mean	SD	Control Mean	SD	t	P
A	7.1	2.3	8.5	2.1	3.82	0.001 *
C	4.8	3.4	8.0	2.7	6.25	0.001 *
E	5.8	2.4	4.5	1.8	2.81	0.02 *
F	6.3	1.6	6.5	2.2	0.22	> 0.5
M	5.4	2.3	4.3	3.3	2.29	0.05

As may be seen from Tables 11.4 and 11.5, the battering parents
were consistently more reserved and detached (Factor A), showed
poorer emotional control and integration (Factor C), were somewhat
more aggressive (Factor E), and were less realistic and practical
(Factor M).   Additionally, the fathers showed a marked decrease
in what Cattell calls 'Surgency' (Factor F).   This means according to this test factor, that battering fathers are less enthusiastic and spontaneous than non-battering fathers of similar age,
status and circumstances.

Table 11.6   16 PF Test profile, mothers

Legend	
Batterers	——— (dashed)
Controls	——— (solid)

STANDARD TEN SCORE (STEN)

Average

LOW SCORE DESCRIPTION		HIGH SCORE DESCRIPTION
RESERVED, DETACHED, CRITICAL, ALOOF (Sizothymia)	A	OUTGOING, WARMHEARTED, EASY-GOING, PARTICIPATING (Affectothymia, formerly cyclothymia)
LESS INTELLIGENT, CONCRETE-THINKING (Lower scholastic mental capacity)	B	MORE INTELLIGENT, ABSTRACT-THINKING, BRIGHT (Higher scholastic mental capacity)
AFFECTED BY FEELINGS, EMOTIONALLY LESS STABLE, EASILY UPSET (Lower ego strength)	C	EMOTIONALLY STABLE, FACES REALITY, CALM, MATURE (Higher ego strength)
HUMBLE, MILD, ACCOMMODATING, CONFORMING, (Submissiveness)	E	ASSERTIVE, AGGRESSIVE, STUBBORN, COMPETITIVE (Dominance)
SOBER, PRUDENT, SERIOUS, TACITURN (Desurgency)	F	HAPPY-GO-LUCKY, IMPULSIVELY LIVELY, GAY, ENTHUSIASTIC (Surgency)
EXPEDIENT, DISREGARDS RULES, FEELS FEW OBLIGATIONS (Weaker superego strength)	G	CONSCIENTIOUS, PERSEVERING, STAID, MORALISTIC (Stronger superego strength)
SHY, RESTRAINED, TIMID, THREAT-SENSITIVE (Threctia)	H	VENTURESOME, SOCIALLY BOLD, UNINHIBITED, SPONTANEOUS (Parmia)
TOUGH-MINDED, SELF-RELIANT, REALISTIC, NO-NONSENSE (Harria)	I	TENDER-MINDED, CLINGING, OVER-PROTECTED, SENSITIVE (Premsia)
TRUSTING, ADAPTABLE, FREE OF JEALOUSY, EASY TO GET ALONG WITH (Alaxia)	L	SUSPICIOUS, SELF-OPINIONATED, HARD TO FOOL (Protension)
PRACTICAL, CAREFUL, CONVENTIONAL, REGULATED BY EXTERNAL REALITIES, PROPER (Praxernia)	M	IMAGINATIVE, WRAPPED UP IN INNER URGENCIES, CARELESS OF PRACTICAL MATTERS, BOHEMIAN (Autia)
FORTHRIGHT, NATURAL, ARTLESS, UNPRETENTIOUS (Artlessness)	N	SHREWD, CALCULATING, WORLDLY, PENETRATING (Shrewdness)
SELF-ASSURED, CONFIDENT, SERENE (Untroubled adequacy)	O	APPREHENSIVE, SELF-REPROACHING, WORRYING, TROUBLED (Guilt proneness)
CONSERVATIVE, RESPECTING ESTABLISHED IDEAS, TOLERANT OF TRADITIONAL DIFFICULTIES (Conservatism)	Q1	EXPERIMENTING, LIBERAL, ANALYTICAL, FREE-THINKING (Radicalism)
GROUP-DEPENDENT, A 'JOINER' AND SOUND FOLLOWER (Group adherence)	Q2	SELF-SUFFICIENT, PREFERS OWN DECISIONS, RESOURCEFUL (Self-sufficiency)
UNDISCIPLINED SELF-CONFLICT, FOLLOWS OWN URGES, CARELESS OF PROTOCOL (Low integration)	Q3	CONTROLLED, SOCIALLY PRECISE, FOLLOWING SELF-IMAGE (High self-concept control)
RELAXED, TRANQUIL, UNFRUSTRATED (Low ergic tension)	Q4	TENSE, FRUSTRATED, DRIVEN, OVERWROUGHT (High ergic tension)

A sten of 10 is obtained by about 2.3% 4.4% 9.2% 15.0% 19.1% 19.1% 15.0% 9.2% 4.4% 2.3% of adults

Printed and distributed by N.F.E.R. Publishing Company Ltd., 2 Jennings Buildings, Thames Avenue, Windsor, Berks, England, by permission Institute for Personality & Ability Testing, Illinois, U.S.A. 16PF, Forms C and D. Copyright 1954, 1956, 1967

Table 11.7   16PF Test profile, fathers

Factor	LOW SCORE DESCRIPTION	HIGH SCORE DESCRIPTION
A	RESERVED, DETACHED, CRITICAL, ALOOF (Sizothymia)	OUTGOING, WARMHEARTED, EASY-GOING, PARTICIPATING (Affectothymia, formerly cyclothymia)
B	LESS INTELLIGENT, CONCRETE-THINKING (Lower scholastic mental capacity)	MORE INTELLIGENT, ABSTRACT-THINKING, BRIGHT (Higher scholastic mental capacity)
C	AFFECTED BY FEELINGS, EMOTIONALLY LESS STABLE, EASILY UPSET (Lower ego strength)	EMOTIONALLY STABLE, FACES REALITY, CALM, MATURE (Higher ego strength)
E	HUMBLE, MILD, ACCOMMODATING, CONFORMING (Submissiveness)	ASSERTIVE, AGGRESSIVE, STUBBORN, COMPETITIVE (Dominance)
F	SOBER, PRUDENT, SERIOUS, TACITURN (Desurgency)	HAPPY-GO-LUCKY, IMPULSIVELY LIVELY, GAY, ENTHUSIASTIC (Surgency)
G	EXPEDIENT, DISREGARDS RULES, FEELS FEW OBLIGATIONS (Weaker superego strength)	CONSCIENTIOUS, PERSEVERING, STAID, MORALISTIC (Stronger superego strength)
H	SHY, RESTRAINED, TIMID, THREAT-SENSITIVE (Threctia)	VENTURESOME, SOCIALLY BOLD, UNINHIBITED, SPONTANEOUS (Parmia)
I	TOUGH-MINDED, SELF-RELIANT, REALISTIC, NO-NONSENSE (Harria)	TENDER-MINDED, CLINGING, OVER-PROTECTED, SENSITIVE (Premsia)
L	TRUSTING, ADAPTABLE, FREE OF JEALOUSY, EASY TO GET ALONG WITH (Alaxia)	SUSPICIOUS, SELF-OPINIONATED, HARD TO FOOL (Protension)
M	PRACTICAL, CAREFUL, CONVENTIONAL, REGULATED BY EXTERNAL REALITIES, PROPER (Praxernia)	IMAGINATIVE, WRAPPED UP IN INNER URGENCIES, CARELESS OF PRACTICAL MATTERS, BOHEMIAN (Autia)
N	FORTHRIGHT, NATURAL, ARTLESS, UNPRETENTIOUS (Artlessness)	SHREWD, CALCULATING, WORLDLY, PENETRATING (Shrewdness)
O	SELF-ASSURED, CONFIDENT, SERENE (Untroubled adequacy)	APPREHENSIVE, SELF-REPROACHING, WORRYING, TROUBLED (Guilt proneness)
Q_1	CONSERVATIVE, RESPECTING ESTABLISHED IDEAS, TOLERANT OF TRADITIONAL DIFFICULTIES (Conservatism)	EXPERIMENTING, LIBERAL, ANALYTICAL, FREE-THINKING (Radicalism)
Q_2	GROUP-DEPENDENT, A 'JOINER' AND SOUND FOLLOWER (Group adherence)	SELF-SUFFICIENT, PREFERS OWN DECISIONS, RESOURCEFUL (Self-sufficiency)
Q_3	UNDISCIPLINED SELF-CONFLICT, FOLLOWS OWN URGES, CARELESS OF PROTOCOL (Low integration)	CONTROLLED, SOCIALLY PRECISE, FOLLOWING SELF-IMAGE (High self-concept control)
Q_4	RELAXED, TRANQUIL, UNFRUSTRATED (Low ergic tension)	TENSE, FRUSTRATED, DRIVEN, OVERWROUGHT (High ergic tension)

STANDARD TEN SCORE (STEN)

Legend:
Batterers – – – –
Controls ————

A sten of 1 2 3 4 5 6 7 8 9 10 is obtained by about 2.3% 4.4% 9.2% 15.0% 19.1% 19.1% 15.0% 9.2% 4.4% 2.3% of adults

Printed and distributed by N.F.E.R. Publishing Company Ltd., 2 Jennings Buildings, Thames Avenue, Windsor, Berks, England, by permission Institute for Personality & Ability Testing, Illinois, U.S.A. 16PF, Forms C and D, Copyright 1954, 1956, 1967.

In addition to the source trait scores, second-order factor
scores were calculated for the factors of Adjustment versus
Anxiety, better known in this country as Neuroticism, and Exvia-
Invia or Extraversion versus Introversion.   These results are
shown in Tables 11.8 and 11.9 respectively.   As may be seen,
while the Neuroticism scores do not differentiate between the two
groups, the battering fathers were significantly lower on Extraversion scores than were the non-battering fathers.

TABLE 11.8   16 PF test second-order factor scores: Neuroticism

	Battering mothers	Control mothers	Battering fathers	Control fathers
Mean score	6.7	5.6	6.6	6.0
SD	2.26	2.11	2.29	2.56
t		1.1066		1.0460
P		05 > P > 0.1		05 > P > 0.1

TABLE 11.9   16 PF test second-order factor scores: Extraversion-
Introversion

	Battering mothers	Control mothers	Battering fathers	Control fathers
Mean score	4.6	5.1	3.4	6.0
SD	3.11	1.96	1.59	1.73
t		0.6513		3.4237
P		> 0.5		0.02 > P > 0.01 *

THE PARENT ATTITUDE RESEARCH INSTRUMENT

The results of this questionnaire have been disappointing.   Not
only did the self-rating technique prove difficult for subjects
to fill in alone, but the length of the test, involving as it did
115 separate statements requiring agree or disagree responses,
proved formidable!   In either its full form or shortened form,
it differentiated very poorly between battering and non-battering
parents.   Confirmation of the relevance of some of Schaeffer and
Bell's factors emerged but the test as a useful tool to elicit
typical 'battering responses' has been a failure in the setting in
which it has been used.   This was particularly disappointing in
view of Elmer's findings (Elmer, 1967a).   Her claim that the
PARI differentiated battering parents in terms of irritability,
marital conflict, homemaking attitudes, ascendant maternal attitudes, seclusiveness in the mother, and her tendency to exclude
outside influences from the home was not substantiated.
    In the present study there were a few interesting trends, but

they did not reach statistical reliability and would certainly
need further support.   Given the difficulties of using the technique with this sort of parent it hardly seemed worth while.

THE HEALTH VISITOR QUESTIONNAIRE

The questionnaire comprised eighteen items.   Of these, the first
merely identified the child (by a code number) and a further eight,
which will be discussed later, failed to show any differences in
the responses made by abusive and non-abusive parents.   The dis-
criminating statements are shown in Table 11.10.

TABLE 11.10 Health Visitor questionnaire. Summary of differentiating statements

No.	Statement	Statistic	d.f.	P	
3	Is the child the natural child of both parents?	$x^2 = 4.5$	1	0.05	*
4	Mother's age Mean age of battering mothers = 24 Mean age of non-battering mothers = 29	$t = 3.55$	28	0.01	*
5	Father's age Mean age of battering fathers = 27 Mean age of non-battering fathers = 34	$t = 2.18$	28	0.05	*
6	Recency of mother's last pregnancy	$x^2 = 8.86$	1	0.01	*
8	Was advice about termination of pregnancy with the injured child sought?	$x^2 = 10.4$	2	0.01	*
15	How well does the health visitor know the family?	$x^2 = 14.43$	2	0.01	*
16	Is there any unusual degree of marital stress in the home?	$x^2 = 7.77$	1	0.01	*
17	Is there any ususual degree of financial stress in the home?	$x^2 = 4.5$	1	0.05	*
18	Is there any unusual degree of stress arising out of housing conditions?	$x^2 = 10.66$	1	0.01	*

  Item 3 shows that there is a greater likelihood that a battered
child may not be the natural child of both parents.
  Items 4 and 5 show a clear tendency for battering parents to be
younger than parents of children sustaining accidental injury in
the home.
  Items 6 and 8 suggest the role of pregnancy in association with
child battery.   On the one hand the result indicates a greater

likelihood that abuse takes place under the influence of a recent
pregnancy, not necessarily the one which led to the birth of the
injured child.   In the second place, it seems that a pregnancy
whose termination had been sought is more likely to give rise to
rejection, or at least later intentional harm to the unwanted child
resulting from that pregnancy.

Item 15 suggests, as have other writers, that battering parents
are hard to get to know by those in authority.

Items 16, 17 and 18 all testify to the role in battering of
present family stresses, whether they derive from difficult marital
relationships, or tensions arising from financial or housing
stringency.

The negative findings from this small survey are also of some
interest.

There was a non-significant tendency for the children's ages
to differ, not so much in terms of their central tendency, as in
the distribution of peak periods for injury.   The differences are
shown in Table 11.11.

TABLE 11.11   Ages of non-accidentally and accidentally injured
children

Age in months	Group B		Group A	
	%	N	%	N
0-6	33.3	5	6.6	1
7-12	6.6	1	13.3	2
13-18	20.0	3	60.0	9
19-24	40.0	6	20.0	3

x^2% = 45.7   0.8 > P > 0.7

Thus Group B, the battered children, showed a bi-modal distribution.   Their most likely age of injury was in the first six
months of life or in the second half of the second year.   The
accidentally injured children, Group A, showed a single peak, at
eighteen months.   Other negative findings include no differences
in the marital status of the two groups, and no difference in the
mother's expressed attitude toward the injured child.   The size
of the family in each group did not differ either.

While it is true to say that some of the questionnaire findings
could have been biased by the fact that the Health Visitors completing the questionnaire often knew which were suspected
batterers and which were not, it is impossible that this could
have affected the age of parents or child or the pregnancy
findings.

It seems impossible too that this fact has affected the judgments regarding housing, financial or marital stress.   Some
positive encouragement concerning the reliability of the questionnaire findings emerges from the fact that battered children were
not thought by health visitors to be less accepted by their parents
than those who were accidentally injured.   From this it may be

supposed that so far as was possible, the interviewers endeavoured, with some success, to maintain an objective approach.

DISCUSSION

Given the small size of the samples employed in the two studies reported here, no absolute generalisations can be made regarding the psychosocial pathology of child batterers.   However, a number of suggestive pointers have emerged quite clearly, despite the limitations of the work.

MATURITY

Despite the fact that the two tested sub-samples were matched for age, there was a non-significant tendency for the battering parents to be younger than their controls.   This tendency was repeated, at a reliable level, in the questionnaire sample, where deliberately no matching was carried out other than that involved in the fact that all children whose parents were interviewed were under two years of age.   There the fathers were seven years and the mothers five years younger than the parents of children receiving accidental injury.   While it is unlikely that these exact differences would be replicated in a national sample, the tendency for parents who batter their children to be younger than those who do not is very likely, and has been observed in one other study in America by Elmer (1967a), and by Smith et al. (1973) more recently in this country.   The greater immaturity of the parent who batters her child is further emphasised by the scores made on the Sixteen Personality Factor Test.   In particular the C scale scores made by the battering mothers reflect a basic deficiency in ego-integration and reality testing.   Confirmed as it is by enhanced M scale raw scores the implication is of immaturity, impracticality and a tendency to flee into fantasy in the face of real problems.   This last finding must remain tentative since judged by American norms the British battering parents scored normally while the controls scored subnormally on scale M.   It is, however, closely in line with Ounsted's description of the battering parent as dominated by his or her own fantasy life (Ounsted et al., 1975).

SOCIAL FACTORS

Thus the young battering mother, under the stress of recent pregnancy, and perhaps faced with the outcome of a previous unwanted one has her job rendered more stressful by her own intrinsic immaturity.   In this situation the additional stress of poor housing and financial stringency, whether it be cause or effect, poses yet further risk for the child growing up in this situation. Clearly immaturity is linked with both the battering parent's greater poverty and the greater likelihood of inadequate housing, since in many ways this is likely to be the lot of the younger members of the population.   Elmer too said of the battering

parent's social milieu, 'The complex of circumstances and personalities characterising the abusive families in our study was
causing them to live under constant stress of a kind unknown to
non-abusive families' (Elmer, 1967a).

TEMPERAMENT

So far the emphasis has been on the mother's role in the battering
situation.   However, there is no support in this investigation
for the idea that battering is undertaken by the mother while the
father passively looks on, nor for the reverse situation.   Most
workers closely involved with battering parents agree that the
battering syndrome is essentially a family one.   The test results
reported here concur in showing abnormalities in both parents.
This has recently received confirmation by Paulson et al. (1974).
The main contributions of the fathers is their own specifically
introverted schizoid personality.   At trait and at second-order
level, and despite slightly enhanced aggression levels, the
fathers represented an abnormally introverted group.   It might
be thought that this was a function of the control group with whom
they have been compared.   A volunteer sample like the fathers in
the control group, is likely to be unusually socially participant.
In fact this was not so.   When both groups were compared (using
the only available population norms, American ones), the control
fathers scored within normal limits, while the battering fathers
scored below the norm.   This was true for the A scale of socia-
bility and the F scale of enthusiasm and sobriety (see Table 11.7).
    Typically, social workers and especially health visitors have
little contact with the fathers in the families they help.   This
is especially regrettable with battering families for whom they
may have to care, since an awareness of the father's inevitably
non-supportive role in family life might enable them to provide
additional support for the women and especially the children at
risk.
    The part played by the father's temperament remains speculative
it is true, but it is not hard to speculate in this area.   Since
it is customary to emphasise the importance of the father's emotional support to the mother during the early dyadic period of
the mother-child relationship, it is easy to imagine her helpless-
ness when absence of support leaves her to withstand the persistent one-way demands of a helpless infant.   Little wonder that
the psychiatric literature ponders at such length upon what they
choose to call the role reversal of the battering mother in relation to her child.   If the father cannot support the mother at
her time of need, it is no great mystery that she turns to her
child for emotional replenishment, illogical as this may be.   The
fathers' combination of a natural introversion with relatively
inadequate verbal facility taken with the mother's immaturity and
impulsivity is unfortunate for the whole family.   It implies that
problems will be shelved rather than talked through, that impulse
will be acted on rather than mediated by thought or language, and
that when outside help is needed it will not be readily sought.
If help is offered it is likely to be rejected because of the

obstacles to easy communication existing in the father himself and
the hostility toward the outside world which both parents share.

ABILITIES

There was little overall difference in the intellectual abilities
of the battering and control parents.   All scored within normal
limits on both sub-scales of the short form of the Wechsler Adult
Intelligence Scale.   Such differences as arose, showed relatively
lower verbal than practical abilities for the battering parents, a
difference in the reverse direction to that of the controls.   Such
a directional trend is very much in line with the work of the
Gluecks (1950).   They have emphasised the essentially concrete
nature of the delinquents' style of thought, a style associated
with poor postponement of impulse shown in a tendency to act out.
Thus the score on scale C of the personality inventory and the
lowered verbal scores on the intelligence test confirm each other.
The balance of scores shows a sex difference with battering
mothers' IQ scores being less significantly different from normal
than their C scores, while the reverse is true for the battering
fathers.   The trend for them both, however, is similar reflecting
a relatively impaired capacity for verbally mediated self control.
  Despite this characteristic style of thought, the battering
parent is otherwise very similar in intellectual 'power' to the
normal parent.   These data in no way confirm Smith's findings that
over 50 per cent of battering parents are of borderline ability
(Smith et al. 1973).   As has been pointed out elsewhere (Hyman,
1973a) this conclusion was probably falsely based upon a mistaken
summation of separate test scores.

THE CHILD

What part the child plays in the battering situation cannot be
told from this kind of investigation.   That he is probably unwanted at the time he was born seems very likely.   That he is most
at risk in earliest infancy or at the late toddler stage of increased autonomy is a possibility as yet unproven.   Whether he
shares his father's unresponsive temperament is also unknown.   The
likelihood is there that the 'unloved' battering parent may repro-
duce himself, not only through the type of environment he creates
but in a genetic sense as well.   Certainly some of the traits
shown to occur exceptionally in the battering father are likely to
be 'true' temperamental traits (Cattell, et al. 1970;   Eysenck,
1956).

CONCLUSION

The present small study suggests that the factors underlying child
battering are complex.   They may include biological factors
associated with immaturity and the hormonal changes occurring in
pregnancy.   They probably include social predisposers arising

from financial and housing inadequacies.   The temperament of the
parent is probably a further instigator to violence against the
child, with heightened aggression, lowered capacity for control
over impulse and the introverted withdrawal of the fathers all
potentially playing a part.   A concrete style of thought which
hinders postponement of action may be another element.   Battering
is almost certainly of complex causation and of shared responsibility within the family.

Chapter 12

A PSYCHOLOGICAL STUDY OF
BATTERED CHILDREN

Part of the psychological research done at Denver House dealt with
the children whose injuries led to their referral. The aim was
to determine in what way, if at all, the injury and parental care
prior to it had affected the child, and whether, after a period of
treatment, there were any lasting results of the trauma. Attempts
were made to see all children but this was not always possible
either because of the severity of the injury or unwillingness on
the part of the parents. However, the group studied remains
small and although the use of controls and standardised tests will
to some extent overcome the problems associated with the sample
size, additional research and replication is obviously desirable.

This study can be looked at in three main sections. The first
deals with the intensive monitoring of children and their mothers
while attending the Denver House Therapeutic Nursery. This comprises schedules filled in by the nursery staff charting the
children's progress and the interaction with their mothers. The
second section is concerned with the results of developmental
tests given to the children on referral and after an interval of
treatment, with comparisons between first and later test scores,
and between those of children in the therapeutic environment and
those in ordinary nurseries. Third, a comparison was made of
several tests given to injured children who were pair matched with
non-injured children on ages of child and parents, size of family,
socio-economic background and ethnic group.

Some of the subgroups in this study overlap and the numbers
vary in each group, but the size and description of each will be
given throughout. All subjects were in social class IV or V so
this is not elaborated upon further.

NURSERY SCHEDULES

Schedules were designed to record the progress of each of the
seven battered children for the duration of their stay in the
therapeutic nursery. They included detailed information on
eating behaviour, toilet training, physical and emotional stages,
interaction with parents and adults, and verbal development.

198

These were filled out by the nursery staff at intervals of approximately three months, and the results were then analysed using the
Statistical Package for the Social Sciences (Nie et al.,1970). In the
final run, cross tabulations were done for each variable by dividing the schedules into age groups of 13-27 months, 29-35 months
and 36-54 months, with approximately 33 per cent in each grouping.

Some of the results which proved significant at the 0.05 level
or less, were self evident and in no way informative, e.g. that as
the child gets older he can eat without help, and tends to cry or
moan less, and begins to be more explorative.   However, it
appears that the children in the older grouping seem less independent than those in the younger section, and are inclined to ask
for help more readily when they need it.   This is probably not
an increase in dependence itself but is more likely to be a reflection of their ease of interaction with the nursery staff, and
perhaps a more developed trust in adults.   The results also show
the expected increase in verbal ability and comprehensibility, as
well as the fact that the children become easier to handle and
need less time and attention as they get older.

Cross tabulations of the variables were also done by dividing
the length of time at the nursery into three equal sections ranging from 1-4 months, 5-13 months and 14-27 months.   These results
were much the same as those above, with the addition of the
variable of fearfulness, which showed that there was a significant
decrease in the children's fear reactions the longer they spent in
the nursery.

The nursery staff also filled in schedules on the mothers which
covered such variables as how frequently she visited the nursery,
how long she spent with her own child and other children, and the
quality of her interaction with them.   These were also analysed
using the above groupings of the age of child and the length of
time the child had spent in the nursery.   There were very few
variables which showed significance in either group, but the mothers
seemed more confident as the child got older and were not so upset
by the demands of an older child.   Their strictness varied a
great deal, showing a form of bimodal distribution, indicating that
they were either very strict or very lenient, or perhaps the same
mother showed inconsistencies and fluctuations in dealings with
her child.

The deficiences in the final results of these schedules were
probably due to the small sample (seven children was the maximum
at any one time) and the large number of variables.   It seemed
that the nursery staff spent a great deal of time over a two-year
period charting the children's behaviour, but that the results in
most cases did not yield a great deal of information which could
be seen as specific to battered children.   Yet both social
workers and nursery staff have verbally identified differences
between this group of children and non-injured ones, so that
obviously future research must attempt to overcome this lack of
information by exploring other means of behavioural observation
and recording.

DEVELOPMENTAL TEST RESULTS

The two tests used were the Bayley Scales of Infant Development for
children under two years, and the Stanford Binet Test Form L-M for
children over two years.   They are both standardised tests of
intellectual development which show the child's level of achievement
in comparison to the norm for a given age.   They consist of a
series of tasks designed to tap a variety of intellectual
behaviours, such as block building, form board completion, number
repetition, comprehension of words and phrases and maze tracing.
     The sample of 25 battered children was made up of 19 children
referred to Denver House from early 1970 to mid 1973, 4 who were
receiving treatment from the NSPCC in Birmingham and two children
under the care of the Social Services Department in Surrey.   All
children were under the age of three years at time of referral but
were not all tested within the first few months of treatment, and
so the age at which the first test was given ranges from 11 months
to 4 years 1 month.   All of the children were given one of the
developmental tests described above.   Controls were found for
only ten of these but an examination of their scores showed that
they were higher than one would have expected (i.e. they were
above the average norm), so they were excluded from the statistical
analysis.   The scores of the whole sample of 25 battered children
range from 50 to 125 with a mean of 80.   In order to compare this
range of scores to what one would expect from a normally distributed sample of the same size, a Kolmogorov Smirnov One Sample Test
(Siegal, 1956) was used and it gave the probability of the sample
being the same as the theoretical distribution as less than 0.01
(i.e. $D = -0.4$, $p < 0.01$ - this result would have been caused by
chance factors alone 1 time out of a 100).   These scores are
presented graphically (see Figure 12.1) and it can be seen at a
glance that the scores of the battered children are skewed to the
left of the normal distribution and that most of the scores are
well below 100, which is the normal average.   As stated above
there was a varying time lapse between referral and the time of
the first test and it is therefore necessary to see if the test
results of those who were seen soon after the battering took place
differed from those who were tested much later.   The time lapses
were divided into two groups - those seen within 8 months of referral and those seen between 14 and 18 months of referral.
Sixteen children were seen within 8 months and they received a
mean score of 81.5 and 9 were seen in the 14 to 18 months group
receiving a mean score of 77.333.   However, a Mann-Whitney test
showed that this difference was not statistically significant
(Mann-Whitney, $U = 38$) but due to chance factors (see Table 12.1).

TABLE 12.1 Time lapse between referral and first test

	Under 8 months	Between 14 and 18 months	Sig. level
Means	81.5 (N = 16)	77.333	not sig.

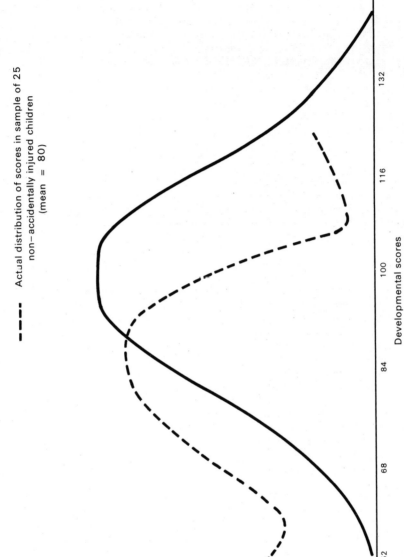

Expected distribution of scores in sample of 25

Actual distribution of scores in sample of 25 non-accidentally injured children (mean = 80)

No. of children

Developmental scores

Figure 12.1

There were also differences in the children's ages at the first test, so the scores of children under two were compared to those of children over two.   The former, of whom there were 11, got a mean score of 70.7272 and those over two (14 in all) received a mean score of 87.2857.   A Mann-Whitney test showed this difference to be significant at the 0.05 level (Mann-Whitney, U = 25) (see Table 12.2).   So it seems that the younger children were more backward than those over the age of two years.   However, it must be remembered that different tests are used on the two groups and this may account for some discrepancy, but it does seem reasonable to assume that a younger child could be more adversely affected by stress and physical violence than an older one.

TABLE 12.2   Age at first test

	Under 2 years	Over 2 years	Sig. level
Means	70.7272 (N = 11)	87.2857 (N = 14)	$p < 0.05$

Out of the sample of 25, 14 were available for retesting at an interval of approximately two years after their first test.   The results showed a great improvement in scores (see Figure 12.2) so that they resembled what one would expect of a 'normal' population i.e. they had a mean score of 100.4 and ranged from 81-121, with most of the scores clustered around the mean.   Therefore one can conclude that with constant and prolonged nursery care, battered children can recover and gain skills which were not in evidence soon after referral.   The families of 14 children who were retested were all receiving social work support from the Denver House team, and of these children 7 were attending the Therapeutic Nursery and 7 were placed in local authority nurseries. These two groups were compared on first and retest scores to see if there was a difference which could be attributed to the Therapeutic Nursery.   On first test after referral the Denver House Nursery children had a mean score of 69 and the others 77.7285, but a Mann-Whitney test showed that this difference was not significant (Mann-Whitney, U = 11) (see Table 12.3).   However, on the retest the Denver House children had a mean IQ of 106 and those in other nurseries a mean of 93.7.   The Mann-Whitney test on those showed the difference to be significant at the 0.004 level (Mann-Whitney, U = 2) (see Table 12.4).   Thus it seems reasonable to conclude that while the scores of all children improve greatly, those in the special nursery setting with a high staff-child ratio and plenty of individual attention, show the greatest improvement.

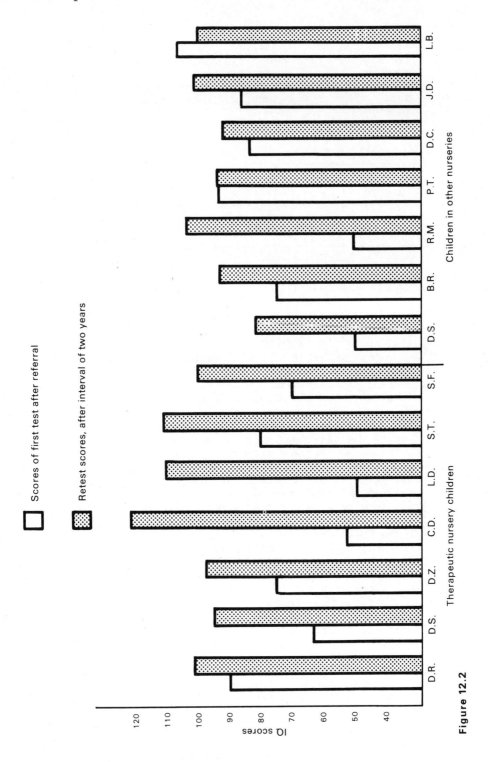

Figure 12.2

TABLE 12.3 First test scores

	Denver House nursery	Other nurseries	Sig. level
Means	69.0 (N = 7)	77.285 (N = 7)	not sig.

TABLE 12.4 Latest test scores

	Denver House nursery	Other nurseries	Sig. level
Means	106.0 (N = 7)	93.7 (N = 7)	$p < 0.004$

PEABODY PICTURE VOCABULARY TEST

This standardised test comprises a graduated series of 150 plates, each containing four pictures. The examiner provides the stimulus verbally, e.g. 'point to the man' - and the child then indicates the picture on the plate which best illustrates the stimulus word. The results can be compared with an age norm.

It was possible to pair match 16 battered children from the total sample of 25 described above on variables of age of child and parents, size of family, class, ethnic group and economic background, with children attending an NSPCC playgroup in Birmingham. Although none of the playgroup children was injured, most came from overcrowded homes, or ones where there was some form of family disturbance, or else environments which were considered lacking in the essential stimulation necessary for young children. The 16 battered children and their matched controls were each given this test, and the results were analysed using a matched pairs t test. This showed the battered children to be statistically higher than controls at the 0.01 level ($t = 3.1768$, $df = 15$). However, an inspection of the raw data indicated that the main difference in scores lay between the Denver House Day Nursery and their controls. When they were compared with their controls on a matched pairs t test, the analysis showed their scores to be significantly higher than their controls at the 0.05 level ($t = 2.6581$, $df = 8$). When this procedure was carried out on the remaining battered children and their controls the difference was not significant ($t = 1.6672$, $df = 6$). In summary it seems that the Denver House children were more verbally advanced than the other children in the sample, a result consistent with the above data on developmental tests. However, again it should be pointed out that the Therapeutic Nursery children's families had all been in treatment and they attending the nursery for at least two years.

FAMILY RELATIONS TEST

Only thirteen of the above sample of matched pairs could be given
this test as it is inapplicable to children under the age of
three years.
    It is designed to provide an objective assessment of the direc-
tion and intensity of the child's feelings towards various members
of his family and his estimate of their reciprocal regard for him.
It comprises various cardboard representations of family figures
from which the child is asked to set up his own family.   He is
then given a series of cards of pre-selected emotional attitudes
which he distributes to the appropriate family member in each case,
and if no member is chosen he can place the card into a 'nobody'
which is included for that purpose.
    These cards are divided into 5 main categories:
 1 Positive feelings coming from the child (e.g. who does N...
    like to play with?)
 2 Negative feelings coming from the child (e.g. who would N...
    like to send away?)
 3 Positive feelings going towards the child (e.g. who likes to
    give N... a hug?)
 4 Negative feelings going towards the child (e.g. who says
    N... is naughty?)
 5 Dependency (e.g. who helps N... get dressed in the morning?)
    This allows the data to be analysed 8 ways - the total involve-
ment (which includes all the above 5 categories), the above 5
separately, the total negatives and the total positives.   A Chi-
squared test was done on all of these because each allocation of
cards is not independent of the others, and it allows for the fact
that a few children did not allocate all the cards.   These
results will be described in terms of differences between the
battered children and their controls, with pointers to the way
the former differ from what one would expect of children in the
same age range.

Total involvement

The total involvement was analysed and showed that the results
were significant at the 0.001 level (x^2 = 40.1681, df = 4).   The
most striking feature of this way of looking at the data was that
the control children had about twice the involvement with the
mother figure as compared to the battered child.   The battered
children had a greater involvement with their fathers than controls, and also allocated more cards to 'nobody'.   Bene and
Anthony describe the allocation of cards to 'nobody' as a denial
tendency, since they tend to 'opt out' of allocating cards which
could perhaps be painful to them.   So it can be seen that
battered children tend not to attach as much importance to the
mother, as one would expect of 'normal' children for that age.

Child's positive feelings

Again this showed a significance level of 0.001 (x^2 = 21.1227, df = 4) and a similar pattern emerged, viz. fewer positive feelings were allocated to mother by the battered children than controls, more were given to fathers and 'nobody', and even more positive feelings to siblings, which is indicative of displacement, since more items went to peripheral rather than to the central characters in the family.   The lack of involvement with the mother is still evident, and some of the feelings which one would have expected to be allocated to her, were distributed between father and siblings.

Child's negative feelings

This analysis was significant at 0.05 level (x^2 = 10.1456, df = 4). In this section the battered children put most of their negative feelings into 'nobody' (twice as many as the controls), but the controls put more negative feelings into mother.   One can see that in the case of the battered child, these cards which probably should have been allocated to mothers were put into 'nobody', since these two categories contained the greatest differences between the two groups.   As this section deals only with the child's negative feelings it tends to highlight the denial tendency described above.

Child's perception of positive feelings directed at him

This showed no significant difference between the two groups of children (x^2 = 5.9148, df = 4).   However, the trends described above were obvious, but did not reach a statistically significant level.

Child's perception of negative feelings directed at him

This result was also not significant (x^2 = 9.1724, df = 4) but as in the above the trend was maintained.

Feelings of dependency

This section was not significant (x^2 = 9.4412, df = 4), and it shows the similar expectations of all the children for things like dressing, feeding, bathing, etc. suggesting that the experience of actual mothercraft in the two groups is not different.

Total positive relationship (incoming and outgoing)

This is an addition of all the positive relationships expressed and is significant at 0.001 level (x^2 = 22.3967, df = 4).   As expected, it shows a displacement of positive feelings towards

the siblings on the part of the battered children, the next
greatest number of cards going to father, then 'nobody', self and
lastly to mother.   The controls followed what one would expect
of the norm, i.e. most went to mother, then father and self,
siblings and least went to 'nobody'.

Total negative relationships (incoming and outgoing)

This addition of negative relationships was significant at 0.01
level (X^2 = 16.5139, df = 4).   Battered children attributed most
negative feelings to 'nobody' (i.e. denial), then to siblings and
mother and least to father.   The controls expressed more negative
feelings towards mother, then siblings, father and 'nobody'.
   Thus it can be seen that in each analysis there were strong
and consistent differences between battered and non-battered children, most notably in that the battered children had less of an
involvement with their mothers, and that their feelings were distributed mostly amongst fathers and siblings, with a denial tendency to attribute most negative feelings to 'nobody'.   This was
the only test in which the Denver House Nursery children did not
differ from the other battered children.

DOLL PLAY

From the sample described above sixteen battered children and their
controls were given a doll to play with in a semi-structured situation.   They were encouraged to identify with it by pretending
to be its mother or father, and were then asked various leading
questions relation to a child's home routine, e.g. 'give your baby
some food - does he eat it all?'.   These sessions were recorded
and transcripts made in order to see if the two groups showed
differences in their play which could be related to their family
experiences.   The results were not analysed using statistical
methods as each session varied according to the child's ability
and inclination to identify with the doll, his involvement in the
situation and other external variables.   It was seen more as a
form of self-expression on the part of the child, and was meant to
give an idiosyncratic supplement to the above test results.
   There were no immediately apparent differences between the two
groups as a whole, but once again the Therapeutic Nursery children
were easily identifiable on several counts.
   Three social workers who did not know any of the children involved were asked to sort the thirty-two transcripts into battered
and non-battered groups using any criteria, and all correctly
placed the seven Therapeutic Nursery children, but no such identification could be made accurately on the remaining twenty-five.
This could be due to the fact that the Denver House children had
expressed much more verbal aggression (defined as proposing punishment, smacks or shouting at the doll) than the other battered and
non-battered children.   However, all but six of the total group
threatened smacking at some stage, so it seems that this form of
discipline is a fairly common occurrence in the lives of these

other children.   The Denver House children also physically struck
the doll many more times than the other children and showed more
violence in shaking and throwing it, and were more frequently
rough while playing with it.

However, these two aspects of aggression must be examined in the
total context of the play and those children were also more involved in the situation, used more expressions of symbolic play of
a make believe kind, used almost twice as many words as the others
and had longer sentences which on average contained more words.
So that while on the surface it appears that they were more aggressive, it could be that they are more verbally and physically
expressive, and therefore these results cannot be interpreted
solely in terms of aggression, but may also reflect an aspect of
their social development and ability to play in an uninhibited
fashion in the presence of an adult.

SUMMARY AND DISCUSSION

This research project set out to obtain a comprehensive picture of
battered children, in order to highlight differences which might
be attributed to the battered children's traumatic experiences.
However, there are obvious limitations in this sort of research -
the sample was fairly small, a psychologist was not employed from
the beginning of intake in Denver House so that some families
receiving treatment were never seen by a psychologist at all, then
the intake decreased and numbers were never made up.   Controls
were also difficult to obtain and not all the children were matched
on each test.   Test results too, rely a great deal on the testing
situation, motivation of the child, his interaction with the
tester and his mood at the time - so that all these considerations
must be taken into account when looking at the results.   There
are also very few tests for this age group and a comprehensive
appraisal of their behaviour and progress is limited by tests
which are available.

The above results show that battered children who were given
developmental tests within eighteen months of referral had scores
lower than the norm, and generally the younger the child the lower
the scores - a result also shown by the studies in the USA by
Elmer (1968) and Martin (1972).   However, there are several
reasons for concluding that these scores are due to environmental
factors rather than intrinsic characteristics: the testing of the
parents by Dr Clare Hyman showed that they had scores within
normal limits and all children greatly improved after some time
in treatment, with those in a therapeutic environment showing the
greatest improvement of all.   These results also emphasise the
importance of a follow-up study and indicate a more hopeful prognosis for the child's future.   It appears that the mental retardation diagnosed on referral (e.g. Smith and Hanson, 1974) is not
necessarily permanent and can be rectified given the appropriate
environment for several years.

The fact that developmental scores after the age of three or
four correlate highly with academic achievement suggests that these
children who have had specialised treatment should find the transi-

tion to school life much easier, and thus another potential source of disturbance should be minimised.

Although the battered children did achieve normal levels of development they still did not view their family relationships in the way one would expect of children in this age group.   There was a great contrast between them and the controls, who were themselves from deprived family situations, so that one would expect this difference to be even greater if compared with children from relatively trouble-free homes.   It seems that battered children have very little involvement with their mothers, at the same time refusing to admit the existence of any negative feelings towards or from her, while dispersing their affection amongst fathers and siblings.

Even though the findings on the cognitive development are encouraging it seems that future research could profitably include some more effective observational and monitoring methods.   It may also be appropriate to get a psychiatric assessment of the children soon after referral, and to make provision for some form of therapy if this appears necessary.   It should also be pointed out that although this study included some children up to school age, there is little or no information on their development after that time, so that any long-term effects remain undiscovered until such time as a much needed follow-up study can be undertaken.

Chapter 13

GENERAL DISCUSSION AND RECOMMENDATIONS

We became aware that we were dealing only with the extreme of a much more widespread phenomenon ....

Steele and Pollock (1968)

In studying the Battered Child Syndrome through a small group of diagnosed families, we have gained a more distinctive impression of detail but our view of the parameters of the problem remains obscure. The definition of child abuse as a discrete entity is problematic. We cannot say with any certainty how child abuse differs from the more generalised harsh treatment of children which is a feature of our cultural pattern, except by degree. There has been little attempt in the literature to examine the fortuitous elements in diagnosis. Why are certain cases identified by certain agencies while others are missed? Research in this area might well help in clarifying the spectrum of abusive behaviour. As it is, we are left with some idea about causal factors associated with the syndrome but little conception of necessary or sufficient causes and no way of explaining why the presence of such factors in other families does not always result in child abuse. Furthermore, we feel that in many respects the confused ethical and legal background against which our project began still remains.

Our findings suggest a mutli-causal model in which a constellation of factors combine to form a dangerous compound. As far as we can tell, no one individual factor is an essential ingredient and a variety of combinations have been noted. Certain factors do seem to be more prevalent than others and some carry more weight. Other factors may simply act as the rider which finally tips the balance, or play a minor role as determinants of abuse. The more important factors include the fragmented and emotionally demanding childhoods of many abusive parents, the fact that most of our study children were unwanted at the time of birth, marital disharmony, overcrowded and inadequate accommodation, social isolation and rootlessness.

Generalisations from a study of this nature should, as pointed out in earlier chapters, be regarded with caution. As a demonstration project we could not aim for the level of exactitude of

an experiment.   None the less, there were pitfalls which, with
hindsight, it appears we could have avoided.   Our attempt at an
exhaustive study could have been replaced by a more focused approach
if, at the design stage, we had been more specific about our aims.
This is not to suggest that a narrow view should have been adopted
at the outset.   The fact that two years were spent in preliminary
research obviated the dangers of a blinkered approach (Lauerman,
1974).   However, the piloting of research instruments before we
took cases and some attempt to project a framework for analysis
might have enabled us to examine more carefully the crucial factors
listed above.   Other more intractable difficulties are a feature
of the syndrome rather than our study.   The problems of sampling
are great in any study where, in epidemiological terms, the incidence is low.   The use of control groups counters bias in sampling
but in child abuse there are great difficulties in finding viable
controls, either in the general population or amongst specific
groups such as families with diseased children (see Elmer, 1967a).

There remains a need for more extensive research.   Many of
the studies referred to in the text have looked, as ours did, at
the diagnostic characteristics of the syndrome in much detail.
Many of the findings remain somewhat speculative.   In our opinion,
there is a great need for more research into other areas, in
particular the epidemiology of the problem and the study of comparative treatment techniques.   Epidemiological studies should
prove a more fruitful proposition now that more cases are being
identified, registers are being established and compulsory reporting laws might be considered.

In our view, the establishment of registries and the mandatory
reporting of cases would provide a valuable secondary research
function.   There are, of course, immense problems in ensuring
common criteria for the referral of cases as well as deciding upon
which kinds of cases to include in a registry.   In addition,
there are problems of confidentiality and access which, however,
can be greatly reduced by computerisation (Diggle and Jackson,
1973).   The real difficulty lies in gaining agreement across the
mixed disciplines about the terms of reference, not least in
deciding what data to include.   Although all of these problems
are probably proportional to the actual size of the area covered
by the registry, we would strongly endorse any movement towards
the establishment of a national register for cases of suspected
child abuse.   Area Review Committees have done much to stimulate
discussion of these issues as well as promoting inter-agency co-
operation and concerted policies for the management of cases.

One particularly important question which area and ultimately
national registries could answer would be the extent to which age
and abuse are correlated.   To date, most studies, with good
reason, have focused on the young child.   Early research revealed
the greater risk to the younger child (Skinner and Castle, 1969;
Gil, 1968).

Nevertheless, as the tragedy of Maria Colwell showed, age in
itself brings no automatic protection.   We need to know defini-
tively whether among older abused children the immature or the
handicapped figure disproportionately.   We need to know whether
the stresses of recent pregnancy, which predispose toward the

battering of babies, are as prepotent in evoking the abuse of older children.

It may be that the older child provides more 'real' provocation to the parent, independent of that parent's inner state of mind. The infant is limited in what he can initiate. The older child has a range of potentially annoying behaviours at his disposal, some by no means accidental. The minority of younger abused children who appear to be scapegoats are probably those who, as they grow older, elicit increasing dehumanisation and perhaps injury from their parents. But we do not know what proportion of these older children have been abused from their infancy.

Steele and Pollock (1968) have also suggested that Oedipal factors play a role in the dynamics of the abuse of older children in contrast to the infant whose dependency appears to be the major source of provocation to the battering parent. Only the detailed and comprehensive data provided from registries can answer these questions, replacing fact with speculation.

Outside specialised agencies such as our own, less attention has been paid to the ongoing treatment of abusing families. Registries could contribute to the prevention of battering by facilitating early case finding which would also aid treatment. Nevertheless, without adequate treatment provision, registries would only contain dead information. Registration provides, in itself, no protection. This, too, applies to case conferences. Protective decisions need to be taken and monitored, as is now the case in some areas with district review committees. As we have shown in this study, there remains a large gap between the provision of an ideal service such as we have attempted, albeit with certain limitations, and the normal facilities available to the battering family without access to a special treatment centre.

Our intensive long-term treatment service operated in near ideal conditions. In our view this was of considerable value to the parents for whom it was provided. It promoted richer, more fulfilling life-styles. This included an improvement in the living circumstances of our families, an increase in their work satisfaction and less frustration in their marital relationships. Our psychological findings suggest that the parents, particularly the fathers, pose a difficult problem in treatment. The fathers indeed were withdrawn and inaccessible as described in chapter 11, and our attempts at their treatment were, for the most part, rebuffed.

However, of the mothers, we managed to engage all but one in a meaningful relationship, in spite of the tendency toward immature, impulsive behaviour which the psychological findings implied. It is of the first importance to state that this supportive care has, in the main, been associated with an absence of rebattering or a reduction in its probable severity. It will be remembered that our criteria in this regard were particularly rigorous (chapter 10). Nevertheless, of the twenty-two children available for re-injury during a three-year period after referral, two only received serious re-injury and three moderate re-injury. None sustained permanent physical or mental disability as a result of post-referral abuse. The remaining injuries, seven in all, were so minor as not to warrant any medical treatment. As was pointed

out in chapter 10, a similar scrutiny applied to any group of
toddlers and young children would be likely to discover a similar
range of minor bruises and small injuries lacking definitive explanation as accidental.

We would emphasise the need to provide, in the initial stages
of treatment especially, the kind of intensive nurturing relationship which we have been at pains to describe in chapter 8.   Without
it, we feel that we might well have lost contact with our parents
before any kind of treatment could have been started.   However,
in the light of our considerable treatment experience, built up
over several years, we are now in a position to see beyond the
immediate presenting needs of our clients.

To go further in attempting to alter the underlying personality
dynamics, especially of parent/child interaction, a more focused
and specific treatment provision should be tried.   Whether this
would be in individual psychotherapy or in some kind of group
treatment with stated goals, would depend upon the individual circumstances.   While still emphasising the need to establish
clients' basic trust and co-operation, we should like to recommend
for the future a wider range of treatment possibilities.   We
would recommend extension of special treatment centres across the
country to provide appropriate therapy for abusive families.
This is not to say that we believe that all families can be helped
by our kind of treatment service or any other.   There were certainly some who appeared not to benefit.   Ultimately, radical
social change is required to intervene in the perpetuation of the
severe social deprivation often associated with battering.   Individual treatment alone is insufficient.   On the other hand some
of our unhelpable clients were not, in fact, grossly disadvantaged.
Neither were they psychotic.   Whether the interaction between a
negative genetic endowment of the kind, for example, which may
contribute to the extremes of introversion and render an individual
inaccessible, and severe emotional deprivation in childhood is
responsible, cannot be known at this stage.   Further work is
required to define the prognostic signs for therapeutic success.

In addition to the therapeutic groups already discussed, there
is a place for groups to combat social isolation.   Where nursery
and treatment facilities are available under one roof, which is
highly desirable, such group meetings would be relatively easy to
establish.   Evening meeting times might help to engage the
fathers.   This would be particularly desirable when their initial
suspicion makes them avoid traditional therapeutic groups.

There is a need, as discussed by Paulson and Chaleff (1973), to
attempt some educational work with the mothers.   Although, as we
have indicated, this is not a first priority, there may be a place
for this, once trust and co-operation have been established.
Better child-rearing techniques might make the children less
frustrated and therefore less provoking to their parents.   It
would be valuable to secure the co-operation of local General
Practitioners and Health Visitors in this work.   Self-help groups,
on the lines of those already developed by parents themselves in
the USA and Canada, have also their therapeutic and educative
value.   One such group has recently been set up in this country
(Brandenburger, 1975).

Other recommendations we would make, would include a system of
built-in psychiatric assessment for all battered children followed
by individual psychotherapy where appropriate.   Undoubtedly the
emotional climate in which battering occurs can have as damaging
an effect in the child's long-term development as the physical
injury itself.   Although we have been able to show that our system
of care has helped to restore the child's overall developmental
status in most cases, personality tests on the children administered
after a period of case work with their families, and nursery care
for the children, reveal a long-term distortion in the child's
relationship with the mother, which appears to be less amenable to
change.   We feel this to be an important finding, stemming as it
does from one of the few follow-up studies undertaken on the
battered child in this country.   Whether the child is removed
from home or remains with his family, it is likely that specific
and intensive therapeutic intervention will be required if there is
to be any chance of undoing this distortion.

We would also recommend the use of specialised day nurseries
providing a therapeutic milieu for the abused child, by catering
for his special emotional needs and by being able to cope with his
behavioural disorder.   We do not share Davies's (1975) view that
special groups for children at risk ... soon gain a notoriety as
something different and defeat their own object.   On the contrary, we have found that the sympathetic reception offered to the
parents in our own therapeutic nursery, unlike that often experienced by battering parents in unspecialised nurseries catering for
a much larger number of children, has done much to ensure the
child's regular attendance and hence his continued physical safety.
We would be in favour of appointing staff to the nursery with
special skill and experience in working with disturbed pre-school
children.

The use of transport for conveying the children to the nursery
would not only encourage maximum attendance, but would also make
the provision of specialised care more economical, by allowing
children to be taken from a wide geographical area.

All abused children, in our opinion, should be required to be
kept under periodic review by medical, psychological and social
work staff, as is standard practice in some day nurseries.   Long-
itudinal studies of a cross-disciplinary nature, which such a
review would provide, would enable assessment to be made of the
long-term effects of various types of treatment procedure.   Information is needed on the relative merits of various types of protective placement in comparison with the home environment.

Apart from treatment consideration as such, we see a need for
a more direct acknowledgment of child-protective functions.   In
this, the role of the police is inevitable.   Their role is essentially that of law enforcement although, at senior officer level,
there is a certain amount of permitted discretion.   It is because
the police must be free to exercise unilateral action that their
presence at case conferences is often viewed with suspicion by
other professionals.   Until there is a uniform national police
policy across the field of child abuse, it will be difficult for
this suspicion to be wholly suspended.   Nevertheless, the access
to police records, which their representation on case conferences

provides, and their access to otherwise inaccessible families, is
of value.

The whole question of balancing parental and children's rights
is a complex one as the debate following the publication of the
Children Act in 1975   has shown.   In the particular case of
abused children, whose rights so far have been insufficiently
acknowledged, we welcome the provisions of the Act which go some
way to strengthen these rights.

Even as the law stands, protection of the child could be
improved by a more effective use of existing legislation.   This
could be fostered by adequate legal education about the syndrome
and co-operation among the various disciplines involved.   Probably
changes in this area would do as much to safeguard children as any
of the proposed legislative changes (see Fontana, 1973).

The Juvenile Court, in any case, exists to protect the child
rather than to punish the adult although confusion over the
different roles of Juvenile and Adult Courts still prevails, as
Cavenagh (1975) discusses (along with the need for special panels
or hearings to deal with child abuse cases).   The work of the
Juvenile Court would be further enhanced by a change in the law
allowing psychiatric reports on the parents to be called for by
the court.

Ultimately, the needs of the child must have priority.   There
will always be cases where therapy for the parents is either unrealistic or, if helpful for them, insufficient to protect their
child absolutely from further abuse.   Permanent separation must
be considered from the outset, despite what is known about the
deleterious effects of separation of the child from his mother
during the period of attachment.   Physical safety must take precedence over personality development.   Even here, our own results
imply that, in some cases, the battered child would have a better
chance permanently and early placed, ideally for adoption, or at
the very least therapeutic fostering.   The need to support and
treat the rest of the family is in no way diminished by such
action.   Future children may be born and older siblings remain at
home.   While it is impossible to lay down rigorous rules of thumb
regarding decisions over permanent removal, the need in some cases
remains, not only to ensure the child's safety, but also to facilitate his development in the broadest sense.

Since this sort of decision needs to be made early in the case
work, if frequent disruptions for the children of the sort their
parents have experienced in their childhood are to be avoided,
there would be much to be said for the setting up of a special
residential assessment centre where the whole family could be
intensively observed.   Ounsted et al. (1975) have shown the great
value of such a setting for treatment and in being able, without
risk, to discuss battering more directly with the parents.   We
would add to this the particular value for proper observation in
a safe place which would be so provided.   The family's capacity
for change could be evaluated as well as the quality of parent-
child interaction.   This provision is of particular importance
where parental consent to adoption may be dispensed with under
the provisions proposed in the new Children Act   (1975), where a
child has been persistently or seriously ill-treated and his rehabilitation in his family is thought to be unlikely.

It follows from all that has been said that, improvement in the provision of contraceptive facilities to forestall battering of unwanted children, requires high priority.   Our own findings, reported in chapters 5 and 11, emphasise the impelling stressfulness of pregnancy in the lives of battering parents.   The need to reduce such stress is urgent.   Another essential recommendation is the need to improve the quality of ante-natal services generally, so that vulnerable families may be identified at this most important stage in their lives.

We have always hoped to be able to draw from our experience specific guidance for those working with battering families in conditions less ideal than ours.   We were well aware that most other workers have neither the time nor the resources that we enjoyed.

However, we feel that it is of the utmost importance, whatever the setting and the pressure of work, that a decision about the child's protection should be taken as early as possible, and that a key worker, with the main therapeutic and liaison responsibility, should be identified both to the family and to the other professionals involved.   Further, we recommend that the primary worker should be prepared to see the family frequently and consistently in the early stages of work;   this appears to be of great importance in establishing a relationship.   In most cases, this level of involvement need not be maintained beyond the first few months, except at later points of crisis.   We would also recommend that workers should offer clients an available telephone number as a life-line, at least in the early period of treatment and at later points of emergency, such as the return of a child home.   Further, we feel that Juvenile Court action should be initiated and taken by a worker other than the main worker and that, if possible, each parent should be offered his or her own worker.   In addition, we recommend that places are kept available at day nurseries for at-risk children at short notice.   Sometimes, a potentially dangerous situation can be averted and the need for a child's removal from home obviated by the provision of an immediate day nursery place;   with a delay of a month or two the situation could deteriorate to the point where such a measure would not be adequate.

Clearly, such recommendations make demands on Social Services Departments at a time when their resources are already overstretched.   However, the management and treatment of battered baby cases is crucial and the experience of many in the field now confirms our view that skill and consistency in the worker and clear co-ordinated management of the total situation are of supreme importance if suffering and tragedy are to be avoided.

NEW DIRECTIONS

With the opening by the NSPCC of the National Advisory Centre on the Battered Child in June 1974, the prospects for more broadly based research following on the small sample studies reported here have improved greatly.

The continuation of controlled psychological testing of battering parents as described in chapter 11 is already proceeding at

the Centre, while plans for extension to all the new Special Treatment Centres in the regions must await further funding.   The
necessity for appointing an educational or clinical psychologist
in every Special Treatment Centre is beyond dispute, given the
need to monitor children's long-term development as well as to
extend the range of research data.   This would provide a nation-
ally representative sample of test results of battering parents on
Intelligence and Personality Tests.   Similar extension of
developmental and personality testing of the children, using the
tests already described in chapter 12, is envisaged.

Modified social history schedules are already in use at the
Manchester and Leeds Special Treatment Units and other units when
opened will be invited to contribute to this attempt to confirm
the diagnostic and treatment data reported in Parts One and Two of
this book.

A long-term follow-up of the consequences of battering to the
child is planned, studying families described in the main part of
this study.

Of perhaps the most significance for long-term prophylaxis,
which is the major goal of all such research, is a study already
under way focusing on direct observations of mother-child inter-
actions.   Again, this is planned as a controlled study with pair-
matched comparison of families attending the Centre with non-
battering control families.

The approach is essentially an ethological one, as described by
Blurton-Jones (1972), requiring the detailed description of
behaviour of mother and child in interaction with each other and
with an observer.   Behaviour in a standard situation is being
recorded on video and will be subsequently analysed by computer
program.   The aim of this observational study is to discover
the essential differences between the interaction of battering and
normally functioning mother-child dyads.   There is evidence
(Kennell et al., 1974) that deviations in normal mother-child
interaction may arise very soon after birth and have long-term
consequences for the mother-child relationship.   It is hoped, in
this project, that some of these later characteristics may be
capable of capture on video tape.   If this were so, such characteristics could be communicated to workers in the field to alert
them to the danger signs in potentially battering mothers.
Despite a burgeoning literature in the field of child abuse,
'hard' data is still hard to come by.   These projected studies,
planned for the long term, should hasten the NSPCC's principal aim.

In the field of treatment new prospects are opening.   Our consultant psychiatrist is extending his services to the therapeutic
nursery where evaluation of the need for children to have individual psychotherapy can more readily be assessed and provision
made.   Treatment for parents is to be diversified with the provision of short-term psychotherapy for self referrals and the
extension of group facilities.   It is intended that the mothers'
group described in chapter 7 may become more goal focused to provide greater therapeutic impact.

With an increasing rate of clients referring themselves, it
should be possible to link treatment developments with research
needs.   Ultimately, all treatment requries critical evaluation.

In our field, such a procedure is fraught with difficulties.   By
attempting random allocation to group or individual treatment with
our less disturbed self-referred clients, it becomes possible to
set up some kind of controlled study.   Naturally case-work
support, as well as more specific treatments, remain freely available to parents referred because of known battering.

Applied research of the kind reported in this book is always
changing its focus.   The research findings of one phase become
the practices of the second stage, while the problems thrown up at
every stage create the working hypotheses for future work.

The first stage of our work has been concluded.   Inevitably,
much remains to be done before the many faceted syndrome we call
child abuse is fully understood and effective preventive measures are
formulated and applied.

APPENDICES

APPENDIX A

Age of child (months)	Referral injuries Details	Evidence of different stages of healing	Degree	Previous injuries Details	Degree	Subsequent injuries Details	Degree
8	Fractured skull, extra-cranial haematoma	No	Severe	None	None	Age 3 yrs – facial bruise	Minor
9	Fracture of lower humeral shaft, facial bruise, bruise to knee	Yes	Severe	None	None	Age 10 m – scratches on face; Age 11 m – bruises on forehead; Age 15 m – bruise on forehead; Age 29 m – black eye	Minor; Minor; Minor; Minor
22	Spiral fracture of the femur	No	Severe	None	None	None	None
2	Fractured skull, fractured humerus, fractured tibia, bony injury to femur, facial bruising	Yes	Severe	None	None	None	None

Age of child (months)	Referral injuries Details	Evidence of different stages of healing	Degree	Previous injuries Details	Degree	Subsequent injuries Details	Degree
15	Flake fracture of the elbow, multiple long bone fractures	Yes	Severe	Age 12 m – bruises on left cheek	Minor	Age 16 m – fractured tibia	Severe
				Age 13 m – bruises on arm and widening of skull sutures	Severe		
2	Bilateral sub-dural haematoma, facial bruising, bruising to ribs	No	Severe	None	None	None	None
11	Fractured right humerus, minor superficial burns between fingers and on knee, fading bruise on cheek	Yes	Severe	None	None	13 m – bump on head, small cut near eye	Moderate
						23 m – faint bruising on bottom and base of spine	Minor
12	Fractured skull, healing burn on leg	Yes	Severe	None	None	None	None

14	Burn on back of right hand, bruises on skin, bruises on trunk		Severe	None	Age 18 m – burn on thigh Age 26 m – bruise on face Age 38 m – extensive burning to legs and body	Moderate Minor Moderate
1	Hairline fracture of skull (more detail?), serious brain damage, bruising to eyelids, multiple bruising to face and rest of body, two scratches on face and body	Yes	Severe	None	None	None
8	Fractured clavicle, bump on head, bruising on right arm	Yes	Severe	None	Age 20 m – tiny abrasion on lip	Minor
14	Fractured skull	No	Severe	None	N/A (child died)	N/A
7	Extensive bruising on face and head, smaller bruises on rest of body. Fractured skull, multiple haemorrhage to eye, mild hemiphegia	Yes	Severe	None	N/A (child remained in care)	N/A

Age of child (months)	Referral injuries Details	Evidence of different stages of healing	Degree	Previous injuries Details	Degree	Subsequent injuries Details	Degree
10	Fracture of right arm, old fracture of left humerus	Yes	Severe	None	None	None	None
32	Abrasions to head and body		Moderate	Age 9 m – serious scald to shoulder; Age 14 m – first degree burns; Age 17 m – fractured skull	Severe; Severe; Severe	Recurring bumps and bruises	Minor
28	Extensive bruising on legs		Moderate	Age 7 m – cut lip	Moderate	None	None
9	Slight bruising on shoulder blade on two occasions	Yes	Minor	None	None	None	None
33	Hand-print on left cheek	No	Minor	None	None	None	None

Case	Presenting injury			Injury episode	Severity
41	Bruise on left cheek	No	Minor	Age 2 m – fractured skull, bilateral subdural haematomas, fractured ribs, bruising to trunk, cheek and ear	Severe
				Age 6 m – mark on face	Minor
				Age 9 m – bruising on forehead, graze on nose, bite mark on wrist	Moderate
				Age 21 m – facial bruise	Minor
				Age 23 m – bruise under left eye	Minor
				Age 29 m – bruise on forehead	Minor
				Age 45 m – weal marks on buttocks	Minor
				Age 46 m – weal marks on thigh	Minor
				Age 47 m – bruises to buttocks	Minor
				Age 57 m – facial bruise	Minor
				Age 59 m – facial bruising	Minor
				Age 61 m – cut over eye	Moderate
				Age 62 m – facial bruise	Minor
				Age 64 m – scald to hand	Severe
				Age 65 m – abrasions on arm, faint bruise on face	Moderate
38	Facial bruising	No	Minor	Age 36 m – bruises and scratches	Minor
				Age 40 m – bruised thumb and bruising on shoulderblades	Minor
31	None		N None	Age 28 m – cut nose	Minor
				Age 33 m – small bruises on neck and shoulders	Minor
39	None		None	History of recurrent bumps and bruises	Minor
				Recurring bumps and bruises	Minor

Age of child	Referral injuries Details	Degree (Evidence of different stages of healing)	Previous injuries Details	Degree	Subsequent injuries Details	Degree
27	None	None	Age 1 yr – bruise on mouth and split lip	Moderate	None	None
1	None	None	None	None	Age 6 m – hand mark on leg, recurring bumps and bruises	Minor
7	None	None	None	None	Age 12 m – faint bruise to forehead	Minor

APPENDIX B1 (for key see p. 227)

Ordinal position	No. of children in family	Type of accom.*	Kind of accom.**	Father's age (years)	Father's birth place	Mother's age (years)	Mother's birth place	Social class	Status of father ***
1	1	P	R	28	W. Indies	25	W. Indies	4	N
1	3	C	S/C	31	England	19	England	3	N
1	1	P	S/C	41	England	37	Gibraltar	3	N
1	1	P	S/C	27	Scotland	22	England	3	N
2	3	P	R	38	England	27	England	3	N
1	1	P	S/C	25	England	23	England	3	N
1	1	P	R	18	England	19	England	4	N
1	2	P	R	40	India	29	Ceylon	4	S
2	2	C	S/C	28	England	25	England	4	N
3	3	P	S/C	28	N. Ireland	30	Eire	3	N
4	5	P	R	32	Eire	29	Eire	4	N
2	2	P	R	25	Eire	18	Eire	3	N
1	1	P	R	22	England	22	England	3	N
2	2	P	S/C	27	India	25	India	3	N
1	1	P	R	23	England	23	Finland	4	N
1	1	P	R	28	Seychelles	26	Seychelles	4	S
2	2	P	R	21	England	24	England	4	N
1	1	O	R	23	England	25	England	4	N
1	1	P	S/C	24	England	18	Hungary	5	T
5	1	P	R	24	Eire	27	Eire	3	N
1	5	C	S/C	36	Pakistan	28	Pakistan	3	N
2	1	P	R	33	Eire	30	USA	5	N
1	2	P	S/C	35	Eire	23	England	4	N
1	1	C	Pt. III	19	England	18	England	4	N
2	2	P	S/C	36	England	33	England	2	N

APPENDIX B2 (for key see p. 227)

Approx. total family income (net)	Hours worked by father	Father's occupation	Marital status ****	SEG Socio-economic group
£15	N.I.	Store-room clerk	C	10
£24	79	Bus driver	C	9
£22	40	Service engineer	M	9
£38	40	Plasterer	M	9
£25	40	Painter decorator	M	9
£24	60	Senior clerk	M	8
£25	40	Milkman	M	10
£23	54	Railway guard	M	9
N.I.	N.I.	Security officer	M	6
N.I.	40	Bookmaker's clerk	M	6
£25	60	Builders' labourer	M	11
£50	70	Building contractor	M	2
£46	60	Electrician	M	9
£37	80	Works organiser	M	8
S.S.	0	Railway labourer	M	10
£34	60	Bus conductor	C	10
£25	75	Trainee postman	M	10
£28	43	Warehouseman	M	12
S.S.	0	Builders' labourer	C	11
£45	70	Plasterer (self-employed)	C	12
£24	58	Shop floor manager	M	2
£22	60	Unskilled steel worker	M	11
£50	40	Builders' labourer	C	11
S.S.	0	Labourer	M	11
N.I.	0	Actor	M	5

KEY TO APPENDIX B1 AND B2

```
  *   P         = Privately rented
      C         = Council accommodation
      O         = Owner occupied
 **   S/C       = Self contained house or flat
      R         = Rooms not self contained
      Pt. III   = Local authority temporary housing
***   N         = Natural father
      S         = Step father
      T         = Temporary father figure
****  C         = Cohabiting
      M         = Married
```

CONTROL CASES

At the end of 1971, when the second phase of intake was about to
begin, it was decided that it would be valuable for research purposes to try to operate a treatment control.   Therefore, as
described in chapter 1, alternate cases referred to the Department
were passed on to the appropriate local agencies for treatment.
This yielded a group of nine control cases and nine Denver House
cases.   These could not be directly compared for treatment, however, since the premature closure of Denver House meant that only
five of our latter cases had a year or more of treatment.
   Our decision to refer some cases as controls was not popular
locally since other agencies were hard pressed for time and
workers and had grown accustomed to our service handling cases of
child abuse in the area.   Since it has now transpired that we
were not able to use the control cases to compare treatment as we
had hoped, we regret that we did not take them on ourselves as
this would have increased our own sample and experience and not
have caused additional work to local agencies.   However, at the
time, since we hoped to have several more years of continued operation, it seemed important and worth while to make an attempt to
compare our specialised service with the routine service normally
provided by other agencies.
   Although a proper comparison has not proved feasible, we thought
it would be of interest to give some information about the control
cases.   Of the nine questionnaires sent out, seven were returned
completed.   One had not been returned, despite several reminders.
In the other case, the Social Services Department involved had not
been able to allocate a worker and the family did not receive any
treatment.   Details and discussion therefore refer to seven control cases, unless otherwise stated.
   As might have been expected, they resembled our cases in respect
of all the following: child's age and sex, severity of the
injury, previous injuries, family size, social class, accommodation,
parents' age and marital status.
   Seven families had been referred to Social Services Departments
and two to local NSPCC group offices.   When followed up by ques-

tionnaire after a year of treatment, there was no information on one family, one had not been seen at all, three had moved out of the area to better housing and four were still being seen regularly by their original worker.

As with our families, inadequate, cramped housing was probably the most important stress factor and workers, appreciating this, helped six out of seven families to move to better accommodation. In all cases this was seen as a most important act of help. For two of the battered children, no kind of protective placement was organised. One child was made the subject of a Care Order and for the remaining four children, local authority day nursery placements were arranged. It was our impression that removal of the child from the home was only considered seriously in one case: a father, who had referred himself, admitted injuring his child and 'boasted of previous assaults'. In the other six cases, including three with serious injuries, use of the Juvenile Court does not seem to have been discussed. However, the need to arrange a day care placement was seen as important in several cases. In general, workers from other agencies could not visit as frequently as we did and, except for the two NSPCC cases, did not offer the same twenty-four availability.

The injuries sustained by the battered children in the year following referral are shown in Table C.1.

TABLE C.1 Reinjuries in year after referral (N = 9)

No information	2
None known	2
Not applicable (child in care)	1
Serious injury	1
Recurring moderate injuries	3

Therefore, four out of a possible six children available for re-injury on whom information was forthcoming, suffered re-injury in the year following referral.

We were interested to see that other workers singled out some of the same practical issues for attention; particularly the importance of re-housing and providing day care. Many workers expressed the sense of bewilderment and frustration so familiar to us. Two quotations from questionnaires well illustrate workers' view of the treatment situation. 'I would see the only possibility of my treatment aims being achieved as being through my offering myself to them as some sort of parental figure over a very long period of time.' 'Mother becoming less defended in relationship with social worker and seems to find relief in talking out problems. Has lately begun to initiate contact with social worker when in need of help. Still remains very defended about her relationship with the child. Needs a lot of time.'

While it was not possible to draw firm conclusions on the basis of such incomplete information, we would recommend that a fully comparative study be conducted in the future in order to assess the

relative value and effectiveness of specialised and costly services
such as ours.

BIBLIOGRAPHY

ANASTASI, A. (1968), 'Psychological Testing', 3rd ed., Collier-Macmillan, London.

Annual Abstracts of Greater London Statistics (1970), vol. 5, Greater London Council.

BELL, S.M. and AINSWORTH, M.D.S. (1972), Infant crying and maternal responsiveness, 'Child Development', vol. 43, pp. 1171-90.

BENNIE, E.H. and SCLARE, A.B. (1969), The battered child syndrome, 'Amer. J. Psychiatry', vol. 125, pp. 147-51.

BLUMBERG, M.L. (1974), Psychopathology of the abusing parent, 'Amer. J. Psychotherapy', vol. 28, pp. 21-9.

BLURTON-JONES, N. (1972) 'Ethological Studies of Child Development', Cambridge University Press, Cambridge.

BOARDMAN, H.E. (1962), A project to rescue children from inflicted injuries, 'Social Work', vol. 7, pp. 43-51.

BONE, M. (1973), 'Family Planning Services in England and Wales. An Enquiry Carried out on behalf of the Department of Health and Social Security', HMSO, London.

BRANDENBURGER, B. (1975), Self help groups, 'Guardian', 6 January 1975.

British Paediatric Association (1966), The battered baby.   A memorandum by the Special Standing Committee on Accidents, 'Brit. Med. J.', vol. 1, p. 601.

BROWN, F. (1968), Bereavement, in J. Gould, ed., 'The Prevention of Damaging Stress in Children, Churchill, London.

BROWN, F. and Epps, P. (1966), Childhood bereavement and subsequent crime, 'Brit. J. Psychiat.', vol. 112, pp. 1043-8.

CAFFEY, J. (1957), Some traumatic lesions in growing bones other than fractures and dislocations: clinical and radiological features, 'Brit. J. Radiol.', vol. 30, pp. 225-38.

CAMERON, J.H., JOHNSON, H.R.M. and CAMPS, F.E. (1966), The battered child syndrome, 'Medicine, Science and the Law', vol. 6, pp. 2-21.

CAPLAN, G. (1961), 'An Approach to Community Mental Health', Tavistock Publications, London.

CARTER, J., ed. (1974), 'The Maltreated Child', Priory Press, London.

CARTER, J. (1974), Child abuse and society, in J. Carter, ed. (1974), 'The Maltreated Child', pp. 11-18.

233

CASTLE, R.L. and KERR, A.M. (1972), 'Study of Suspected Child Abuse', NSPCC, London.

CATTELL, R., EBER, H.W. and TATSUOKA, M.M. (1970), 'Handbook for the Sixteen Personality Factor Test', Institute for Personality and Ability Tests, Champaign, Ill.

CAVENAGH, W. (1975), The battered child cases in the courts in A.W. Franklin, ed. (1975), 'Concerning Child Abuse', pp. 140-6. Children and Young Persons Act (1969), HMSO, London.

COURT, J. (1969a), Battering parents, 'Social Work', vol. 26, pp. 20-4.

COURT, J. (1969b), The battered child, 'Medical Social Work', vol. 22, pp. 11-20.

COURT, J. (1969c), Battered child research project, 'Child Care News', July, pp. 2-4.

COURT, J. (1971), The battered child syndrome. 1. The need for a multi-disciplinary approach, 'Nursing Times', 3 June, pp. 659-61.

COURT, J. (1973), Some reflections on non-accidental injury to children, 'Social Work Service', no. 3, pp. 6-10.

COURT, J. and KERR, A. (1971) The battered child syndrome. 2. A preventable disease?, 'Nursing Times', 10 June, pp. 695-7.

COURT, J. and OKELL, C. (1970), An emergent programme to protect the battered child and his family, 'Intervention', no. 19, pp. 16-21.

CROSSE, V.M. (1971), 'The Pre-Term Baby and Other Babies with Low Birth Weight', 7th ed., Churchill Livingstone, Edinburgh.

DAVIES, J.M. (1975), A health visitor's viewpoint, in A.W. Franklin, ed.(1975), 'Concerning Child Abuse', pp. 78-81.

DAVOREN, E. (1968), The role of the social worker, in R.E. Helfer and C.H. Kempe, eds. (1968), 'The Battered Child', pp. 153-68.

DE FRANCIS, V. (1963), 'Child Abuse. Preview of a Nationwide Survey', Children's Division of the American Humane Association, Denver.

DELANEY, J.J. (1972), The battered child and the law, in C.H. Kempe and R.E. Helfer, eds. (1972), 'Helping the Battered Child and his Family', pp. 187-207.

DHSS (1972), The 'battered baby' syndrome: an analysis of reports submitted by Medical Officers of Health and Children's Officers, DHSS, London.

DHSS (1974a), Memorandum on non-accidental injury to children, LASSL(74)13 and CMO(74)8, DHSS, London.

DHSS (1974b), 'Report of the Committee of Inquiry into the Care and Supervision Provided in Relation to Maria Colwell', HMSO, London.

DHSS (1974c), 'Health and Personal Social Services Statistics for England ... 1974', HMSO, London.

DIGGLE, G. and JACKSON, G. (1973), Child injury monitoring system, 'Brit. Med. J.', vol. 3, pp. 334-6.

DOPPELT, J.E. (1956), Estimating the full scale score on the Wechsler Adult Intelligence Scale from scores on four subtests, 'J. Consulting Psychology', vol. 20, pp. 63-6.

DRILLIEN, C.M. (1964), 'The Growth and Development of the Prematurely Born Infant', Livingstone, Edinburgh.

ELMER, E. (1966), Hazards in determining child abuse, 'Child Welfare', vol. 45, pp. 28-33.

ELMER, E. (1967a), 'Children in Jeopardy. A Study of Abused Minors
and Their Families', University of Pittsburgh Press, Pittsburgh.
ELMER, E. (1967b), Child abuse: the family's cry for help, 'J.
Psychiat. Nursing', vol. 5, pp. 332-41.
ELMER, E. (1968), Fifty families study. Part 2. Infant accident
study. Final report. Neglected and abused children and their
families, Children's Hospital of Pittsburgh, Pittsburgh.
ELMER, E. (1971), Child abuse: a symptom of family crisis, in
E. Pavenstedt and V.W. Bernard, eds., 'Crisis of Family Disorgani-
sation', Behavioral Publications, New York, pp. 51-8.
ELMER, E. (1972), Stress and support among abusive and non-abusive
families, paper presented at the Regional Meeting of the American
Association of Orthopsychiatry, Galveston.
ELMER, E. and GREGG, G.S. (1967), Developmental characteristics of
abused children, 'Pediatrics', vol. 40, pp. 596-602.
ERLANGER, H.S. (1973), Social class differences in parents' use of
physical punishment, in S.K. Steinmetz and M.A. Straus, eds.,
'Violence in the Family', Dodd, Mead, New York.
EYSENCK, H.J. (1956), The inheritance of extraversion-introversion,
'Acta Psychologica', vol. 12, pp. 95-110.
FANAROFF, A.A., KENNELL, J.H. and KLAUS, M.H. (1972), Follow-up of
low birth weight infants. The predictive value of maternal visit-
ing patterns, 'Pediatrics', vol. 49, pp. 287-90.
FONTANA, V.J. (1973), 'Somewhere a Child is Crying: Maltreatment,
Causes and Prevention', Macmillan Publishing, New York.
FRANKLIN, A.W. (1973), 'Tunbridge Wells Study Group on Non-
Accidental Injury to Children: Report and Resolutions', available
from the DHSS.
FRANKLIN, A.W., ed. (1975), 'Concerning Child Abuse: Papers Pre-
sented by the Tunbridge Wells Study Group on Non-Accidental Injury
to Children', Churchill Livingstone, Edinburgh.
GALDSTON, R. (1966), Observations on children who have been
physically abused and their parents, 'Amer. J. Psychiatry', vol.
122, pp. 439-43.
GALDSTON, R. (1969), Dysfunction of parenting: the battered child,
the neglected child, the exploited child, in J. Howells, ed.,
'Modern Perspectives in International Child Psychiatry', Oliver &
Boyd, Edinburgh, pp. 571-88.
GALDSTON, R. (1970), Violence begins at home, paper presented at
the annual meeting of the American Academy of Child Psychiatry,
Denver.
GALDSTON, R. (1971), Violence begins at home: the Parent's Centre
Project for the study and prevention of child abuse, 'J. Amer.
Acad. Child Psychiatry', vol. 10, pp. 326-50.
GALDSTON, R. (1973), Preventing the abuse of little children,
paper presented at the annual meeting of the American Psychiatric
Association, Hawaii.
GELLES, R.J. (1973), Child abuse as psychopathology: a sociologi-
cal critique and reformulation, 'Amer. J. Orthopsychiat.', vol.
43, pp. 611-21.
GIBBENS, T.C.N. and WALKER, A. (1956), 'Cruel Parents', Institute
for the Study and Treatment of Delinquency, London.
GIBSON, C. (1974), The association between divorce and social
class in England and Wales, 'Brit. J. Sociology', vol. 25, pp. 79-93.

GIL, D.G. (1968), Incidence of child abuse and demographic charac-
teristics of persons involved, in R.E. Helfer and C.H. Kempe, eds.
(1968), 'The Battered Child', pp. 19-40.
GIL, D.G. (1970), 'Violence Against Children, Physical Child Abuse
in the United States', Harvard University Press, Cambridge, Mass.
GLUECK, S. and E. (1950), 'Unravelling Juvenile Delinquency',
Commonwealth Fund, New York.
GOLDSTEIN, J., FREUD, A. and SOLNIT, A.J. (1973), 'Beyond the Best
Interests of the Child', Collier-Macmillan, London.
Government Statistical Services (1970-2), 'Social Trends', nos. 1-3,
HMSO, London.
Government Statistical Services (1974), 'Social Trends', no. 5,
HMSO, London.
Greater London Council (1974), '1971 Census Data for London',
Greater London Council.
GREEN, A.H. (1968), Self-destructive behavior in physically abused
schizophrenic children, 'Arch. Gen. Psychiat.', vol. 19, pp. 171-9.
GREEN, A.H., GAINES, R.W. and SANDGRUND, A. (1974), Child abuse:
pathological syndrome of family interaction, 'Amer. J. Psychiatry',
vol. 131, pp. 882-6.
GREGG, G.S. (1968), Physician, child abuse reporting laws, and
injured child, 'Clinical Pediatrics', vol. 7, pp. 720-5.
GREGG, G.S. and ELMER, E. (1969), Infant injuries: accident or
abuse?, 'Pediatrics', vol. 44, pp. 434-9.
GRIFFITHS, D.Ll. and MOYNIHAN, F.J. (1963), Multiple epiphysal
injuries in babies, 'Brit. Med. J.', no. 5372, pp. 1558-61.
GWINN, J.L., LEWIN, K.W. and PETERSON, H.G. (1961), Roentgeno-
graphic manifestations of unsuspected trauma in infancy, 'J.A.M.A.',
vol. 176, pp. 926-9.
HAYS, W.L. (1963), 'Statistics for Psychologists', Holt, Rinehart
& Winston, New York.
HELFER, R.E. and KEMPE, C.H., eds. (1968), 'The Battered Child',
University of Chicago Press, Chicago.
HELFER, R.E. and POLLOCK, C.B. (1968), The battered child syndrome,
in 'Advances in Pediatrics', vol. 15, Year Book Publishers,
Chicago, pp. 9-27.
HENRY, J. (1972), 'Pathways to Madness', Cape, London, p. 66.
HOLTER, J.C. and FRIEDMAN, S.B. (1968), Principles of management in
child abuse cases, 'Amer. J. Orthopsychiatry', vol. 38, pp. 127-36.
House of Lords (1974), 'Children's Bill', no. 42, Clause 11, sub-
section 2f.
HOWE, M.W. (1974), Casework self evaluation: a single subject
approach, 'Soc. Serv. Review', vol. 48, pp. 1-24.
HUGHES, A. (1967), The battered baby syndrome: a multidisciplinary
problem, 'Case Conference', vol. 14, pp. 304-8.
HUNT, J. McV. and KOGAN, L.S. (1952), 'Measuring Results in Social
Casework. A Manual on Judging Movement', Family Service Association
of America, New York.
HYMAN, C.A. (1973a), I.Q. of parents of battered babies, 'Brit.
Med. J.', vol. 4, p. 739.
HYMAN, C.A. (1973b), A psychological study of battering parents,
Ph.D. thesis, University of Surrey.
ISAACS, J.L. (1972), The role of the lawyer in child abuse cases, in
C.H. Kempe and R.E. Helfer, eds. (1972), 'Helping the Battered
Child and his Family', pp. 225-41.

JOHNSON, B. and MORSE, H.A. (1968a), The battered child: a study of children with inflicted injuries, Denver Welfare Department, Denver.

JOHNSON, B. and MORSE, H.A. (1968b), Injured children and their parents, 'Children', vol. 15, pp. 147-52.

JONES, C. and JONES, R. (1974), Treatment: a social perspective, in J. Carter, ed. (1974), 'The Maltreated Child', pp. 89-99.

JONES, R.A. (1973), Battering families, 'Health and Social Services Journal', 10 January 1973.

KAUFMAN, I. (1962), Psychiatric implications of physical abuse of children, in 'Protecting the Battered Child', American Humane Association, Denver, pp. 17-22.

KAUFMAN, I. (1966), Helping people who cannot manage their lives, 'Children', vol. 13, pp. 93-8.

KELLSALL, R.K. and H.N. (1971), 'Social Disadvantage and Educational Opportunity', Holt, Rinehart & Winston, London.

KEMPE, C.H. (1968), Some problems encountered by welfare departments in the management of the battered child syndrome, in R.E. Helfer and C.H. Kempe, eds. (1968), 'The Battered Child', pp. 169-71.

KEMPE, C.H. (1969), The battered child and the hospital, 'Hospital Practice', October, pp. 44-57.

KEMPE, C.H. (1970), Tea and sympathy. The 'therapeutic person' in the treatment of the battered child and his family, 'Child's Guardian', March, pp. 7-9.

KEMPE, C.H. (1971), paediatric implications of the battered baby syndrome, 'Arch. Dis. Child', vol. 46, pp. 28-37.

KEMPE, C.H. and HELFER, R.E., eds. (1972), 'Helping the Battered Child and his Family', Lippincott, Philadelphia.

KEMPE, C.H. and HELFER, R.E. (1972), Innovative therapeutic approaches, in C.H. Kempe and R.E. Helfer, eds. (1972), 'Helping the Battered Child and his Family', pp. 41-54.

KEMPE, C.H. et al. (1962), The battered child syndrome, 'J.A.M.A.', vol. 181, pp. 17-24.

KENNELL, J.H. et al. (1974), Maternal behaviour one year after early and extended post-partum contact, 'Develop. Med. Child. Neurol.', vol. 16, pp. 172-9.

KERR, A. and COURT, J. (1972), Battered babies, 'London Doctor', February, pp. 34-6, 38.

KLAUS, M.H. and KENNELL, J.H. (1970), Mothers separated from their newborn infants, 'Pediatric Clinics of North America', vol. 17, pp. 1015-37.

KLEIN, M. and STERN, L. (1971), Low birth weight and the battered child syndrome, 'Amer. J. Dis. Child', vol. 122, pp. 15-18.

KOEL, B.S. (1969), Failure to thrive and fatal injury as a continuum, 'Amer. J. Dis. Child', vol. 118, pp. 565-7.

LAUERMAN, M.W. (1974), Examining the role of the social services researcher, 'Social Work Today', vol. 4, no. 21, pp. 658-62.

LOEB, M.B. (1960), The backdrop for social research: theory-making and model building, in L. Kogan, ed., 'Social Science Theory and Social Work Research', National Association of Social Workers, New York, pp. 3-15.

MACDONALD, M. (1959), Compatability of theory and method: an analysis of six studies, in 'Use of Judgements as Data in Social

Work Research', National Association of Social Workers, New York, pp. 22-35.

MCDONALD, R.L. (1968), The role of emotional factors in obstetric complications: a review, 'Psychosomatic Medicine', vol. 30, pp. 222-37.

MACFARLANE, A. (1974), If a smile is so important ..., 'New Scientist', vol. 62, no. 895, pp. 164-6.

MCHENRY, T. GIRDANY, B.R. and ELMER, E. (1963), Unsuspected trauma with multiple skeletal injuries during infancy and childhood, 'Pediatrics', vol. 31, pp. 903-8.

MARTIN, H. (1970), Antecedents of burns and scalds in children, 'Brit. J. Med. Psychol.', vol. 43, pp. 39-47.

MARTIN, H. (1972), The child and his development, in C.H. Kempe and R.E. Helfer, eds. (1972), 'Helping the Battered Child and his Family', pp. 93-114.

MAXWELL, E. (1957), Validities of abbreviated WAIS scales, 'J. Consulting Psychology', vol. 21, pp. 121-6.

MELNICK, B. and HURLEY, J. (1969), Distinctive personality attributes and child abusing mothers, 'J. Consulting Psychology', vol. 33, pp. 746-9.

MERRILL, E.J. (1962), Physical abuse of children: an agency study, in 'Protecting the Battered Child', American Humane Association, Denver, pp. 17-22.

MILOWE, I.D. and LOURIE, R.S. (1964), The child's role in the battered child syndrome, 'J. Pediat.', vol. 65, pp. 1079-81.

MORRIS, M.G. and GOULD, R.W. (1963), Role reversal: a concept in dealing with the neglected battered child syndrome, in 'The Neglected Battered Child Syndrome', Child Welfare League of America, New York, pp. 26-46.

MORRIS, M.G., GOULD, R.W. and MATTHEWS, P.J. (1964), Toward prevention of child abuse, 'Children', vol. 11, pp. 55-60.

MORSE, C.W., SAHLER, O.J.Z. and FRIEDMAN, S.B. (1970), A three-year follow-up study of abused and neglected children, 'Amer. J. Dis. Child', vol. 120, pp. 439-46.

NEWSON, J. and E. (1963), 'Patterns of Infant Care in an Urban Community', George Allen & Unwin, London.

NEWSON, J. and E. (1968), 'Four Years Old in an Urban Community', George Allen & Unwin, London.

NIE, N.H., BENT, D.H. and HULL, C.H. (1970), 'Statistical Package for the Social Sciences', McGraw-Hill, New York.

NOYES, A.P. and KOLB, L.C. (1963), Psychophysiological autonomic and visceral disorders, in 'Modern Clinical Psychiatry', Saunders, London, pp. 379-420.

NURSE, S. (1964), Familial patterns of parents who abuse their children, 'Smith College Studies in Social Work', vol. 35, pp. 11-25.

Office of Population Censuses and Surveys (1968), 'Registrar General's Statistical Review of England and Wales for the Year 1965. Part 3. Commentary', HMSO, London.

Office of Population Censuses and Surveys (1970), 'Classification of Occupations, 1970', HMSO, London.

Office of Population Censuses and Surveys (1971), 'Registrar General's Statistical Review of England and Wales for the Year 1969. Part 2', HMSO, London.

Office of Population Censuses and Surveys (1972), 'Registrar General's Statistical Review of England and Wales for the Year 1970. Part 2', HMSO, London.

Office of Population Censuses and Surveys (1974), 'Census 1971. Great Britain. Summary Tables (1% Sample)', HMSO, London.

OKELL, C. (1969), The battered child syndrome: a tragic breakdown in parental care, 'Midwife and Health Visitor', vol. 5, pp. 235-40.

OKELL, C. (1971), Childhood accidents and child abuse, 'Community Medicine', vol. 126, pp. 124-7.

OKELL, C. (1972), The battered child syndrome: recent research and implications for treatment, paper presented at the Royal Society of Health Congress, Eastbourne.

OLIVER, J.E. and COX, J. (1973), A family kindred with ill-used children: the burden on the community, 'Brit. J. Psychiatry', vol. 123, pp. 81-90.

OLIVER, J.E. and TAYLOR, A. (1971), Five generations of ill-treated children in one family pedigree, 'Brit. J. Psychiatry', vol. 119, pp. 473-80.

OLIVER, J.E. et al. (1974), 'Severely Ill-treated Young Children in North-East Wiltshire', Oxford Regional Health Authority, Oxford.

O'NEILL, J.A. et al. (1973), Patterns of injury in the battered child syndrome, 'J. Trauma', vol. 13, pp. 332-9.

OUNSTED, C., OPPENHEIMER, R. and LINDSAY, J. (1974), Aspects of bonding failure: the psychopathology and psychotherapeutic treatment of the families of battered children, 'Develop. Med. Child Neurol.', vol. 16, pp. 447-56.

OUNSTED, C., OPPENHEIMER, R. and LINDSAY, J. (1975), The psychopathology and psychotherapy of the families: aspects of bonding failure, in A.W. Franklin, ed. (1975), 'Concerning Child Abuse', pp. 30-40.

PARRY, W.H. and SEYMOUR, M.W. (1971), Epidemiology of battered babies in Nottingham, 'Community Medicine', vol. 126, pp. 121-3.

PAULSEN, M.G. (1968), The law and abused children, in R.E. Helfer and C.H. Kempe, eds. (1968), 'The Battered Child', pp. 175-200.

PAULSON, M.J. and CHALEFF, A. (1973), Parent surrogate roles: a dynamic concept in understanding and treating abusive parents, 'J. Clin. Child. Psychology', vol. 11, pp. 38-40.

PAULSON, M.J. et al. (1974), The MMPI: a descriptive measure of psychopathology in abusive parents, 'J. Clin. Psychol.', vol. 30, pp. 387-90.

PEAK, H. (1953), Problems of objective observation, in L. Festinger and D. Katz, eds., 'Research Methods in the Behavioral Sciences', Dryden, New York, p. 249.

PIAGET, J. (1967), 'Play, Dreams and Imitation in Childhood', Routledge & Kegan Paul, London.

PIZZEY, E. (1974), 'Scream Quietly or the Neighbours Will Hear', Penguin, Harmondsworth.

POLLOCK, C. and STEELE, B. (1972), 'A therapeutic approach to the parents', in C.H. Kempe and R.E. Helfer, eds. (1972), 'Helping the Battered Child and his Family', pp. 3-21.

REINER, B.S. and KAUFMANN, I. (1959), 'Character Disorders in Parents of Delinquents', Family Service Association of America, New York.

RICHARDS, M.P.M. (1974a), 'The Integration of a Child into a Social World', Cambridge University Press, London.

RICHARDS, M.P.M. (1974b), The one-day old deprived child, 'New Scientist', vol. 61, no. 891, pp. 820-2.
RICHARDS, M.P.M. and BERNAL, J.F. (1972), An observational study of mother-infant interaction, in N.J. Blurton-Jones, ed. (1972), 'Ethological Studies of Child Development', pp. 175-97.
Royal College of Psychiatrists (1974), Memorandum. Battered Wives, February 1974.
RUNCIMAN, W.G. (1966), 'Relative Deprivation and Social Justice: A Study of Attitude to Social Inequality in Twentieth Century England', Routledge & Kegan Paul, London.
RUTTER, M. (1974), A child's life, 'New Scientist', vol. 62, no. 903, pp. 763-6.
RYLE, A. (1967), 'Neurosis in the Ordinary Family: A Psychiatric Survey', Tavistock Publications, London.
SAVINO, A.B. and SAUNDERS, R.W. (1973), Working with abusive parents: group therapy and home visits, 'Amer. J. Nursing', vol. 73, pp. 482-4.
SCHAEFFER, E.S. and BELL, R.Q. (1958), Development of a Parental Attitude Research Instrument, 'Child Development', vol. 29, pp. 337-61.
SCOTT, P.D. (1974), Battered wives, 'Brit. J. Psychiat.', vol. 125, pp. 433-41.
SEARS, R.R., MACCOBY, E.E. and LEVIN, H. (1957), 'Patterns of Child Rearing', Row Peterson, Evanston.
SEASHORE, M.J. et al. (1973), The effects of denial of early mother-infant interaction on maternal self confidence, 'J. Personality and Social Psychology', vol. 26, pp. 369-78.
SELLITZ, C. et al. (1965), 'Research Methods in Social Relations', Methuen, London.
SIEGAL, S. (1956), 'Nonparametric Statistics for the Behavioural Sciences', McGraw-Hill, London.
SILVER, L.B., BARTON, W. and DUBLIN, C.C. (1967), Child abuse laws: are they enough?, 'J.A.M.A.', vol. 199, pp. 65-8.
SILVER, L.B., DUBLIN, C.C. and LOURIE, R.S. (1969), Child abuse syndrome: the 'gray areas' in establishing diagnosis, 'Pediatrics', vol. 44, pp. 594-600.
SILVERMAN, F. (1968), Radiological aspects of the battered child syndrome, in R.E. Helfer and C.H. Kempe, eds. (1968), 'The Battered Child', pp. 59-76.
SIMONS, B. et al. (1966), Child abuse: epidemiological study of medically reported cases, 'N.Y. State J. Medicine', vol. 66, pp. 2783-8.
SKINNER, A.E. (1970), 78 battered children, 'Social Work' (South Africa), vol. 6, pp. 3-4, 7.
SKINNER, A.E. and CASTLE, R.L. (1969), '78 Battered Children: A Retrospective Study', NSPCC, London.
SMITH, S.M. and HANSON, R. (1974), 134 battered children: a medical and psychological study, 'Brit. Med. J.', vol. 3, pp. 666-70.
SMITH, S. and HANSON, R. (1975), Interpersonal relationships and child-rearing practices in 214 parents of battered children, unpublished.
SMITH, S.M., HANSON, R. and NOBLE, S. (1973), Parents of battered babies: a controlled study, 'Brit. Med. J.', vol. 4, pp. 388-91.

SMITH, S.M., HANSON, R. and NOBLE, S. (1974), Social aspects of
the battered baby syndrome, 'Brit. J. Psychiat.', vol. 125,
pp. 568-82.
SPINETTA, J.J. and RIGLER, D. (1972), The child-abusing parent: a
psychological review, 'Psychological Bulletin', vol. 77, pp. 296-
304.
STEELE, B.F. (1966), Proceedings of a conference on patterns of
parental behaviour leading to physical abuse of children, unpublished paper, University of Colorado School of Medicine.
STEELE, B.F. (1970), Parental abuse of infants and small children,
in E.J. Anthony and T. Benedek, eds. 'Parenthood: Its Psychology
and Psychopathology, Little, Brown, Boston, Mass., pp. 449-78.
STEELE, B.F. and POLLOCK, C.B. (1968), A psychiatric study of
parents who abuse infants and small children, in R.E. Helfer and
C.H. Kempe, eds. (1968), 'The Battered Child', pp. 103-47.
TEN BROECK, E. (1974), The Extended Family Center. A home away
from home for abused children and their parent, 'Children Today',
vol. 3, pp. 2-6.
TERR, L.C. (1970), A family study of child abuse, 'Amer. J.
Psychiatry', vol. 127, pp. 665-71.
WASSERMAN, S. (1967), The abused parent of the abused child,
'Children', vol. 14, pp. 175-9.
WECHSLER, D. (1958), 'The Measurement and Appraisal of Adult Intel-
ligence', 4th ed., Williams & Wilkins, Baltimore.
WOOLLEY, P.V., and EVANS, W.A. (1955), 'Significance of skeletal
lesions in infants resembling those of traumatic origin, 'J.A.M.A.',
vol. 158, pp. 539-43.
YOUNG, L. (1964), 'Wednesday's Children. A Study of Child Neglect
and Abuse', McGraw-Hill, New York.
YOUNG, L. (1966), An interim report on an experimental program of
protective services, 'Child Welfare', vol. 45, pp. 373-82.
ZALBA, S.R. (1966), The abused child. 1. A survey of the problem,
'Social Work', vol. 11, pp. 3-16.
ZALBA, S.R. (1967), The abused child. 2. A typology for classification and treatment, 'Social Work', vol. 12, pp. 70-9.

INDEX

As this book is devoted to aspects of the battered child syndrome and child abuse these headings have not, as far as possible, been used in the index

abuse of the older child, 211-12
adoption, 41, 215
Adult Court proceedings, 13, 106-7
aggression
  in children, 125, 207-8
  in parents, 67, 83-4, 188, 195, 197
ante-natal care, 38-9, 216
anxiety
  in parents, 39, 89, 91-2, 141
  in professionals, 2, 5, 98-9, 100-4, 105, 114, 135, 145-6, 151
Area Review Committees, 105, 211

Battered Child Research Department
  establishment of, 1-7
  staff of, 2, 4, 5, 102, 136-7, 165-6
battered child syndrome
  as diagnostic label, 1, 2, 210-11
  recommendations on, 210-18
battering incident, 18-28
  explanation of injuries, 23-5
  identification of abuser, 25-6
  see also injuries
Bayley Scales of Infant Development, 200-4

birthweights, 42-7
brain damage, 21

Calouste Gulbenkian Foundation, 1
Care Order, 109, 112, 113, 121, 123, 129, 131-2, 161, 162, 163
case conferences, 12, 100-1, 103, 105, 160, 214
caseloads, 2, 104
case management, 3, 97-105, 216
case records, 4, 12, 99-100, 102, 164
casework strategy, 3, 134-5
Castle, R., 4
Cattell's Sixteen Personality Factor Test, 183-4, 188-91, 194
Chase Charity, 1
childbirth and postnatal experience, 39-41
Child Guidance Clinics, use of 161-2
children
  age of, 30, 185, 186, 193, 202, 211-12, 221-6
  behaviour, 27-8, 41-2, 48-9, 60-2, 125, 173-4, 198-9
  characteristics of, 27-8, 42 50, 60-2, 173-4, 196

development of, 41-50, 62-
3, 173-4, 198-9, 200-4, 214
emotional disturbance, 60-2,
125, 128, 161-2, 174
feelings towards family,
61, 205-7
neonatal period, 40, 42-9
ordinal position, 31, 185
placement of, 100, 115-25,
215
protection of, 97, 100, 106-
32, 214-15, 216
psychology of, 198-209
sex of, 29
treatment for, 128, 161-2,
214
Children and Young Persons Act,
1969, 109, 110
Children's Bill, 215
Children's Department, 3, 97,
100
Colwell, Maria, 211
Committee of Inquiry, 102,
130, 132
confidentiality, 100, 105, 211
contraception, 85-6, 175, 216
co-operation
inter-agency, 3, 97-101,
103-5, 106-7, 108-9, 113-15,
159-62
within BCRD, 5-6, 102
co-ordination, problems of, 23,
100-2, 103, 104-5, 109,
110-11, 113-15
co-therapy and co-therapists,
158-64
Court, J., 2, 4
crisis intervention, 98, 99,
137-9
crying, 27, 43-6, 48-9

data analysis, 14-16
data collection, 4, 12-14
day care, 122-5, 214, 216, 231
parents' reactions to, 122-
4, 126
see also therapeutic day
nursery
day nurseries, see day care
Denver House Day Nursery, see
therapeutic day nursery
Department of Health and Social
Security, 105

dependency needs
of child, 52-6
of parents, 52-3, 79-80, 86,
87, 90, 133-4, 156-7, 195
depression, 71, 73, 88, 91
developmental testing, see
psychological testing
diagnosis, differential, 18-28
diagnostic schedules, 12-13,
167-9, 198-9, 217
see also data collection;
treatment data
discipline
parent's attitudes to, 58-9,
171
children's response to, 61-2
doll play, 207-8
drop-in foster mother, 4, 120,
165

epidemiological studies, need
for, 211
extended family, 79-80, 169,
176

failure to thrive, 49-50
family functioning, 13, 14, 50-
9, 81-7, 167, 170-2, 174-6,
177
Family Relations Test, 205-7
family size, 30
father-child relationship, 51,
55, 171, 206
fathers
characteristics of, 51, 55,
86-7, 90-2, 149-50, 177,
188-91, 195-6
childhood and adolescence,
65-8, 72-4
drinking problem, 83, 92,
169
inaccessibility of, 16, 149-
50, 158-9
personality of, 90-1, 188-91,
194, 195-6
psychology of, 90-1, 183-97
follow-up studies, need for,
209, 217
fostering, 118-19, 120, 215
Friends of Violet Melchett
Infant Welfare Centre, 1

general practitioners, 3, 19,
    97, 101, 213
grandparents, 66-73, 79, 80
Griffiths, D.Ll., 1
group therapy, 213

Health Department, 3, 19, 97
Health Visitor questionnaire,
    184, 186, 192-4
Health Visitors, 19, 98, 99,
    160, 184, 186, 213
Helfer, R., 2
hospital care, 115-17
    parents' reactions to, 116-17
hospitals, 3, 19
    staff of, 98, 101, 110, 116
housing, 35, 37-8, 76-8, 170,
    185, 192-3, 194, 227, 229,
    231
Hughes, A., 2

illegitimacy, 36-7, 192
injuries
    accidental, 3, 18-19, 26
    degree of, 19-21, 30,
    221-6
    diagnosis of, 3, 18, 22
    history of, 22, 221-6
    long-term effects, 21
    see also children, develop-
    ment of; children, behaviour
    of; physical handicap
intake
    closure of, 4, 12
    opening of, 4, 11
Inter-Agency Co-ordinating
    Committee, 3, 97

Joseph Rowntree Charitable
    Trust, 1
Juvenile Court proceedings,
    13, 97, 106, 107-15, 158,
    159, 215, 216
    discussion of evidence,
    110-11
    parents' reactions to,
    111-12

Kaufman, I., 156-7
Kempe, C. Henry, 1, 2, 3, 13

Kempe, Ruth, 3

legal advice, 112-13
legal intervention, 106-15
legal profession, 110-11, 112-13
loss of parents, 73-4

mandatory reporting, 2, 211
marital violence, 83-4, 171
maternal behaviour, 40, 41-2,
    217
mental retardation, 21
mother-child interaction, 40,
    41-2, 176, 217
mother-child relationship, 41-2,
    51-5, 56, 57-8, 171-2, 176,
    205-7, 209
mothercraft, 56-7, 171-2, 213
mothering-aide, 4, 164-5
mothers
    attitude to child, 40-1,
    51-5, 57-8, 88-9, 171-2,
    175-6
    attitudes to pregnancy and
    birth, 36-7, 39-41
    characteristics of, 51-9,
    86-90, 140-4, 150-1, 176-7,
    188-91, 194, 195-6
    childhood and adolescence,
    65-6, 68-74
    personality of, 87-8, 188-91,
    194, 195-6
    psychology of, 87-90, 183-97
mother's group, 126-8, 176, 217
Moynihan, F.J., 1

National Advisory Centre on the
    Battered Child, 5, 216
NSPCC, 1, 5, 19, 200, 216, 217,
    230, 231
    special units, 6, 7, 216-17
neglect, 50, 57
nurturing problems, 27-8, 42-50

over-protectiveness, 57

paediatricians, role of, 101, 110
Parent Attitude Research Instru-
    ment, 183-4, 191-2

parent-child interaction, 50-
64, 171-2
parenthood, 88-9, 90-1, 175-6
parents
    admission of abuse, 23-4,
    147-9
    age of, 32, 82, 185, 186,
    192, 194, 227
    care and handling of child,
    52-8, 171-2, 175-6
    criminal history, 81
    employment and income, 74-6,
    169, 228
    ethnic origin, 32-3, 185,
    227
    help sought by, 22-4, 38-9
    intelligence of, 187, 196
    lack of concern, 25, 26, 27
    marital relationship, 81-7,
    170-1, 174-5, 192-3, 195-6
    medical problems, 91-2, 177
    provocation of partner, 26
    social isolation, 80-1, 90,
    169
    social class, 33-4, 66, 68-
    9, 227
    see also fathers; mothers
Peabody Picture Vocabulary
    Test, 204
physical handicap, 21, 49
Place of Safety Order, 100,
    106, 109, 113, 116, 117
play, 57-8
police, role of, 3, 97, 106-7,
    214-15
pregnancy, 36-9, 192-3, 194,
    211-12, 216
    unplanned, 82-3
prematurity, 42
psychiatric assessment, 162-3,
    214
psychiatric consultant, role
    of, 2, 162-4
psychiatric treatment, 160-2,
    163
psychological testing, 183-92,
    198, 200-7, 216-17
    samples, 184-6, 198, 200
psychotherapy
    for children, 214, 217
    for parents, 213, 217

radiological signs, 22

referral
    criteria for, 3, 4, 11, 97
    procedures for, 3, 98-100
    sources of, 19, 98, 99
registers, 6, 211-12
Reiner, B.S., 156-7
re-injury, 2, 107, 172-3, 212-
    13, 221-6, 231
research project, see therapeu-
    tic study
residential care, 118-22, 129,
    131-2
    parents' reaction to, 119,
    121-2
    return of children from, 129-
    30, 131-2
retrospective study, 2
role reversal, 52, 195
Royal Borough of Kensington and
    Chelsea, 1

Scientific Advisory Committee, 1
self-help groups, 213
self-referrals, 217-18
separation
    effects on mother-child bond,
    47
    of parent and child, 100,
    107-8, 116, 117, 118, 121,
    132, 215
    of therapeutic and legal
    roles, 97, 108-9, 110-11,
    113-15, 216
sexual identity, 89-90, 176
sexual relationship, 85-6, 171
siblings, 31, 63-4, 173
Social Services Departments, 3,
    19, 97, 108-9, 114-15, 118,
    119, 158, 159, 161, 216,
    230-2
social workers
    assessment of children, 13,
    60-4
    assessment of parents, 13,
    87-93, 141-4
    contact with children, 144-7
    frequency of visits, 139,
    151-2
    witnessing rough handling,
    56, 145-7
Stanford Binet Test, 200-4
Statistical Package for the
    Social Sciences, 14, 199

stress, 35, 37-8, 74-8, 82-6,
   192-5

therapeutic day nursery, 1, 4,
   124-8, 198-9, 214
   effects on children, 125,
   128, 202, 204, 208-9
therapeutic relationship, 133-
   57, 213
therapeutic study
   critique of, 16-17, 211
   methodology of, 11-17, 167-9
   sample, 11-12, 18, 29-35
transfer of cases, 5, 104,
   136-7
treatment
   evaluation of, 14, 15, 167-
   80
   first phase, 50-64, 100-1,
   137-51
   second phase, 152-3
   third phase, 153-4, 169-80
   fourth phase, 154-5
   termination of, 155

treatment centre, residential,
   215
treatment control group, 4, 12,
   14, 230-2
treatment data, 13-14, 15, 167-9
treatment philosophy, 3-4, 133-4
twenty-four hour service, 98,
   102, 134, 136, 152

University of Colorado Medical
   Centre, 2, 3, 13

verbal skills,
   of children, 197, 204
   of parents, 187, 195-6

Wechsler Adult Intelligence
   Scale, 183, 187